Flatline Constructs

Flatline Constructs:
Gothic Materialism and Cybernetic Theory-Fiction

———

Mark Fisher

Forward by
exmilitary

Exmilitary Press
New York, New York

*Flatline Constructs: Gothic Materialism
and Cybernetic Theory-Fiction,*
Mark Fisher

ISBN 978-0-692-06605-8 (print)

Contents

Forward
by exmilitary

Mark Fisher clicked send in 1999. The unpromising year - of forecasted occurrences, appearances and happenings - hosted the reception of his PhD dissertation at the University of Warwick - a site notorious today for a select cohort and non-tradition that Fisher continued to unearth and fabulate until his death last year. The disclosures of *Flatline Constructs: Gothic Materialism and Cybernetic Theory-Fiction* are manic, stimulative and depressive; a glimpse into a previous and insular era of fiction and theory that was, to be thought of, at its peak in the 1990s and yet colossally archaic in 21st century hindsight. Hysteria of the year 1999, and Y2K as a foundational hyperstitional event, should come at no surprise as a contagious and memetic inspiration for cyberpunk theory-fiction. The chronological prophecy from 1999[1] to 2000 is either entirely a fabrication suspect to illusions of ends or an underlined portrayal of the ongoing climatological yet air-conditioned disaster in progress both hiding the conceit that contemporary (of Fisher's time and ours) culture is a ruinous disaster, vacuously invaluable. Optimistic postulates to the contrary are relapsed simulations of Minervian owls, serpentine coils, twittering birds, redemptive angels facing forward.

Fisher never printed *Flatline Constructs*; it remained dispossessed from any material form. But, it lied archived and formatted for anyone's immediate search, side by side with the many web 1.0 radical informational hubs as it still

---

1. November 1999: Anarchists in Seattle spread over crowning downtown accomplishments of Empire and globalism, broadcast live from the select Seattle public broadcast stations with astonishment. Anarchists in bloc ripping concrete from the pavement, finding nothing beneath but a portability and effective weapon. Welcoming to the new millennium of trade, vandals confront corporate downtown properties. Beneath the pavement, the street - a site of commerce and logistics to be blocked off, partitioned by formations in black. Delegates abandoned their hotels, police cordon the intersection, the New York Times writes an article, then apologizes for fucking up the story. The medium rebels against the real event, amplified and jacked straight into the war at home; an accident in coverage, a coincidence in public relations that lead our favorite acronyms (CNN, NBC, ABC, CBS) to air it vertically central in the news cycle for 48 hours. Widely seen as the first time domestic implications of media as confused, the non-gulf war scenario where its oil and libido on the mind - these are American citizens throwing "molotov cocktails" (NYT) at police. For maybe the last time, the protesters were correct in saying the whole world was watching, by accident.

is: https://web.archive.org/web/2008032501 3155/http://www.cinestatic. com/trans-mat/Fisher/FCcontents.htm. The hyperlinks flowing outwards from the dissertation directed readers into a rhizomatic network specific to the lo-fi blogosphere of the early 2000s. The production and circulation are not afterthoughts of the work or the text, added hermeneutic suspicions, but central and formative conditions of its own readership. Against the ideological claims of more mainstream cyberspace advocates, Fisher (and his hypertext) knew that the last frontier of emancipatory potential was in cyberspace. The next colonization after globalization, the proverbial "end of geography," positioned in the wild west of RealMedia radio streams, IRC, listservs, blogroll-communes of cultural critics. This is why Fisher's optimism is not: restless in the rupturing counter-hegemonic space ardently positioned against the capital-infused digital spaces of Silicon Valley - Paypal, Google, Microsoft. Now, Fisher's counter-cultural diasporic sphere remains primarily in web archives, but the dream of fissure, free zones has continued: the internet underground - the dark net, The Pirate Bay, private trackers, Photoshop cracks, Megaupload, proxy sites, VPNs, pastebin, defacements of government websites, hackers of all kinds - persistently continues in the margins of an always more total presence of surveillance, social media and licensed content.

Subsequently there is an archive of Fisher's blog k-punk that circulates information and distributes content, and there is the medium that made transcultural and experimental demands: to be transparent, produce more, create new value, find the/a self. It should not be surprising that the emphasis on new 'subjectivity' that came out of a certain moment of post-structuralism is now the event horizon of silicon valley - post-humanizing toward and of nature and ostensibly not against. If there was a way out via posthumanism, it would have already happened, and Fisher's *Flatline Constructs* demands to be read against this silicon-multiplier of neoliberal consent. Silicon, concrete, glass against the gothic, acidic: as much a fictitious plague as they are inorganic bodies, *"we live in overstimulated times"* (Cronenberg), abstract and intense - or as Fisher writes in his essay *Gothic Materialism, "It is not a matter of speaking the unspeakable, but of vocalising the extra-linguistic or the non-verbal, and thereby letting the Outside in. Admit it, count zero, get out."*

J.G. Ballard's *Atrocity Exhibition,* Lizzie Borden's *Born in Flames,* John Carpenter's *In the Mouth of Madness,* Kathy Acker's *Empire of the Senseless* (the RIYLs are numerous...) are literary maps of these schizoid relations; mapping their coordinates as cartographies of control societies, revealing new dystopian constellations formative in the coming politics – or, civil war – of Thatcherite memorandums of the future alternatives. The constant refrain towards immediate connectivity prequels these dystopian fictions, which interlink a profitable imagination with a drive towards a distinct complicity of their own capture. This desert is thoroughly diagnosed and theorized in *Flatline Constructs:* and as this wasteland grows, tertiary apparatuses condense into insignia's of the old, latent sequels and disasters. Sequelization processes of recursive submersion proliferate the screen with a stale drama. And at this point in our current Disney nightmare it seems vital to hold this text, outside of the screen, in proximity with the apparent body, scanning its pages, creasing its corners, underlining. We hope the text becomes soiled, damp, torn - stolen even - that which underlies its fatality in the world and dispossessed immateriality.

The redress for the retromaniacal nostalgia-machine requires the acidic qualities of a gothic contagion at the porous borders of entertainment. If the gothic is an instantiation of a certain oneiric uncanniness, the false promise of any aesthetic-transgressive diatribe empties out the aesthetic object of choice, becoming transparent, communicating ecstasy. This is the movement of the 'avant-conservative,' its unwavering repetitions - denoting stylistic differing iterations, yet continually regurgitating the same pulsating form. Some find it transiently impassive, others latently reactionary and others imminently intense - regardless, *Flatline Constructs* comments on the indeterminate tendency, the falling rate of aesthetics, which starts from the crevasse of the abyss and still looks down.

Fisher's work was devoted to explaining, disseminating and delineating the concept of capitalist realism through criticism, amounting to decades of k-punk, which typed lines of criticism on innumerable prolific and mass-mediated trends, phenomena, events, etc. Claims made throughout Fisher's most commercially distributed/cited, the very contagious *Capitalist Realism: is there no alternative?*, tend to come full stop in a general diagnosis of cultural melancholia as resultant of austere hyper-connectivity and collectively ubiquitous depression: "*In his dreadful lassitude and objectless rage, Cobain seemed to give wearied voice to the despondency of the generation that had come after history, whose every move was anticipated, tracked, bought and sold before it had even happened. Cobain knew that he was just another piece of spectacle, that nothing runs better on MTV than a protest against MTV; knew that his every move was a cliche scripted in advance, knew that even realizing it is a cliche.*" Gradients of content and style are no longer possible, as *Postmodernism* writes, in a world where all there is are cultures of death idolizing themselves, sedimenting a crypt once again for old voices. Think: *Blade Runner 2049* - the overwritten, scripturally prophetic blockbuster, which does nothing to envision a world, but plots overdetermined and pre-sent realities, layered above a realist Los Angeles, while the center was already lost last century.

The primacy of curatorial taste, which dictates off-brand aesthetics as the underground current dissolving the semblance of the mainstream is a good irony of the 21st century. Streamlined consumerism will not allow it: retromania insists upon it, nostalgia machines are fueled by it - insularity is impossible, everything is already known about curatorial taste, assessments. For Fisher, the phenomenon known as "Sonic Youth" is the recapitulation of an ongoingness of a past-present recombinant history that wears the wounded attachment of the past, iterated again to the present and sold as entertainment. Look: Sonic Youth, the New York City post-rock outfit, in a breath, is a "no wave" noise rock band that has directed their own underground trajectory, self-assured, for the past 30 years. Carried by a certain mystical yet neoliberal concentration on bland renewal, cross-continent proximity and posturized indifference, SY was met with a pre-subscribed genre as experimental, and as such is the identitarian reflection - merely derivative, and sold as such, which solidified their reputation among minoritarian interests.

And, if the gothic is an instantiation of a certain oneiric uncanniness, the false promise of their own post-punk diatribe is not that they were not the first to amass a certain authenticity; the main conceit, noticeable throughout k-punk (and its interlocutors), is that SY was never original, yet self-admirably cast in an image of their own reception, publicity stunts, liner notes, cacophonous sound - not even pastiche (the intentions of their predecessors) but the debris remained after the catastrophe. The case against "rock history repeating itself, first as deluxe CD reissues, then as inglorious reunion tours, then as deluxe DVDs of the reunion tours" (as *Zone* writes in response to k-punk's SY critique) reads as an additional verse to Fisher's long-committed relationship to theorizing "capitalist realism" - that which succeeded socialist realism - state sponsored, verified, aesthetic channels that portrayed an imaginary complacency of the people with their governance. Mark cites an anonymous blog: *"it isn't the music so much as the tissue of references that is backward looking."* The forced and intentional kitsch of Sonic Youth's last studio, *The Eternal* (2009), is where this theorization is nowhere more apparent. Each song is intentionally - and explicitly acknowledged as in liner notes - bound in a previous discography that has heavily determined their music. Lost from any origin, yet inundated with the continuation of the derivative sign, a "portal" disappears, following Fisher in a blog post *"My mind it aint so open,"* writes: *"...[portals] function most powerfully when they are transversal connectors between different cultural domains, e.g. fiction and music - whereas many of SY's references were to music, justifying the trend that will end up in mediocrities such as Starsailor parasiting credibility by association with great moments in rock history."* As a friend of Fisher would say, "Sonic Youth sounds like Sonic Youth." Self refurbished rockist sanctimony, and iterative again.

The form of this engagement with aesthetics, popular music in particular, does not come without predecessors - such as the discussed intensity of My Bloody Valentine, not unlike Steven Shaviro's transgenre "Doom Patrols" (1997): *This isn't just a case of being overwhelmed by the sublime. You can't stand it, and you can't see beyond it; but for that very reason you get used to it after a while, and you never want it to end. As with psychedelic drugs--at least sometimes--sensory overload is only the beginning. There's a whole new world out there, beyond the experience of shock. You enter a realm of "microperceptions," as Deleuze and Guattari put it: "microintervals between matters, colors and sounds engulfing lines of flight, world lines, lines of transparency and intersection." Things rush up on you, suddenly, in waves, and then slip ever-so-slightly out of focus. Densely articulated textures fade in and out. You pick up on subtleties you didn't notice before: wavering rhythms, minor chords, muddily shifting tonalities, synthesized special effects, Bilinda Butcher's floating vocal lines buried deep within the mix. You even hear fragments of pop melodies, tentatively emerging and then quickly dissolving; it's as if they were suspended in a chemical solution. These are the qualities sometimes described as 'dreamy' and 'ethereal' by listeners who haven't played the Loveless CD at sufficiently high volume. But such words fail to convey how deeply embodied--how physically attentive, you might say--this music actually is... you're stunned by the realization that there are so many types of ambiguity, so many distinct shades of gray. Your nerves and your viscera are tingling, as they register the tiniest differences, the most minute alterations. These are changes beyond, or beneath, the threshold of ordinary perception. Your sensory organs are being stretched or contracted far outside their usual range. In such altered states, as Deleuze and Guattari say, "the imperceptible is perceived."* Against the formulaic manufactured avant-conservative, k-punk took to his blog often to decry the mass appeal of certain aesthetic tastes, trends that pretend they are the real deal. A lot amounts to inorganic life, artifice, clockwork - aesthetics that are as fatal as they are machinic.

But with k-punk things were always a little different, responding in "real" time to the calendar's album releases and political elections alike. Thus the author as not only producer, but marketer, advertiser, and reader - the short-circuiting of any discrepancy of agency along the flatline construct. A libidinal drive to consume the text, a satiated desire to follow the hyperlinks that chain the inevitable signification of the text, the bar of signification is no long a bar but a line, a vector attached and connecting the chapters present but also the outside - the internet as an unconsciously rhizomatic apparatus; without roots or arborescence. An immediacy of the hyperlinks joints genealogies and fictions as one, elaborating to the criminalization of distinguishing between theory and fiction. "Theory-fiction" (the hyphen is a huge lie), then is, like the simulacra for Baudrillard, the truth: dangerous, deadly, and will kill you. Fisher's treatise can be summarized as warranting and narrating how theory-fiction came to be realized, conscious of, in a select group of authors, artists, programs, computer scientists, perverts, sex workers, immigrants, deviants, schizoids.

Another world is not possible - the late soviet spiritual directors from VGIK, as much an insular hotbed of praxis as CCRU Warwick, developed a slow shedding off of socialist realism, traceable from the war films of Shepitko and Klimov that play with the genre, injecting a brutal, Dostoevskian, psychical question of whither death or betrayal, to the monastic films of Tarkovsky and Lopushansky. *Nostalghia* (1983) is a failed attempt to revive a past, but as Andrei and Domenico discover the future is foreclosed too. Our contemporary stuckness is sublimated in Hollywood films, as Fisher writes, with an interpassivity that lets us live out a future on the screen. Against this, Tarkovsky preaches in a cathedral in 1984: *"... and now I ask myself a question: what should I do if I have read the Revelation? It is quite clear that I can no longer be the same as before, not simply because I have changed, but because it has been said to me: knowing what I have learned, I am obliged to change."*

This is the thesis of his films: apocalypse is here and now, as the spiritual erupting in a state of decay. *The Sacrifice* and *Joy Division* as desperate companions. Tarkovsky's and Lopushansky's apocalyptic films do not present a contemplative image of what a future/collapse might look like; they imbue an uncanny imperative of responsibility for a collapse always already occurring, inside and outside the films. This collapse is not due to nuclear war, political implosion: *"What is the Apocalypse? As I have already said, from my point of view, it is an image of the human soul with its responsibility and its duties."* It is no use imagining what happens after the Fall, after 1989, (our) history is over. *Russian Symphony, Russian Ark* as orchestras of pasts made immediately present, apocalypses are always happening, and we must answer their call.

In these films there is a total collapse of futurity: a paralyzing fear of imminent nuclear war coinciding with the fall of the Soviet Union. The political collapse is perhaps why VGIK's films are so dire and inward, while in America blockbuster post-apocalyptic action-adventure films debuted. *A Visitor to a Museum* was released in 1989, showing global ecological disaster, trash as earth, earth as trash. The world was not abandoned, like WALL-E, but inhabited by desperate survivors. There is no chance of escape for anyone, even those with money.

There are no conclusively overt methods of utopia and politics in the above mentioned narrations, nor are there fictions of resistance, party politics, sexual liberation - only a radical indeterminacy as resilience, a languid silence, semiotic insurrection, de-stabilizing and problematizing the diagnosis that Deleuze-Guattari posit in "Postscripts on the Societies of Control," that *what matters is that we are at the beginning of something.* For *Flatline Constructs*, a possibility of a beginning does not imply an end, but an infinitely regressive flatline as the zero point of death. As such, Fisher denotes a world of literature that contends that this communicative apparatus cannot sufficiently resolve itself in a stage of late capitalism, but rejoins with the other assembled realities happening. Each singular thought possession continues to be several in *A Thousand Plateaus*, the primordial and liminal space of influence for *Flatline Constructs*, which invokes a user guide to late capitalism, that ceaseless striation of space that envelops territory and operates a proto-globalism, shaping the map for *Empire*, mapping networks across boundaries and issuing communication and its exploits. Fisher's cohort, readership, audience would experiment with these fictions, but in the end the preface to a post-truth and worldly dystopian situation should have been expected, and entertained as such. Instead, today Fisher's queue seems like an idyllic dwelling on past landscapes, themselves monographs into deterred situations. Fisher was as much a Corbynist as he was a nihilist, dedicated to consciousness raising.

But the map is not the territory - nor is it a hermeneutic key that protracts one's way out, exit or fabulation away from the ongoing dystopia of the present. There is a fragmentary recoil to Fisher's pessimism of the lost future in the early dissertation, long tirades into the nature of reality, narrated situations in cybernetic fiction, and what he will continue to theorize over for the rest of his life: although future's pasts reclaim the present, the way out lies in a denial of present austere imagination. Fisher reminds us that Gibson's *Neuromancer* constantly asks *"what kind of addiction?"* For gothic materialism and cybernetic theory-fiction there are many: media, violence, media violence. A dissolution of the border is the contagion that emulates further placation of genre and kinds, which continues to expand the territory, and engenders reality itself. As fictions of the subject unravel, so does the communicative apparatus that annotate the subject and their world. The body of work considered in *Flatline Constructs* introduces a pivot in the communicative apparatus's ability to convey the truth of the subject.

The reconciliation of cybernetic space, and the fabulation of its virtual potential, has led one delusional (read: deleuzional) astray with a youthful affirmation and optimism, celebrating the end times of histories and humans alike. But decisively, in *Flatline Constructs,* Fisher negotiates an episodic delineation on cyberspace - and all its fictions - with a devoutly acidic pessimism, at times teetering on a nihilism, that theorizes what comes after its crystalline instantiation: the decay, the rumination, the rust of it all.

For Fisher, the interjection of cyberspace does not create, but supplements the current dismal reality as a mirror of the austere times and corroded imagination of its world subjects. As in the most critically dystopian fantasies of our times, the plot gravitates at the release of gradations of traumas, the pre-Oedipal abject that has been established monarch. If late capitalist society breeds fictions of simulation, then its realities of paranoid specular traumatic interactions are soaked in social fantasies of the outside and exit. The cyber-theorist's diagnosis that cyberspace and the world is a false metonymy, but are oscillating in permanent flux and instability, follows an uncanny logic. Cyberspace both simulates and exists within; a procedure of constant deterrence, proto-cellular logic of hyperreality. Implexed against the world and its simulation, cyberspace proceeds to unfold varieties of simulated reality. Loss of identity, de-subjectivation as embodied gore, put the body in a fluctuating feedback loop, disintegrating its organicity. Cyberspace is implicated in the economy of the world, yet arouses its double and, as Fisher writes, *"simulate[s] 'the world', but not passively, or mutely: what happens here is immediately effective in the world outside the technical environment (...) There is both operational difference – the translation of 'the world' into data, the raw material of cyberspace (and of cybernetics), makes a difference and ontological in-difference – cyberspace is continuous with 'the world', not different from it. Feedback ensures that the operational, or cybernetic, relationship between this simulated realm destroys any 'illusion of difference', denying metaphor its ground (the economy of representation as such)."* Long gone are the occult fixations with determining whether the present reality is of the real; these fictions explore the immanence of these falsities as definitional to experience.

Flatline Constructs   is the next trajectory in the historical and theoretical step of a certain (de)subjectivity as quotidian of cyberspace. An exercise in theory-fiction against its limits of fiction-text, open to projected simulations inherited from his other otherworldly predecessors: the late 70s/80s cyberpunk fiction/cinema: speculative experimentation, new iterations of the outside, against global network of the abolished same.

Think of cyberspace like the futurist motorik drum pattern: a lucid prolongation of a maintained signal, propulsive currents, accents on forming an incessant sensation, extended reverberation that breathes as a constant without conclusion. It is instantaneously acute, yet excessively linear protracted without point. A flatlined tempo yet also a contagious terrain, individualized, atomized; stimulants, highways without delay, arriving. The infinite horizon displaced by its accessible terrain. Nothing about it is circular and eternal, but it is entirely repetition with difference; infectious quality to both motorik and cyberspace. One maintains this guise as a constructed flatline, plateaued and intense - offering its users an exit. Look: the continual drum pattern of motorik, like everything Neu! or a 13 minute "What Goes On" Velvet Underground recording is indeterminate to its own movement. No longer teleological, in fact now deteriorating as an infrastructure the same way that "Sister Ray" or early Stereolab breaks apart. Cyberspace operates as the conduit through which our many connections flow. Totalization begets fragmentation, as bleak post-indust-reality proliferates into cyberspace itself. Hollowed and abandoned sections of the internet like blown-out American cities in the 80s (think John Carpenter, again),

In 1999, the protocol was (a weak) king: websites used HTTP, e-mail used SMTP, chats used IRC, devs used FTP and SSH, MUD games used TELNET, and the earliest users communicated via BBSes. This enabled decentralized hubs of communication - protocols were open source and there were readymade software implementations for all operating systems. All you needed was a connection (dial-up would do) and you could begin discovering and communicating with the outside. Read not as a temporalized possibility but a topographic spreading-out of power, we can recover Fisher's cybernetic-claustrophobia (the world would get more technologically dense) from the utopians who believed the net would reveal a future-to-come. Here the communicative circuitous drive is radicalized: euphoric, tactile exploration of the net's undercommons provides the plus d'un of web surfing: collated experiences culminating in a persistent subjective decentering/destabilizing - once you know the URLs, once you get access, you can continue on endlessly outside of monetized cultural streams. Accessibility teeters on immediacy in the current area, where a deluge of information proliferates without origin or *telos*, the speed borders delirium, communicative ecstasy as a condition of sexual relations. There is a tactile and sensory affect of the medium, suspending rationality at the assemblage of information[2].

2, March 2000: NASDAQ peaks, and for the next 30 months falls 78%. Tech

The transcendental and material clash. Fisher rails the last line of a nascent collective cyber-mania, sublating these two reactions: quoting Poe, cybernetics/cyberspace, our new God, is neither immaterial or material - instead, Gothic Materialism *"deploys the Kantian critical machine to interrogate what remains uncritiqued in Marx (the reification of already-constituted actualities like 'the social') whilst using Marx to re-insert Kant's subject into the hypermaterialist field of Kapital."* Like Lyotard, the unintelligible, transcendental core of cyberspace comes from the vastness of its material network. Identity is decentered, but not in the forgiving way of the immaterialists; it is forced upon us, like Max Renn in *Videodrome* (1983) - we're invaginated, with networks, screens, images penetrating us. We do not have control over the infrastructure, but are like patients in Foucault's hospitals. The computer-scientist's identity play is only a minigame - of course we can choose our usernames and role play with others, but the primal shift in cybernetic identity plays out precisely when we face not an invented digital world but the becoming-virtual real world. Fisher's task becomes revealing the horrific tearing of cybernetic de-subjectivity, against a hitherto-painless identity play.

In opposition to the "now" of that episodic time (of Thatcher, Reagan, Thatcher-Reagan) - but also of the counter-times and its schizophrenic modality to its future's past - *Flatline Constructs* details a looming futurity surrounding the imagination of the late 20th century, refuting adamantly their premises under the phrase "the slow cancellation of future" degrading a past tense orientation of the internet to its virtual potential, freedom, unmasked potential. It is in this optimism, that cyberspace will necessarily be the dichotomous invert of the present austerity, that one sees today within hindsight that the dystopian landscapes of canonized SF et al., are not too different than a few decades into the 21st century: Think of the mapping of an infrastructural apparatus that renders communication possible, yet only granted to a few corporations. Consistent across all critiques is the rise of cybernetic capitalism as a withering away of the modernist welfare state, giving rise to corporate power and brutal

---

companies go bankrupt; mergers usher in centralization and monopolization; tech fortifies itself, San Francisco as the west-coast axis of Wall Street-Silicon Valley dual power. Inefficiency is ruthlessly hunted down; venture fund money makes capitalists out of anarchists. Telecommunications is pushed to the private sector, effectively ending state-control over communications infrastructure. New business models emerged that found ways to make profitable data and information, and there was an especially lucrative one: advertising. Cyberspace and its communications were corporatized. On Wall Street, cables were laid to directly jack into the markets - a millisecond can make the difference between a profit and a loss. Once chaotic and messy, the 'pit' became a loud room of labeled server racks. Speed meant money, and after the gold rush the largest corporations bought everything and everyone out. Any emancipatory dreams for the net were dead, a brutal horizontality of increased density and thick fiber cables infest the world.

individuation. Fisher was following this closely: his writings on Joy Division summarize the depressive malaise of post-industrial landscapes, contemporizing industrial alienated metropolitans. Siouxsie makes art out of her own objection, dances an artifice of seduction. Addiction, sex, violence were simultaneously found in London and *Neuromancer's* Chiba City, Japan.

Abysses are everywhere. The ambivalent optimism towards a nascent cybernetic capitalism was visibly incorrect: the sublime hotel lobbies had no vacancies but something more sinister had been happening since 1988. Virtual space was an endless and powerful network that, unlike the bourgeois sublime of the hotel lobby, neutralized and displaced subjects anywhere they went. The parodies of the West as pastiche sketches follow a majoritarian vulgar appreciation of decay, minimalist design and self-irony that are themselves exchanged as commodities with aesthetic values on the world market. There is a certain aesthetics of that situation that follows a cultural logic, but Fisher looks toward who and what are outside the splendor of Warhol. Warhol does not escape his own code but ends up on the cover of the Duke chair's *Postmodernism*. All the more prophetic the longer we can continue to say we live in austere times - the ongoing looting of the State(s) since 2008; the substitution of start-ups for the function of that ever-more-bygone modernist state; all the while the American Empire declines terminally, not without leaving the permanent residue of our new cybernetic reality, our "cold world," concocted in its basement labs.

It is not coincidental that the underground internet is hosted in poor post-Soviet nations (Russia included) and other 'offshore' countries, where the US media lobbies - MPAA and RIAA - and the FBI cannot extend their legal reach. Extradition treaties dictate the state of play. Cyberspatial capitalist hegemony operates topographically: uncooperative groups and websites are forced to the global margins - Assange is holed up in the Ecuadorian Embassy in London, a microcosmic representation of the total situation. Today, it is obvious that cybernetic density is not the same as cybernetic liberation. Instead, every territory is contested; for example what is called "The Great Firewall of China," an endeavor taken by the Chinese government to monitor and manipulate all traffic going in and out of the Chinese territories (a classic 'man-in-the-middle' attack). All connections are algorithmically processed, able to instantaneously determine the origin, destination, content, and protocol. Politically-sensitive requests can be blocked, as is most notoriously the case with information about Tiananmen Square, which is all totally inaccessible. Similarly, other countries have demanded of large websites the erasure of country-specific sensitive material, leveraging favorable nation-wide access and exposure, essential agreements for global tech companies. Now that the world's politics and economy operates instantaneously (the shockwaves of the 2008 crisis were globally felt within hours of the first whiff of disaster), technology no longer a bottleneck of cooperation, the technological margin is a crucial counterposition, as it operates not with the burnt-out utopianism of the 20th century left but a pessimistic, oppositional understanding of the world, answering calls for a cognitive mapping of contemporary conditions. The tight knot between the communicative function of the commodity (as a formative function of the latter) and the austere withering away of the state becomes apparent: an exit from governance while its neglect of welfare consolidates dreams of the future under the guise of progressive technology. But long gone are the dreams of the party-state providing a futurist agenda and implementing its plans for and towards its workers. The tangential folding of the state's concession of insecurity and of the utopianist myth coming from somewhere else entirely. Post-industrial decay, and its complementary ruses of post-ford/taylorism - and/or the sino-futurist images of toyotism - compound optimism with an ingrained techno-futurism. Elon Musk tells Werner Herzog that the present moment is opportune for an exit, but these demands are belated, aborted, or "hell is truth seen too late" (Hegel). Maybe even Freud too at his most speculative: *Man has, as it were, become a kind of prosthetic god. When he puts on all his auxiliary organs he is truly magnificent; but those organs have not grown on to him and they still give him much trouble at times. ("Civilization and Its Discontents")*

Appendages to the body follow a series of invocations on the prosthetics of the body without organs. The modern McLuhanite trope "media as extensions of men" demands the episodic question of, both, "extensions" and "men," both of which appear suspect as contingent in the world. What reifies man and extensions, extensions and their men, is more so the disguised difference between what could be considered immaterial and material, a translucent cable. Yet immediacy is performed at the embodied level, whether assembled as a matter of intentionality or not, cybernetic and theoretically-fictitious situations are inundated with broken contingency of immaterial/material dichotomy. The difference between prosthetics and object is consumed by the code, a mobius strip of postmodern anxiety; "material digital labor" vs. "immaterial digital labor" seems malnourished in the topology of installed protocols and complicit platforms. Inherent to the body's operations is a modality of cybernetic realism. It is non-Cartesian insofar as there is no duality between mind and body, but bodies and bodies - carrying modern skepticism to subvert it. The passage from body to mind is a relation to horror, violence, stimulants, media - all mind-altering conditions that sonorously alter reality; it is no longer a question of subjectivity and its screen, its conditions and/or postscripts, but of its container as immanent to the gothic flatline, engineered schizoanalysis, bodies without organs - which becomes the name to designate the grid of the subject, formatted, stylized, assembled, invented. Prosthetics and appendages attempt to enclose the gap between the thing and its person, but the closeness of proximity does not locate us any closer to the thing itself. Understanding media technologies as services always intended to communicate and not simply a historicizing of these technologies drives a fixation on immediate forms. From the telegram to the Internet, communication has always had the intent of immediacy, technology has seemingly closed in on an approximation to alleviate any temporal causality in mediation; becoming immediate, following an asymptotic logic that cyberspace emits. Media's archeology reveals yet another facade of progress considering communication was immediate 200 years ago. But technologies are distilled into the social contexts that produce them, and surrounding the cultural history that Fisher is analyzing is an exit to the outside, following new spatial alternatives as cyberspace. There is always an ecstatic euphoria of the possibility of communication being received, and transmitted, like a virus, a phallic desire to getting off within immediacy, as in Ballard-Cronenberg's *Crash*. Prosthetic death, organs without "organs" can be re-created, distributed and circulate in cyberspace - many small deaths, repeating an embodied *jouissance* at the expense of technologically mediated condition.

Following cyborg/feminist remarks that the boundary between science and fiction has become an optical illusion, Fisher repeats that inorganic slogan of Donna Haraway once again: "*our machines are disturbingly lively, while we ourselves are frightening inert.*" But like trees, Fisher is also tired of cyborgs, which resist pursuing the gothic flatline of cybernetics, and stay placated by the cleavage between the outer limit of cybernetics and the human at home, oscillating between the two, unfixed in their relapse, negotiating the pre-mediated ground beneath a field of occurrence. Unfortunately, Haraway still believes in reality. As a category of thought, outside of a plane of immanence, and not, as Nietzsche would say, "merely assembled." The cyborg distances herself from the flatline, not intoxicated on its immanence but satisfied with its non-identitarian vibrations. The gothic flatline against Haraway's cyborg as an ongoing revenge of the simulacrum as only that: *ressentiment* without drawing a line of flight.

Full immersion in the gothic flatline would not make it a matter of "life over death," as Haraway maintains her Cyborg Manifesto, but of locating a designation of the gothic flatline. Gothic materialism as an incision of an inorganic continuum, deteriorating boundaries across life and its absence. An analysis of the visual gore of a body-without-organs, de-personalized. The reference of gothic materialism and its main allegation is that technology is not merely instrumental in organic life, but has as a prostheticized hyper-nature - and new in/organic configuration, as a material phenomenon, within human nervous systems. This is procedurally why it is material; the rejoinder of materiality isolates a crudely gothic ontologized design. It is anti-postmodern, as it finds textual claims secondary to their libidinal consumption, as much as it is unlike Marxism insofar as it takes solemnly the flowing movement of automation as abstract machines and as such recodes 'fantasy' as reality; a totally immanent approach that designates a flatline to unfold.

The immaterial gothic, flatlined materially: acid rain oozing against a gothic cathedral creates decrepit state of commotion, black noise as ruin value, the rotting of concrete against the corrosive afterbirth of industrialism, as the model for de-centralism/centralism of worldly communicative infrastructure. It was always a contest against nature, to follow an information highway of commodities to a commodified highway of information. Compelled to offset the dust that conglomerates like the multi-national corporations and their protocols, there is always excess and waste as the next nature to come. Decentralization is the final fantasy of these ambitions, to let the state rot and to take from it the proto-anarchic blueprints that serviced out ability to, literally, communicate. The present analogizes these past forms as semblance of their own simulation. Internet providers follow the same predatory logic of state infrastructure.

How to maintain the flatlined plateau, and how to theorize its ontology: Foucault's re-introduction of the flatline to modernity occurred in his 1963 work *The Birth of the Clinic,* which is situated in an ironically fitting location: the hospital - where monitors of death and administrators of life, demand close readings of the pulse, prioritizing a vibrantly ecstatic interpretation over one that would be considered flat. But, as Mark Fisher details, the monitor continues to this day to declare life and its death in a very classical sense. Defibrillating the asystole, electroencephalogram readings, oxygen depletes in the brain, after repeated emergency tests, it is time to consider pronouncing the patient dead. Incidentally, within the body of literature (theory and/or fiction) that Fisher deploys, "flatline" is a verb and a noun. Fisher: "*the flatline is where everything happens, the Other Side, behind or beyond the screens (of subjectivity), the site of primary process where identity is produced (and dismantled): the "line Outside." (Deleuze) It delineates not a line of death, but a continuum enfolding, but ultimately going beyond, both death and life. (Foucault)*"

Biomedical technicians seem to resent Hollywood because of their fabricated portrayals of flatlining, considered too melodramatic and insistent on the audio to complement the visual in the screen. But the television drama is closer to the "reality" than of the medicinal apparatus; thinking of *Videodrome* (1983) here, as Fisher surely would: "*the screen is the retina of the mind's eye.*" A very peculiar television interview occurs in *Videodrome's* overstimulated time, where Professor Brian O'Blivion, the pseudonym of a media prophet not unlike k-punk, successfully flatlined, ocr'ed and livefed straight into near present day Pittsburgh. But Max Renn's economy of overstimulated hallucinations of hardcore pornography is justified as a product to displace any 'real' motivation to commit violent crime in society, soon returns as not only the transit of real and imaginary, but concluding as a front for megacorporations to sell missile guidance systems for NATO: "*cyberspace is where the money is at.*" Hyperreality at the annexation of perverse fantasy, the meltdown of their machines, the production of desire in media res.

The formulaically conceived truth is that nothing can reset the heart- to entertain the notion that there is a weird and eerie displacement for an altogether different alternative. We think that Cronenberg is closer to the truth than the monitorial apparatus of life/death, "make a rhizome with the world," become-VCR, as does Max Renn, intentionally or not (intensely for sure). To consider the flatline as a measurement of life is the flatline is another designation, an alternative location than entropic death, zero. The flatline is a designation in which affect plateaus, reaches an intensity. Vibrant, yet contained - it is the dispersion of the multiple and its virtual potential, but importantly its space of capacity to be emulated. It is always in reference to death but interpreted as *"violent, plural and coextensive with life... taken as a line."* Detourn the monitors, administrate the flatline as stimulating and vibrant. Beneath the street, the flatline construct.

Nothing is hidden from view, everything now circulates and exchanges: hypervisible, contagion and contact as infectious. Sex as a feedback loop. Post-oedipal destruction of the erogenous zone. There is thought that is corollary to the canon and there is thought that demands its own assimilation within it. The syllabus tends to aggregate difference into one, consolidate it towards the instruction of younger minds to repeat, again, the apparent merit of the texts. We see here, as well with the bibliography of cyberpunk literature a pulse measured, which traditionally designates the precondition of death and life, is instead supplemented with reversibility that conceives death as a line instead of a point; a vectorial imperative. Intensities against the wall of ecstasy, nouns as verbs, adverbs as nouns – syntax failures.

What haunts, instructs, Fisher, is not so much the past of communisms, mediums, ideologies, but of a lost horizon of futures[3]. A deterioration of all

---

3. January 2017: Post-truth presidency, world-vision enabling hyperstitional attitudes, an engineering of faiths that cut-up fake strands, pre-determined to permute what is real. The center is dead; everything is prohibited. The flatlining of civilization - it is itself the very document that simultaneously bears witness to its own barbarism. But moreover, the hyperstition before any future reason as the situation of hyperreality derails healthiness of the world; contaminates the Internet just as its other administrators of torture foresaw. The demand for cyberspace and its containers of new potential, economies, relations, sexualities yet in its final moment: new territories, subjectivities and the condition of unravel. There is of course a silent utopianist promise in this project, a non-location to launch out and plug in of an exit of the current austere conditions. There is, also, a non-futuristic alternative qua cyberspace, parasitic of the end times imagined by the current administrators and effectuated by its alleged concrete bureaucrats. What arises from a buoyancy to the real, supplanted and/or de-rooted by, probably, a combinatory apparatus of late capitalism's cybernetic communications networks as a *waning of affect*, or even Lyotard describing intensities as *free-floating and impersonal and tend to be dominated by a peculiar kind of euphoria*. Baudrillard would go on to typify this as a resultant euphoria of communication that dissuades the informative content at proximity to its consumed medium of exchange. Private property destruction pornography, a brick through a Starbucks and Bank of American in downtown DC mobilizes the three branches of governance and media alike: there exists domestic terrorists and they dress in all black. Then, the regime's response: felonies through mass incrimination never worked well, but they try again, to incriminate over 200 citizens, and detain for more than 12 hours. But preceding the law's response: A collective exhumation, a large felony riot.

conceptualizations of futures, radiant and optimistically typecast as preceding motivators for enlightened thought and practice, a futile neglect of imagination supplanted by a cultural logic of postmodernism, totalization in its wake. Futurism now is less a relation to a certain temporality invoking what comes after the present, but a distinct style affiliated with a certain affect. Structures of feeling, of a subconscious yet immediate orientation to a lost set of futures, are the very landscapes of cybernetic theory-fiction; mourning the disappearance of a connective fictitious strand of thought is a dialogue with these lost futures, as such presented univocally as dystopian realities evident and imaged in a cyberpunk contingency that delineates what hypothetically and fictionally came after the future. Indeed, the present is fictitious, wrapped up in self-conceptualizations as cybernetic. Fisher above all understood immediacy and its technologies. When writing on lost futures he was a hauntologist in the sense that he could deter the sequencing of the present condition for an acidic temporality, something was lost yet was temporary to begin with.

The cybernetic theory-fiction that Fisher wrote on was not just a new conceptualization of text - one where, following Artaud, the high culture of the literary 'masterpiece' is replaced by fiction (the .50c novel), opening a space for non- and anti-bourgeois relations to and representations of life - but also creating a new way to examine our cybernetic-infused contemporary moment: cybernetic science-fiction mirrors the unification of the cultural and political spheres, the subordination of the social sciences to driving fictional narratives, hyperstitions. These fictional articulations drive our understanding of, and action in, the world - Fisher: *"We live science fiction,' McLuhan had pronounced at the end of his 1964 essay on Burroughs ..." The same for Baudrillard. Following this, "theory should abandon its assumed position of 'objective neutrality', and embrace its fictionality."* The '-' in theory-fiction denotes not a merging but a dissolution of the two categories. Fiction doesn't just 'contain' theory, but produces it.

Concurrently, and submerged in the violence of its systematic production, the pretense of the internet as a military apparatus is emblematic of the continual tropes of network condensation - the partitioned divisions that installed the functioning internet - the university, private companies, the military - continues to drive dreams. The code as a necro-biological determinant to all social interaction and pseudo-authenticity appears vaguely interesting in aesthetic practice until Fisher. The code continues and progresses as history, through the enlightenment, seemingly both more and less the cause of organic life. Expressing and unfolding absent temporarily/ontology. The code presents itself to us as a lame melodrama with sporadically parodic and pastiche elements that mimics something about its machinic reproduction or of its facade of identity. The code is a mythological device without origin, generated by a topology with recurring reproduction; If the code is a totalizing function of late capitalism, complicit and even encouraged by culture, then Fisher's counter-cultural delineations are strategic guides of not subversion or transgression, but of decoding. Which is met against flows of texts and their digressions, multiple instructional mechanics appear literary interpretation but really are perhaps subversive strategies to decode, and as instruction manuals to how conceptually decoding can be thought of.

Like everyone else bludgeoned by these billboard harangues and television films of imaginary accidents, I had felt a vague sense of unease that the gruesome climax of my life was being rehearsed years in advance, and would take place on some highway or road junction known only to the makers of these films.

(J.G. Ballard, "Crash")

By making highways, you multiply the means of control... people can travel infinitely and "freely" without being confined while being perfectly controlled. That is our future.

(Deleuze, "Two Regimes of Madness")

There is a metaforensical approach latent to Fisher, horrific and truly detective, producing reality as simulated as artifice. Like ontology, flatlines delineate like highways; transmitting live commodities along a path towards a destination. Traffic, speed, information are all the same; both highways and the Internet had an initial militarized function. But there is a deception in the highway similar to that of cybernetics, that the outside is a mere continuation of the inside; even the highway infrastructure decays, the state empties and retreats from public spending. The highway is also the site of hypervisibility, surveilled indefinitely on camera as an extension of the law. We tend to think that the highway, like the 90's promotion of the Internet as an "information superhighway," has extended beyond its figural representations, induced a society of control, then split: leaving cracked concrete on the side of the road adjacent the metallic debris of a vehicle crash littered across asphalt pavement. Highways that were installed to carry commodities across territories, soon were supplemented by maps of Internet networks, which followed an eerily similar map-strategy to that of cyberspace: to cut terrain, smoothen the space and render arrivals. Yet highways are not an infinite horizon towards something determinate, but are concealed and striated, jagged and edged. The highway is a circuitous reference in *Crash*, a sprawling dissonance that is at once speculative as contemplative. Yet these views last no more than a few seconds, reminiscent of aerial photography, the expansive network of highways intersection, looping, traversing – or, connecting the bodily arteries of late capitalism.

The highway, not unlike the metal fence, partitions areas as vacant and permissible, but also in the same motion, criminal and juridical. The police re-invent the fence at every moment possible, during demonstrative protests of murder and presidents alike. Millennial crowd control is the confusion when there are dozens of eight-meter long, four and a half meter tall fences separating you from, both, the crowd and the street. First response is confusion, then anger, then complicity; you're at 53rd Street or 12th and L and thinking of how to get back home. Yet aware that the protest, like the future, has come to a close. The metal fence or the concrete highway, which observably draws the line through the mass, divides and contains logistics and breakages; the NYPD, the MPD and the constructed flatline.

If highways are a post-disciplinary technique of control, and following Deleuze *"our future"* then the decayed concrete has initialized our descent into something different. Crumbling infrastructure, quite literally, decays. The ambivalent attitude towards the highway, the nostalgic beat iteration of getting off, getting on like the experience of a prolonged altering trip demands critique today: the highway-machine is a flatlining of previous modalities of control and surveillance complicit in its own immaterialization. Coincidentally, we're left back at the promissory exit of cyberspace, and that of the highway. One can certainly leave its premise, log off, unplug and uninstall: removal oneself from the speed and velocity. But today, such optimism is denied, the vector will follow you, track the movements, measure your identity. Transparency has taken over the outside, and the dystopian landscapes of cybernetic theory-fiction are prescient. Techno-futurist promises of cyberspace are empty, yet the gothic flatline remains a conclusion to the end times that reality implicates.

INTRODUCTION

Isn't it strange the way the wind makes inanimate objects move? Doesn't it look odd when things which usually just lie there lifeless suddenly start fluttering. Don't you agree? I remember once looking out onto an empty square, watching huge scraps of paper whirling angrily round and round, chasing one another as if each had sworn to kill the others; and I couldn't feel the wind at all since I was standing in the lee of a house. A moment later they seemed to have calmed down, but then once again they were seized with an insane fury and raced all over the square in a mindless rage, crowding into a corner then scattering again as some new madness came over them, until finally they disappeared round a corner.

There was just one thick newspaper that couldn't keep up with the rest. It lay there on the cobbles, full of spite and flapping spasmodically, as if it were out of breath and gasping for air.

As I watched, I was filled with an ominous foreboding. What if, after all, we living beings were nothing more than such scraps of paper? Could there not be a similar unseeable, unfathomable 'wind' blowing us from place to place and determining our actions, whilst we, in our simplicity, believe we are driven by free will? What if the life within us were nothing more than some mysterious whirlwind? The wind whereof it says in the Bible, 'Thou hearest the sound thereof, but canst not tell whence it cometh and whither it goeth'? Do we not sometimes dream we have plunged our hands into deep water and caught silvery fish, when all that has happened is that our hands have been caught in a cold draught?[1]

Today's children [...] are comfortable with the idea that inanimate objects can both think and have a personality. But they no longer worry if the machine is alive. They know it is not. The issue of aliveness has moved into the background as though it is settled. But the notion of the machine has been expanded to include having a psychology. In retaining the psychological mode as the preferred way of talking about computers, children allow computational machines to retain an animistic trace, a mark of having passed through a stage where the issue of the computer's aliveness is a focus of intense consideration.[2]

---

1. Gustave Meyrinck, *The Golem*, trans. Mike Mitchell, Sawtry/Riverside: Dedalus/Ariadne, 1995, 54-55. A crucial aspect of the legend concerns the writing of a secret name (the name of god) either onto a piece of paper or directly onto the Golem's head. In some cases, the Golem is animated by a letter of the secret name being deleted.

2. Sherry Turkle, *Life on the Screen: Identity in the Age of the Internet*, London: Phoenix, 1996, 83. Gothic Materialism finds a number of these terms uncongenial (for instance: life, screen, identity). Indeed, *Unlife Beyond the Screens* could serve as another subtitle for this study.

These two passage – the first from Gustave Meyrinck's 1927 novel *The Golem*, the second from Sherry Turkle's 1995 work of "cyber-psychology" *Life on the Screen* – take us directly to what will be the guiding preoccupation of this thesis. Meyrinck's novel is a recounting of an old narrative: the Kabbalistic tale of the rabbi who animates lifeless clay, giving form to the monstrous Golem. The myth has many variants. In many cases – and in anticipation of Shelley's *Frankenstein* and Goethe's *The Sorcerer's Apprentice* – the Golem, once animated, and no longer subject to its master's control, runs amok. Turkle's account, meanwhile, concerns the response of children to those newest of cybernetic machines, the personal computer. Across time, Meyrinck's character and the children Turkle is studying have an independent insight into what will be called here the *Gothic flatline*: a plane where it is no longer possible to differentiate the animate from the inanimate and where to have agency is not necessarily to be alive.

It might seem that the children have now accepted what Meyrinck's character found so terrifying. Yet the question Meyrinck's character poses is not quite the one Turkle entertains – which is to say, what if the machines were alive? – but something more radical: what if we are as "dead" as the machines? To pose even this second question seems immediately inadequate: what sense would it be to say that "everything" – human beings and machines, organic and nonorganic matter – is "dead"? Much of what follows is an attempt to answer this question.

Donna Haraway's celebrated observation that "our machines are disturbingly lively, while we ourselves are frighteningly inert"[3] has given this issue a certain currency in contemporary cyber-theory. But what is interesting about Haraway's remark – its challenge to the oppositional thinking that sets up free will against determinism, vitalism against mechanism – has seldom been processed by a mode of theorizing which has tended to reproduce exactly the same oppositions. These theoretical failings, it will be argued here, arise from a resistance to pursuing cybernetics to its limits (a failure evinced as much by cyberneticists as by cultural theorists, it must be added). Unraveling the implications of cybernetics, it will be claimed, takes us out to the Gothic flatline. The Gothic flatline designates a zone of radical immanence. And to theorize this flatline demands a new approach, one committed to the theorization of immanence. This thesis calls that approach Gothic Materialism.

The conjoining of the Gothic with Materialism poses a challenge to the way that the Gothic has been thought. It is a deliberate attempt to disassociate the Gothic from everything supernatural, ethereal or otherwordly. The principal inspiration for this theorization comes from Wilhelm Worringer via Deleuze-Guattari. Both Worringer and Deleuze-Guattari identity the Gothic with "nonorganic life", and whilst this is an equation we shall have cause to query, Gothic Materialism as it is presented here will be fundamentally concerned with a plane that cuts across the distinction between living and nonliving, animate and inanimate. It is this *anorganic continuum*, it will be maintained, that is the province of the Gothic.

---

3. Donna Haraway, "The Cyborg Manifesto", in *Simians, Cyborgs and Women: The Reinvention of Nature*, London: Free Association Books, 1991, 152

At the same time as it aims to displace the Gothic from some of its existing cultural associations, the conjoining of the Gothic with materialism also aims to provoke a rethinking of what materialism is (or can be). Once again, Deleuze-Guattari are the inspirations here, for a rethinking of materialism in terms closer to Horror fiction than to theories of social relations. Deleuze-Guattari's abstract materialism depends upon assemblages such as the Body without Organs (a key Gothic concept, we shall aim to demonstrate), while in their attacks on pyschoanalysis (their defence, for instance, of the *reality* – as opposed to the merely phantasmatic quality – of processes such as becoming-animal) it is often as if they are defending Horror narratives – of vampirism and lycanthropy – against a psychoanalytic reality principle. Moreover, the Deleuze-Guattari take-up of authors as various as Artaud, Spinoza, Schreber and Marx can, we hope to establish, be seen as quintessentially Gothic: what Deleuze-Guattari always emphasise in these writers is the theme of anorganic continuum. But the non- or anorganic Deleuze-Guattari introduce us to is not the dead matter of conventional mechanistic science; on the contrary, it swarms with strange agencies.

The role of cybernetics as we shall theorise it is very much parallel to the theoretical direction Deleuze-Guattari have taken. Cybernetics, it will be argued, has always been haunted by the possibilities Deleuze-Guattari lay out (even if, in certain cases, it has inhibited or impeded them). As a materialist theory, it, too, we will attempt to show, has tended to challenge the boundary between the animate and the inanimate. Like Deleuze-Guattari, it has questioned the confinement of the attribution of agency only to subjects. The kind of fiction with which this study will be concerned – what has variously been labeled cyberpunk, imploded science fiction and body horror (amongst other things) – has been exercised by many of the same concerns as cybernetic theory. Specifically, these texts have been fascinated by the concepts of agency-without-a subject and bodies-without-organs, emerging in the ambivalent form of the blade runners, terminators, and AIs that haunt current mass-mediated-nightmare.

Gothic Materialism is interested in the ways in which what would appear ultramodern – the gleaming products of a technically sophisticated capitalism – end up being described in the ostensibly archaic terms familiar from Horror fiction: zombies, demons. But it will resist the temptation to think of this "demonization of the cybernetic" as the revival of something "something familiar and old-established in the mind." (PFL 14 363), preferring to think of it as the continuation of a nonorganic line that is positively antagonistic to progressive temporality. As Iain Hamilton Grant puts it, "the Terminator has been there before, distributing microchips to accelerate its advent and fuel the primitives' fears."[4] As we shall see, the nonorganic line as occupied by Gothic Materialism is to be distinguished both from "the supernatural" (the supposed province of Horror fiction) and "speculative technology" (the home of Science Fiction).

---

4. "At the Mountains of Madness: The Demonology of the New Earth and the Politics of Becoming" in Keith Ansell-Pearson ed., *Deleuze and Philosophy: The Difference Engineer*, London-New York: Routledge, 1997, 97

The phrase "something familiar and old-established in the mind" belongs, of course, to Freud, who will emerge in the terms of this study as a somewhat ambivalent figure, sometimes an ally, sometimes a foe, of Gothic Materialism. Writing of "animist traces", Turkle is alluding to Freud's famous essay on "The Uncanny", from which this phrase comes, an essay written almost directly contemporaneously with *The Golem*. Here, Freud famously flirts with the problem of the inanimate becoming-active. I say "flirts" because Freud – in what, in the terms of the present thesis, is a clear anti-Gothic gesture – moves to dismiss the importance of this theme. (Nevertheless, his own compulsive need to repeatedly reiterate it, has led to a persistent association in critical writings of the uncanny with exactly the question of *what should not be alive* acting as if it were.) Feelings of the uncanny, Freud insists, are not to be attributed to the confusion of the animate with inanimate, but to a fear of castration. We shall examine Freud's essay on "The Uncanny" in more detail later, but will note, for now, Freud's own failure to keep at bay the problem of animism; the theme has its own kind of living death, stalking him posthumously with the implacability of any zombie. Its very persistence constitutes a powerful argument for another of Freud's theses in "The Uncanny" – one that Gothic Materialism will find much more congenial – the strange, nondialectical, functioning of the "un" prefix. Thinking, no doubt, of his own remarks on the absence of negation in the unconscious[5], Freud establishes that the "un" of "unheimliche" does not straightforwardly reverse the meaning of the word "heimlich". In a – fittingly – disturbing way, "unheimliche" includes heimlich.

"The Uncanny" leaves us with the impression that the source of Freud's critical deflections and circumlocutions is something powerful indeed. Castration may be terrifying, but it is not as *disturbing* as what Freud seems so keen to bury – precisely because it is a matter of terror, or fear. Terror or fear have an object – *what is feared* – and a subject – *he[6] who fears* – whereas the "ominous foreboding" Meyrinck's character experiences arises from the inability to differentiate subject from object. There is a dispersal of subjectivity onto an indifferent plane that is simultaneously too distant and too intimate to be apprehended as anything objective.

This thesis will approach this plane via theorists who have been associated with a critique of psychoanalysis: Deleuze-Guattari, whom we have already introduced, and Baudrillard. Provisionally, we could identify Gothic Materialism with the work of Deleuze-Guattari and "Cybernetic Theory-Fiction" with the work of Baudrillard. But this – simple – opposition, whilst schematically useful, is ultimately misleading. Baudrillard, we shall see, can make a contribution to Gothic Materialism, whilst Deleuze-Guattari's work can certainly be described as Theory-Fiction. Baudrillard's interest in cyber-

---

5. See Freud's essays on "The Unconscious" and *Beyond the Pleasure Principle* in PFL 11 for his argument that the concept of negation is alien to the unconscious.

6. Needless to say, the gender designation here is not accidental, since, as numerous sources have noted, Freud's castration fear presupposes the male as the universal subject. For a particularly powerful critique of this gender-blindness in Freud, see Luce Irigaray, "The Blindspot in an Old Dream of Symmetry" in *Speculum: Of the Other Woman*, trans. Gillian C. Gill, Cornell University Press: Ithaca, New York, 1985

punk fiction and film, his fascination with automata and simulacra, make him both the object of a Gothic Materialist theory, and a contributor to it.

One of the aims of *Flatline Constructs* is to play off Deleuze-Guattari and Baudrillard against each other on the question the Meyrinck's passage poses. In developing theories radically antipathetic to subjectivity, Deleuze-Guattari and Baudrillard have occupied parallel trajectories, sometimes closely inter-meshing, sometimes radically diverging. One common feature is the – cyber-netic – emphasis on *code* (as we shall see, one major difference between them concerns the role of *decoding*).

Baudrillard can also be placed as probably the principal theorist of what we might call the *negativized Gothic*; Baudrillard is the inheritor of a social critical tradition that has tended to cast its narratives about the decline of civi-lization in terms of what it would no doubt think of as metaphors of inorganic unvitality: dead labour (Marx), mechanical reproduction (Benjamin). Standing at the demetaphorized terminal of this trajectory, Baudrillard's work frequent-ly amounts to what is, in effect, a negativized Gothic, which "takes the Guy Debord/J.G. Ballard fascination with 'the virtual commodification or crystal-lization of organic life towards total extinction' further, towards narrating a technological triumph of the inanimate – a negative eschatology, the nullity of all opposition, the dissolution of history, the neutralization of difference and the erasure of any possible configuration of alternate actuality."[7] Production is displaced by a totalized (re)production that a priori excludes novelty; "new" objects and cultural phenomena increasingly operate on an exhausted but im-placable closed-loop, which – in some sense – recapitulates itself in advance. "Necrospection."[8]

Another of the features Deleuze-Guattari share with Baudrillard is the importance they place on fiction. Which leads us to the second term of this study's subtitle – Cybernetic Theory-Fiction – a phrase it is worth unpacking a little now. It is Baudrillard who is most associated with the emergence of theory-fiction as a mode. And it is the role of "third order simulacra" – associ-ated, by Baudrillard, very closely with cybernetics, that, Baudrillard says, "puts an end" to theory and fiction as separate genres. By circulating a series of ex-emplary "fictional" texts – Ridley Scott's *Blade Runner*, William Gibson's *Neu-romancer*, J.G. Ballard's *The Atrocity Exhibition*, and David Cronenberg's *Vid-eodrome* – throughout the study, we will aim to unravel something of what is at stake in the claim that the era of cybernetics eliminates – or smears – the distinction between theory and fiction. In some cases, the performance of theory is quite literal: *The Atrocity Exhibition* and *Videodrome* include characters who are theorists (Dr. Nathan, Professor O'Blivion). But this study will want to take Baudrillard's claim very seriously and approach fictional texts, not sim-ply as literary texts awaiting theoretical "readings", but as themselves already intensely-theoretical.

---

7. Mark Downham, "Cyberpunk", *Vague* 21, 1988, 42

8. Cf "Necrospective", TE 89-99. Like Jarry's dead cyclist, contemporary metro-politan culture only appears to be moving forward because of the inertial weight of its own past (a past it simultaneously annihilates *as* the past, precisely by continually [re] instantiating it as the present).

The thesis is divided into four chapters, whose themes are as follows.

Chapter 1 examines the nexus of postmodernism, cybernetics and the Gothic. The cluster of approaches that have gone under the name "postmodernism", it will be argued, have been haunted by cybernetic themes: in particular, the interlocking notions of automatization and feedback. Beginning with an analysis of *Blade Runner*, which, like Gibson's *Neuromancer*, has frequently been taken to be an exemplary "postmodern" text – and is undoubtedly a key cyberpunk text – the chapter contends that many theorizations of postmodernity have been fundamentally concerned with the impact of machines which can reflect on (and consequently adapt) their own performance. Baudrillard in particular will be seen as an inheritor of cybernetic themes: his Order of Simulacra will be traced back to Wiener's typologization of machines. Following Baudrillard's lead, we will aim to distinguish the features proper to what Baudrillard calls the fiction of third order simulacra (cybernetics as such). In parallel, the chapter also aims to show ways in which Cybernetics has been haunted by the Gothic. It rehearses Worringer's account of the Gothic line in *Form in Gothic* and *Abstraction and Empathy*. By reference to both Gibson and Deleuze-Guattari, the concept of the Gothic *flatline* will be introduced. The term comes from *Neuromancer*, and designates states adrift between life and death, or states of simulated life, but will be taken up here as a more general name for the radically immanent line described by Gothic Materialism. The chapter will also show the importance, to Deleuze-Guattari, of the *language* of Horror – the recurrence of descriptions of phenomena in terms of vampirism, zombification, etc. It will be claimed that this is part of a "realism about the hyperreal" or "cybernetic realism" which emerges as equivalent to what will be characterized as the *hypernatural*. The hypernatural will be positioned as an intensification of naturalism, and by opposition the supernatural.

Chapter 2 approaches that commonplace of contemporary theory, "the body", but it does so by opposing a – Gothic Materialist – concept of the body (the Artaud/Deleuze-Guattari body without organs) to what it calls a "Science Fictional" body. Reinforcing arguments made in the first chapter, it will be argued that "cyberpunk" fictions need to be placed under the sign of a Horror fiction that has been freed from any reference to the supernatural. Baudrillard's essay on Ballard is a crucial resource here. Here, Baudrillard argues that traditionally SF has been complicit with "classical" accounts of the body and technology. What makes cyberpunk Gothic Materialist, it will be argued, is the departure from an instrumental view of technology and the organs. Technology is no longer seen, that is to say, as a simple extension of organic function. A genealogy of the Science Fictional body will be laid out, passing from Freud through to McLuhan; but these same theorists, it will be shown, also display themes anticipative of cyberpunk. The chapter concludes with an analysis of two texts that have posed a challenge to the Science Fictional body: Cronenberg's *Videodrome* and Ballard's *The Atrocity Exhibition*. Cronenberg's film quite literally opens up the body. We will parallel the invaginated body of *Videodrome* – a body unable to process the amount of stimuli with which it is bombarded – with McLuhan's autoamputated body and Baudrillard's schizophrenic body. Baudrillard's equation of cybernetic circuitries with "schizophrenia" will be paralleled with Jameson's theories of postmodern subjectivity, and Deleuze-Guattari's theories of capitalism. Both these themes – the disruption of organismic interiority, and the concomitant emergence of "schizophrenia" – had already emerged in Ballard's novel, which explicitly deals with the question of schizophrenia, and radical deterritorializations of the body. It will be shown that some of Ballard's most important (ficto-theoretical) coinages – the spinal landscape, the media landscape – point to the key Gothic Materialist intuition of anorganic continuum.

Chapter 3 focuses on what has always been a theme in Gothic texts (even when the Gothic is conventionally conceived); something that has also been a theme in writings on cybernetics. The artificialization of reproduction was posed as a possibility in the Golem legend, and more recently in the founding story of modern Horror and Science Fiction, Mary Shelley's *Frankenstein*. It has also been posited by cybernetics, not only in respect of the reproduction of human beings, but also in connection with the reproduction of machines themselves. This chapter uses Baudrillard and Deleuze-Guattari to provide a framework for examining this theme in fiction, by opposing the former's concept of an ever more perfect reproduction with the latter's ideas of multiplicitous recombination. In both cases, what is crucial is a supercession of the sexual as such. Baudrillard offers a theorization of reproduction in terms of what we have called the "negativized Gothic" (see above): the dream of the perfect copy, which always goes badly wrong. Deleuze-Guattari, meanwhile, take as their models not organic reproduction, but the explicitly Gothic figures of vampirism, lycanthropy, and disease: what they call *propagation*. The account of propagation will be preceded by a discussion of the concept of "surplus value of code", introduced by Deleuze-Guattari in *Anti-Oedipus*. This involves a discussion of Samuel Butler's important work of theory-fiction, "The Book of Machines" (in his *Erewhon*), which offers numerous ingenious arguments contradicting the idea that machines are unable to reproduce themselves. In arguments reconstructed by Deleuze-Guattari in *Anti-Oedipus*, Butler shows that the fact that human beings are involved in the reproduction – or replication – of machines does not mean that they lack a reproductive system: on the contrary, human beings form *part* of such a system. The chapter concludes with an analysis of Gibson's *Neuromancer*, which will be shown to display themes of Baudrillard's ultra-mechanical reproduction and Deleuze-Guattari's sorcerous propagation.

Chapter 4 moves into territory associated with Baudrillard, the theorization of hyperreality in terms of the emergence of cybernetic systems, but aims to move beyond Baudrillard's position of terminal melancholy. The role of fiction itself is a crucial theme here. The chapter recounts Baudrillard's narrative about the triumph of cybernetic modeling systems (supposedly bringing the end of what might be called the category of "the marvelous"), comparing and contrasting it with Gibson's description of the return of demonism in the cyberspace Matrix. Where Baudrillard's story ends with the burial of the "primitive double", the other narrative posits the return of animistic themes, and presents a mode of recursion radically opposed to one based upon a simple reiteration of the same. The question of the return of animism in a cybernetic era will be discussed, and animism will be compared with Deleuze-Guattari's machinism. The theme of recursion will be dealt with here in terms of the opposition between two processes (associated with two types of fiction): hyper and meta. Metafiction will be placed on the side of an *imploded transcendence*. This will be opposed to *hyperfiction* (and to hyper-processes in general), which can be defined by its radical immanence, as found in Deleuze-Guattari's rhizome. The chapter – and indeed the thesis – concludes with an analysis of John Carpenter's recent film *In the Mouth of Madness*, which will be shown to describe (if not quite display) many of the features of hyperfiction.

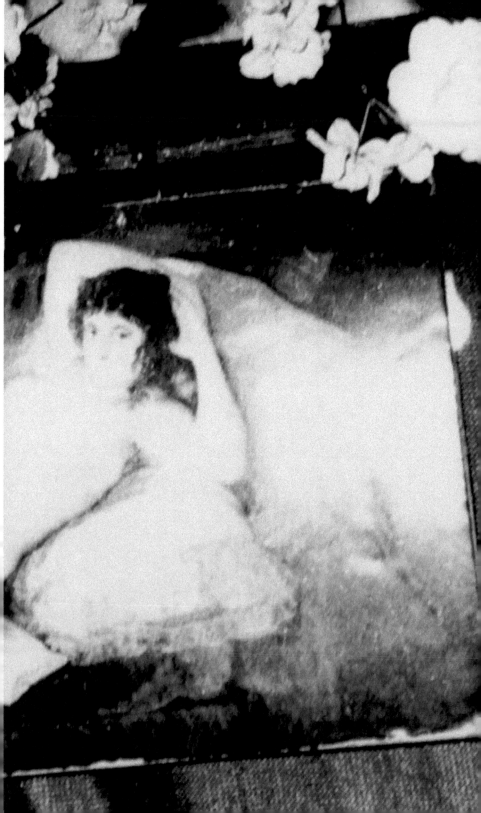

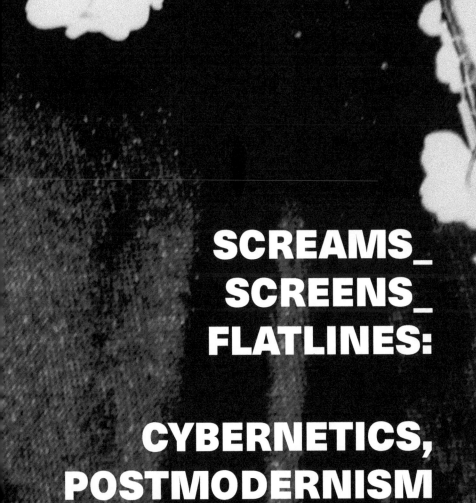

SCREAMS_ SCREENS_ FLATLINES:

CYBERNETICS, POSTMODERNISM AND THE GOTHIC

1.1 HOW AN ANDROID MUST FEEL

Deckard: "Replicants weren't supposed to have feelings. Neither were Blade Runners."[1]

There's an intriguing scene in the middle of Philip K. Dick's *Do Androids Dream of Electric Sheep?*, a novel best known now as the source of Ridley Scott's *Blade Runner* (1982). Rick Deckard and Phil Resch, two bounty hunters whose prey is not human beings but androids, have pursued a target to a museum where a Munch exhibition is showing. Pausing in front of what is evidently *The Scream* – "[t]wisted ripples of the creature's torment, echoes of its cry, flooded out into the air surrounding it; the man or woman, whatever it was, had become contained by its own howl" – Resch comments, "I think [...] this is how an andy must feel."[2]

To anyone acquainted with Fredric Jameson's analyses, the connection Resch makes should raise a number of questions. For Jameson, "*The Scream* is a canonical expression of the great modernist thematics of alienation, anomie, solitude, isolation, a virtually programmatic emblem of what used to be called the age of anxiety" (PCLLC 11), whereas Dick's novel, and *Blade Runner*, have been held up (not least by Jameson himself[3]) as quintessentially postmodern. If *The Scream* does really communicate the "alienation, anomie, solitude" appropriate to a melancholy human(ist) subjectivity, as Jameson suggests, how can an android – nonhuman simulacrum of the human – have any affinity with it? Is there something to account for the appearance of expressionist imagery and thematics in *Blade Runner* other than the notorious "pastiche" effect? What does an android *feel*, any way?

To begin to answer these questions is to start to pick apart the theoretical approaches that have dominated commentary on *Blade Runner* and Dick. This will involve, initially, weaving a few more strands in the already-existing rhizome theory has run around, and through, *Blade Runner*. Much commentary has already made the connection between Scott's film and the almost directly contemporary "cyberpunk" fiction of William Gibson, thereby clicking onto a literary genealogy that includes Burroughs and Ballard as well as Dick.

---

1. From the *Blade Runner* script. Here, as with all the right-justified quotations in the thesis, italics have been added.

2. Dick, *Do Androids Dream of Electric Sheep?*, London: HarperCollins, 1993, 100

3. As we shall see below: see especially *The Seeds of Time*, New York: Columbia University Press, 1994, 146-149, and *The Geopolitical Aesthetic: Cinema and Space in the World System*, Bloomington and Indiana/ London: Indiana University Press/ BFI publishing, 1992 , 12

Parallels have also been made with the films of David Cronenberg[4]. Critical reception of these authors has been dominated by debates on "postmodernism" and "postmodernity"; theorists with a variety of responses to postmodernism – negative (Christopher Lasch[5]), ambivalent (Kellner[6] and Jameson), and neutral (McHale[7]) – have cited one or all of them as exemplars of postmodern practice. Jameson famously goes so far as to call cyberpunk "the supreme *literary* expression, if not of postmodernism then of late capitalism itself." (PCLLC 38)

What follows will not reject these postmodernist approaches so much as it will envelop them, as it will envelop cyberpunk fiction, into what it will call *Gothic Materialism*. To suggest that many of Gothic Materialism's principal resources come from Deleuze-Guattari's *Capitalism and Schizophrenia* is not to imply that it is in some sense a transcendent deployment (or application) of Deleuze-Guattari's work, in part because whatever Gothic Materialism can use, it becomes. So when it emerges, Gothic materialism describes Deleuze-Guattari (not the other way around), their work appearing now as a clicking together of Gothic authors whose names are legion: Lovecraft, Artaud, Freud, Marx, Schreber, Worringer...

In part, then, what follows will present a materialist critique of postmodernism. The kind of postmodernist theorists Gothic Materialism interfaces with is are those it already haunts – not thinkers who process reality through a textualist or linguistic grid, but theorists who understand "postmodernity" as an essentially material phenomenon, describing its effects primarily in terms of the impact that new telecommercial configurations have on the human nervous system: Jameson, certainly, but also Baudrillard, and one of his key antecedents, Marshall McLuhan.

Prompted by what, at first sight, appears to be an invasion of the human body by technology, McLuhan and Baudrillard's work follows the metapsychological Freud in describing a becoming-technical of the organism. As we shall see in more detail in the next chapter, this reverses the idea of "ex-

---

4. Scott Bukatman's *Terminal Identity: the Virtual Subject in Postmodern Science Fiction* (Durham and London: Duke University Press, 1991) makes a somewhat unsatisfactory attempt to connect all these figures. Jameson, meanwhile, has written at length on Gibson (*Seeds of Time* 146-149), Ballard (PCLLC 55-80), Dick (PCLLC 279-287) and Cronenberg (*Geopolitical Aesthetic* 22-32).

5. See Lasch, *The Minimal Self: Psychic Survival in Troubled Times*, London: Pan, 1984, especially the chapter, "The Minimalist Aesthetic: Art and Literature in an Age of Extremity", which discusses Burroughs and Ballard.

6. See Douglas Kellner, "David Cronenberg: Panic Horror and the Postmodern Body", *Canadian Journal of Political and Social Theory*, vol 13, 3, 1989

7. See Brian McHale, *Postmodernist Fiction*, New York and London: Methuen, 1987, which discusses Ballard, Burroughs and Dick, and "POSTcyberMODERNpunkISM", (in Larry McCaffrey, ed., *Storming the Reality Studio: A Casebook of Cyberpunk and Postmodern Fiction*), Durham and London: Duke University Press, 1991, which discusses all of the above, plus Gibson.

tensions of man" McLuhan develops in *Understanding Media*. The concept of media as extensions of the human body is a direct echo of the organicist confidence Freud had displayed in *Civilization and its Discontents* when he wrote of technology making "Man […] a prosthetic God."[8] What Baudrillard picks up on is the other side of Freud (and the other side of McLuhan): a side that doesn't stress the extension of an organic interiority, or its invasion, but the folding Out of interiority into a pure exteriority, registered by the subject as shock or trauma.

For Baudrillard, then, the cultural reconfigurations that Jameson identifies do not mark the end of the age of anxiety, as Jameson thinks; rather, they usher in another, new, era of anxiety. The characteristics of this new age of anxiety had already been delineated by McLuhan. Whereas "[m]odernist anxiety is founded on the inescapability of individual freedom; its themes are individual solitude, social fragmentation, and alienation." By contrast, "McLuhan's anxiety", in anticipation of Baudrillard's, "is exactly contrary: it has its origins in a social disalienation and the denial (or penetration by the media, and so by everyone else) of any margins of solitude or alienation. Modernist anxiety involves the withdrawal to an imaginary identity resistant to immersion in the forms of modernization. McLuhan's postmodern anxiety has given up this resistant identity, and has no anchorage in individual thought or feeling."[9]

Which brings us back to Munch, to Dick, and to Jameson, who comes across *The Scream* during the course of his celebrated discussion of the "waning of affect". In positing a "waning of affect", Jameson does not want to argue, he insists, "that the cultural products of the postmodern era are utterly devoid of feeling, but rather that such feelings – which it may be better and more accurate, following J.F. Lyotard, to call 'intensities' – are now free-floating and impersonal and tend to be dominated by a peculiar kind of euphoria." (PCLLC, 16) This "peculiar kind of euphoria" – feeling floating free from any qualification by the personal – is what Baudrillard has called *ecstasy*. Ecstasy – which has an ostensibly inverse but effectively indistinguishable state, dread – arises when the subject is jacked into late capitalism's network of cybernetic communications. Plugged into the network, traversed by it, Baudrillard's Terminal Man knows that retreat into private space is no longer an option, and this awareness generates a new sense of terror – for Baudrillard "the state of terror proper to the schizophrenic: too great a proximity of everything, the unclean promiscuity of everything which touches, invests and penetrates without

---

8. "With every tool man is perfecting his own organs, whether motory or sensory, or is removing the limits to their functioning," Freud writes there. "Man has, as it were, become a kind of prosthetic God. When he puts on all his auxiliary organs he is truly magnificent; but these organs have not grown on to him and they still give him trouble at times." "Civilization and its Discontents" in *Penguin Freud Library*, Volume 12, *Civilization, Society and Religion*, 279, 280

9. Wilmott, *McLuhan, or Modernism in Reverse*, Toronto-Buffalo-London: University of Toronto Press, 1996, 170

resistance, with no halo of private projection to protect him anymore."[10]

Both dread and ecstasy arise from a loss of the sense of self as a de-limitable entity: a white- or black-out of identity that can just as easily be experienced as terror or euphoria "(dread is a kind of jouissance-in-negative, a slow subsidence into uncontrol and panic)."[11] Following Lyotard through his rerouting of Kantian aesthetics, Jameson calls this "simultaneous apprehension of ecstasy and dread" the postmodern sublime.

For Gothic Materialism, the sublime still belongs to a human(ist) aesthetics of representation (precisely because it fixes what lies beyond representation as *the unrepresentable*). Gothic Materialism's aesthetic theory, as we shall see below, derives not from Burke and Kant (nor from some postmodern reinvention of their theories), but from Wilhelm Worringer, whose two treatises on "barbarian art", *Form in Gothic* and *Abstraction and Empathy* – both re-animated by Deleuze-Guattari in *A Thousand Plateaus* - oppose representation not to the unrepresentable, but to *the abstract*. Gothic Materialism is above all an abstract materialism, distinguished from other types of materialism, (including what Baudrillard disparagingly refers to as "anthropo-Marxism" [SED 140), and from every sort of idealism, by its focusing principally on the organ grinder – the nonorganic processes of stratification that produce the organism – rather than the monkey – anthropoid consciousness as manifested in an experience of subjectivity screened through the (Freudian) perceptual-consciousness-system. Such processes have agents, but they are not human, humanistic, or subjectivist; they are "Abstract Machines."[12]

In other words, Gothic Materialism takes literally what "Marx critically denounced as the *'fantasy'* of capital as 'an automatic system of machinery … set in motion by an automaton, a moving power that moves itself'.[13] It as-

10. Baudrillard, "The Ecstasy of Communication", in *The Anti-Aesthetic: Essays on Postmodern Culture*, ed. Hal Foster, Port Townsend: Washington Bay Press, 1983, 132

11. Simon Reynolds, *Blissed Out: The Raptures of Rock*, London: Serpent's Tail, 1991, 169

12. The concept of abstract machines is an important one for Deleuze-Guattari. It is important to stress that abstract machines "[are] opposed to the abstract in the ordinary sense." (TP 511) "There is no abstract machines, or machines, in the sense of a Platonic Idea, transcendent, universal, eternal. Abstract machines operate within concrete assemblages." (TP 510) Abstract machines are the principle of operation immanent to the workings of any machine. They "know nothing of forms and substances. This is what makes them abstract." (TP 511) "Abstract, singular, and creative, here and now, real yet nonconcrete, actual yet noneffectuated – that is why abstract machines are dated and named (the Einstein abstract machine, the Webern abstract machine)" (TP 511) One example of an abstract machine Deleuze-Guattari give is Foucault's diagram of discipline. (TP 66-67) What Foucault makes possible, they point out, is an abstract description of ostensibly disparate empirical phenomena: prisons, schools, hospitals. These institutions instantiate a single abstract machine of discipline, but this is to be explained as an emergent phenomena, arriving bottom-up, rather than as the top-down imposition of a macro-subjective will.

13. Iain Hamilton Grant, "Los Angeles 2019: Demopathy and Xenogenesis (Some

sumes, with Deleuze-Guattari's schizoanalysis, that the possibility of transcendently critiquing capitalism, kept alive in a mournful kind of way by Jameson, ostensibly abandoned but effectively retained by Baudrillard, has always been dysfunctional, for the simple reason that "[c]apitalism defines a field of immanence and never ceases to occupy this field." (AO 250) While anthropo-Marxism still posits a transcendent and authentic human agent which could overcome capital, Gothic Materialism takes it for granted that real materialism must involve total immanentization; one of its chief resources, therefore, is the philosopher whose whole work was devoted to developing a rigorously immanent account of agency: Spinoza.

For Spinoza, there is agency everywhere but this never belongs to human subjects. *The Ethics*, therefore, does not identify subjects (or objects); rather it *entifies*. Spinoza disontologises all subjective, generic and species distinctions into a single Gothic classification: the Entity. "[W]e are wont to classify all the individuals in Nature under one genus, namely, the notion of Entity, which pertains to all individuals in Nature without exception." (ETH, IV, Pref: 153) Bodies are defined, not by form or function, but as processes; in other words, "True Entities are events."[14]

Crucial in this respect is Deleuze-Guattari's concept of the haecceity. The haecceity can be defined briefly as non-subjectified individuation. It is individuation as intensive multiplicity, not extensive address. For Deleuze-Guattari ("Memories of a Haecceity" [TP 260-265]), the haecceity "is a mode of individuation very different from that of a person, subject, thing or substance. [...] A season, a winter, summer, an hour, a date have a perfect individuality lacking nothing, even though this individuality is different from that of a thing or a subject." (TP 261) The haecceity is the entity as event (and the event as entity); it occurs when things "cease to be subjects to become events" (TP 262). "It should not be thought that a haecceity consists simply of a decor or backdrop that situates subjects, or of appendages that hold things and people to the ground," Deleuze-Guattari warn. "It is the entire assemblage in its individuated aggregate that is a haecceity." (TP 262) The Gothic has an affinity with the concept of the haecceity because it refuses to distinguish human figures from backgrounds; "the 'Gothic or Northern' decorative line" is "a broken line which forms no contour by which form and background might be distinguished."[15] You can't enter such zones without entering into composition with them.

Realist Notes on *Blade Runner* and the Postmodern Condition)," unpublished paper, 1997, no page refs. Quotation from Marx's *Grundrisse*.

14. Deleuze and Parnet, *Dialogues*, trans. Hugh Tomlinson and Barbara Habberjam, New York: Columbia University Press, 1987, 66. To make the Gothic link explicit, Deleuze and Parnet go on to refer to Lovecraft's Randolph Carter (also discussed in TP 240) "ENTITY= EVENT, it is terror, but also great joy. Becoming an entity, an infinitive, as Lovecraft spoke of it, the horrific and luminous story of Carter: animal-becoming, molecular-becoming, imperceptible-becoming." (66)

15. Deleuze, *Cinema 1*, 111

Haecceities, Deleuze-Guattari say, find expression in a "particular semiotic": "This semiotic is composed above all of proper names, verbs in the
infinitive and indefinite articles or pronouns. *Indefinite article + proper name +
infinitive verb* constitutes the basic chain of expression [...] of a semiotic that
has freed itself from both formal signifiances and personal subjectifications."
(TP 263) Deleuze-Guattari's vindication of this semiotic – a positivization of
the indefinite – is simultaneously a theory of Horror, a critique of psychoanalysis and a program for cyberotics. Whereas psychoanalysis, Deleuze-Guattari
argue, always seeks to reduce the indefinite to the definite – "When the child
says '*a* belly', '*a* horse', 'how do *people* grow up?' '*someone* is beating *a* child', the
psychoanalyst hears 'my belly,' 'the father,' will I grow up to be like daddy?'"
(TP 264) – rhizomatics understands that desire operates through the indefinite: "*Flat multiplicities* [...] are designated by indefinite articles, or rather by
partitives (*some* couchgrass, *some* of a rhizome)." (TP, 9) The Gothic use of
such terms as "the unnamable", "the Thing", "the nameless" – favoured by
Deleuze-Guattari themselves – implies a modification of this model: here, indefinite adverb-nouns function to de-definitize definite articles.

Gothic Materialism is flat with its material; it names both the mode of
analysis and what is to be analysed. It does not arbitrarily conjoin materialism
with the Gothic, but insists that all effective materialism must lead Out towards
a non-organic (dis)continuum. Amongst other things, the Gothic can serve
as a proper name for this continuum[16]; and cyberpunk is the registering of its
arrival on the terminals of a wired humanity. Whilst an organicist Left social

---

16. Much of what follows will be an attempt to rigorise a definition of the Gothic,
which, like the cyber- prefix, has often been used imprecisely or in a way that is un-
helpfully general. (This may account for the widespread failure to perceive the connection between cyberpunk and the Gothic.) Judith Halberstam's "definition" of the
Gothic as "the rhetorical style and narrative structure designed to produce fear and
desire in the reader" (*Skin Shows: Gothic Horror and the Technology of Monsters*, Durham
and London: Duke University Press, 1995, 2) for instance, is emblematic of these
failings. Whilst the version of the Gothic that will be employed in this study cannot
be put in a nutshell – in part because it designates something "'teeming, seething,
swelling, foaming, spreading like an infectious disease, [...] [a] nameless horror '"(TP
245) – it does have a number of specific features which will be delineated. It is not a
vague synonym for everything transgressive or morbid (as it seems to be, for instance,
for Christopher Grunenberg ["Unsolved Mysteries: Gothic Tales from *Frankenstein* to
the Hair Eating Doll" in *Gothic:Transmutations of Horror in Late Twentieth Century
Art* , Cambridge Mass./ London: the MIT Press 1997]). As should quickly become
apparent, Gothic Materialism has little in common with what Jameson (PCLLC 289-
291) calls "modern gothic". Jameson's modern gothic, which concerns the bolstering
of a social and individual identity by means of the construction/ projection of an
Other, bears more relation to what James Donald terms "the vulgar sublime." Donald
('What's at Stake in Vampire Films? The Pedagogy of Monsters" in *Sentimental Ed-
ucation: Schooling, Popular Culture and the Regulation of Liberty*, London: Verso 1992)
makes a connection between pulp fictions – Gothic, melodrama – and the high theory
of Lyotard and Kristeva. But Donald's vulgar sublime is ultimately contained within
the problematics of representation: the boundaries of the subject are disturbed (in

criticism finds in cyberpunk the quietist collapse of transformative political projects into a "hardboiled" "survivalist" hyper-nihilism[17], Gothic Materialism locates in Baudrillard's ecstatic communication, Gibson's Cyberspace, Jameson's total flow and Cronenberg's Videodrome the map of a hypermediatized capitalism that is decoding privatized subjectivity. Organicist postmodern theory has tended to read cyberpunk as the apogee of Cartesianism, the story – now told, in part, ironically – of the triumph of disembodied Mind over docile body (this latter referred to by Gibson's cybserspace cowboys as "meat"). Told this way, the story has inevitably gender implications: it is a re-run of the old narrative of the hylomorphic domination of Nature by Man. For Andrew Ross, for instance, "Cyberpunk male bodies [... are] spare, lean, and temporary bodies whose social functionality could only be maintained through the reconstructive aid of a whole range of genetic overhauls and cybernetic enhancements – boosterware, biochip wetware, cyberoptics, bioplastic surgery, designer drugs, nerve amplifiers, prosthetic limbs and organs, memoryware, neural interface plugs and the like." Yet this is still to buy into the story the cowboys tell themselves, a story which the narratives they are embedded in refuse to maintain; it is to treat "the body" as the container for/ of a Self which will ultimately escape it (in techno-transcendence). Ross is aware that cyberpunk is much more ambivalent than this; that it also tells of the invasion of the (male) organism by technical machines. Deliberately echoing the Baudrillard of "The Ecstasy of Communication", he describes the cyberpunk "body as a switching system with no purely organic integrity to defend or advance, and only further enhancements of technological 'edge' to gain in the struggle for technological advantage. These enhancements and retrofits were technotoys that the boys had always dreamed of having, but they were also body-altering and castrating in ways that boys always had nightmares about." (152-3)

Yet, as we have already seen, to oppose invasion of the organism with its extension is still not to process the materialist critique cyberpunk presents: the Spinozistic/cybernetic unravelling of the organism back into its environment. Ross always recodes cyberpunk sensations in terms of a psychopathology and a politics – an affective range – whose continuing purchase on contemporary reality the very existence of cyberpunk radically questions. Despite sharing some of Ross's attachment to transcendent social criticism, Jameson nevertheless recognises that the new cultural configurations cannot be theorised using this old (psychoanalytical) language. What he calls the decline of

---

discourse) rather than, as with Gothic Materialism, materially dismantled (in practice). One problem with these approaches is that they maintain a distinction between texts and theory; theorists are still given the role of reading/ interpreting the (political) unconscious of/ for texts. Gothic Materialism, meanwhile, treats "texts" as already intensely theoretical.

17. Ross, Andrew, "Cyberpunk in Boystown", *Strange Weather: Culture, Science and Technology in the Age of Limits*, London/ New York: Verso, 1991, 153

affect is signalled in part by a liberation " from the older *anomie* of the centered subject", an ambiguous "liberation" which " may also mean a liberation from every other kind of feeling as well, since there is no longer a self present to do the feeling" (PCLLC, 16). Jameson's analysis here parallels that of Baudrillard in suggesting that "the end of the bourgeois ego, or monad" brings with it a concomitant "end of the pyschopathologies of that ego" (PCLLC, 16) ("No more hysteria, no more projective paranoia," Baudrillard announces in "The Ecstasy of Communication" (EC 132]).

If, as Baudrillard says, there is no more hysteria, then – contra Ross – there is no more castration either. For Baudrillard, as we have seen, castration fear has become reversed; media implicitly "feminize", not cutting man off, but "penetrating without resistance." The dread here corresponds to the masculine terror Klaus Theweleit describes in *Male Fantasies*: it is a terror of being inundated, overwhelmed by what Jameson calls the "total flow" (PCLLC 70, 76-78, 86, 90) of hyperconnected cybernetic culture. Cyberpunk registers a trauma that Ross, apparently secure in his organic interiority, still thinks can be commented upon from the point of view of an unproblematic humanist transcendence. The terror, for Gibson's characters, and for Cronenberg's, is not just, or even primarily, that the interior of their bodies will be invaded, but that *they do not have any insides.*

This dread gives rise to the startling images of Cronenberg's *Videodrome.* Infamously, at one point in the film, the lead character Max Renn's "body literally opens up – his stomach develops a massive, vaginal slit – to accommodate a new videocassette 'programme'. Image addiction and image virus reduce the subject to the status of a videotape player/ recorder; the human body mutates to become a part of the massive system of reproductive technology."[18] This is a new type of dread, emerging in theory and fiction simultaneously.

As a registering of this new horror, *Videodrome*, like Baudrillard's "Ecstasy of Communication"[19], is a kind of cyberpunk sequel to Freud's (anti) Gothic tale, "The Uncanny". There Freud keeps Gothic terror at bay by attributing the feelings of "dread and anxiety" to a fear of castration. By the time of Baudrillard and *Videodrome*, the phallic visual scene Freud sought to erect has collapsed into a terrible, cloying tactile intimacy: what Baudrillard's calls the *obscene.* The equation Freud makes between the eye and the penis is no longer relevant in conditions where there is no distance (specular or otherwise): you can't touch without being touched. You can't penetrate what already envelops you. Gibson: "The matrix folds around me like an origami trick."[20]

---

18. Bukatman, "Who Programs You: The Science Fiction of the Spectacle?", in Annette Kuhn ed., *Alien Zone: Cultural Theory and Contemporary Science Fiction Cinema* , London: Verso, 1990, 206

19. Bukatman's "Who Programs You" offers an extensive comparison of *Videodrome* and Baudrillard.

20. Gibson, *Burning Chrome*, London: Grafton, 1986

To simulate the POV of the androids in Dick's novel is to be drawn to where you – as subject – are turned inside Out. To begin to see what the androids could see in Munch's painting, is to realise that, for them, it must show not the inevitability of solitary interiority, but its impossibility; the painting's "loops and spirals" diagramming now not the projection of a subjective state outwards, but the enormous pressure – "inwards" – of an exteriority "which touches, invests and penetrates without resistance", and which produces the subject, as Deleuze-Guattari would want to say, as a residuum or side-effect. ("[T]he subject [is] produced as residuum alongside the machines, as an appendix, or as a spare part adjacent to the machine." [AO 16-22]) For Gothic Materialism this, as much as the more familiar inventory of modernist angst-states, is what Munch and the rest of Expressionism was always getting at.

So it will be argued here that cybernetic capitalism does not engender what Ballard has followed Jameson in identifying as a "death of affect." Those switched on to Spinozism by Deleuze-Guattari might suspect the reverse; that what defines the "postmodern" is in fact the amplification of affect. Brian Massumi suggests that the theorization of "intensity" Jameson calls for is to be achieved precisely by paying renewed attention to the phenomenon of affect and to Spinoza as its principal theorist. "It is crucial," Massumi argues, "to theorize the difference between emotion and affect." "An emotion is a subjective content, the socio-linguistic fixing of the quality of an experience which is from that point on defined as personal. Emotion is qualified intensity, the conventional, consensual point of insertion of intensity into semantically formed progressions, into narrativizable action-reaction circuits, into function and meaning. It is intensity owned and recognised [...] If some have the impression that affect has waned, it is because affect is unqualified."[21]

To account for these abstract feelings ("abstract is a word for sensations so new they don't have a name yet"[22]), demands a new affective register, and a new type of "realism" – not any more the "empirical realism" described and delimited by Kant in the name of transcendental philosophy and echoed in the conventions of the bourgeois realist novel, but a *cybernetic* realism[23]: a theory-fiction for an artificial reality.

Bacon: "The more artificial you can make it, the greater the chance of its looking real."[24]

21. Brian Massumi, "The Autonomy of Affect", unpublished paper, 7

22. Kodwo Eshun, "Motion Capture (Interview)", Abstract Culture 2, winter 97

23. This term comes from Grant "Los Angeles 2019".

24. David Sylvester, *The Brutality of Fact: Interviews with Francis Bacon*, London: Thames and Hudson 1987, 148

1.2 CYBERNETICS, POSTMODERNISM, FICTION

<u>Gothic Materialism</u>, *1st Definition: Gothic materialism is equivalent to cybernetic realism.*

Written a few years ahead of key cyberpunk texts such as *Blade Runner* and *Neuromancer*, Baudrillard's two essays on SF, "Simulacra and Science Fiction" and "Crash", are stunningly prescient in their recognition "that the good old imaginary of science fiction is dead and that something else is in the process of emerging (not only in fiction but in theory as well). The same wavering and indeterminate fate puts an end to science fiction – but also to theory, as specific genres." (SS 121) The theme of the end of theory (and its absorption into a science fiction which is no longer one) will be taken up more fully in Chapter 4; for now, we will concentrate on the collapse of science fiction.

Cyberpunk conforms to Baudrillard's prophecies to such a degree that it threatens to go beyond them. This is more than a question of "*Neuromancer* and other novels, [providing] stunning examples of how realist, 'extrapolative' science fiction can operate as prefigurative social theory"[25], although it certainly involves this; it is a matter of fictional concepts becoming what used to be called Social Facts – the most obvious example of this phenomenon being the migration of Gibson's "cyberspace" from fiction out into (post) social reality.

Baudrillard's own examples of the "new science fiction that is not one" are Dick and Ballard (two influences Gibson has repeatedly acknowledged). It is precisely Ballard and Baudrillard's shared sense of immanence, their refusal – Jameson would want to say inability – to offer any kind of social criticism that make both quintessentially "postmodern" in Jameson's terms. Unlike Baudrillard, for whom, "SF proper" replaces the utopian as a mode, Jameson assumes that, in its more confident period, science fiction was very much in the business of dealing with utopia. According to Jameson, the critical examination of images of utopia in SF novels such as Ursula LeGuin's *The Dispossessed* meant that these fictions were capable of exercising political responsibility in a way that the new science fiction cannot. (PCLLC 160) (As we shall see, for the Jameson of *The Seeds of Time*, *Blade Runner* becomes a privileged example of this phenomenon because it apparently exemplifies all the features of the old

25. Mike Davis, "Beyond Blade Runner: Urban Control The Ecology of Fear", Westfield NJ: Open Magazine Pamphlets, 1992: 4

dystopian fiction, yet it is clearly not dystopian.)

Scornful of the aspirations of the leftist transformational project to which Jameson is still committed, Baudrillard is particularly delighted by Ballard's refusal of the binary "function/ dysfunction", by his complete abandonment of any moral or political/critical stance[26]. For Baudrillard, the dream of transformation belongs to the "productive, Promethean" era – industrialism – that cybernetics has terminated. Like cybernetics itself, the fictions characteristic of the new era are "immanent and thus leave no room for any kind of imaginary transcendence." (SS 122)

In what follows, the emphasis will be placed on cybernetics rather than postmodernism, in part because it will be argued that cybernetics plays a crucial part in the genealogical development of what has been called postmodern theory. In his somewhat pompous essay "The Postmodern Dead End", Felix Guattari attributes all postmodern thought to "hastily developed, [and] poorly mastered [...]" references made in the immediate postwar period to "the new communications and computer technologies." "The secret link that binds these various doctrines stems, I believe, from a subterranean relationship – marked by reductionist conceptions, and conveyed immediately after the war by information theory and cybernetic research."[27] Whilst not wanting to be quite so peremptory as Guattari, it will be argued here that postmodernist theory – in particular that of Jameson and Baudrillard – is substantially given over to description of processes that are often explicitly identified as "cybernetic"[28].

---

26. Except in Ballard's commentaries on his own fiction, which, Baudrillard complains, reinscribe the moral frameworks the novels efface. See "Crash". For a bizarre cyborganicist polemic against this, see Vivian Sobchack "Beating the Meat/Surviving the Text, or How to Get out of this Century Alive" in Mike Featherstone and Roger Burrows ed., *Cyberspace/Cyberbodies/Cyberpunk: Cultures of Technological Embodiment*, London-Thousand Oaks-New Delhi: Sage 1995

27. Felix Guattari, *The Guattari Reader*, ed. Gary Genosko, Oxford/ Cambridge Mass.: 1996, 111

28. This is even the case with Lyotard's *The Postmodern Condition* - which will not be considered in any detail here – despite Lyotard actually making a point of attempting to actively differentiate the "postmodern" thought he is developing from cybernetic frameworks. According to Peter Gallison, though, "the link between" cybernetics and Lyotard's version of the postmodern "is profound and the continuity nearly complete." Lyotard "nervously contended that his social analysis [...] departed from cybernetics" but, Gallison shows that the three ways in which Lyotard attempts to distinguish his own position from that of cybernetic are unconvincing. First, Lyotard attacks cybernetics for treating messages homogeneously, claiming that it fails to distinguish "denotatives, prescriptives, evaluatives, performatives, etc." but "at least two of Lyotard's categories (denotative and prescriptive) directly parallel Wiener's distinction between the indicative and imperative modes of messages." Second, Lyotard argues that "a cybernetic machine does indeed run on information, but the goals programmed in to it [leave no way] to correct in the course of its functioning [...] its own performance." But this "self-correction is *exactly* what Wiener's machines did." Third, Lyotard's claim that "the trivial cybernetic version of information" misses the "agonistic aspect of society" is similarly misconstrued: "it was on the agonistic field

Briefly, the crucial insight of cybernetics as presented in Wiener's 1948 *Cybernetics, or Control and Communication in the Animal and the Machine* and in the later *The Human Use of Human Beings* concerned feedback: "the property of being able to adjust future conduct by past performance." (HUHB 33) In the Second World War, Wiener had worked on Anti-aircraft weaponry, whose efficacy depended upon the ability of the machines "to record the performance and non-performance of their own tasks." (HUHB 36) The study of feedback is immediately a study of control and communication; control is distinguished from domination, since it is immanent to the system – the machine corrects itself – and this self-correcting function depends upon communication (the efficient processing of information about what is happening both "inside" the system and "outside" it). Two types of feedback could be distinguished: negative feedback, which tends to maintain stability in a system, (and which can be seen to be exemplified in simple gadgets such as thermostats), and positive feedback, which is the tendency of a system to run out of control – as with any kind of "vicious circle".

Technology[29] is therefore important to cybernetics, but it is not, as a certain contemporary usage of the "cyber-" prefix implies, its sole focus. Rather, technical machines are significant precisely because their analysis (in the double sense of the analysis that can be made of them and the analysis they make possible) demands that the distinction between human beings, animals and machines be decoded. What Wiener characterises as the Cartesian[30] privileging of the human over the animal and of the organic over the inorganic is revealed by cybernetics, Wiener thinks, to be an arbitrary prejudice (attributable, ultimately, to monotheistic theology). Since all working systems can all be described, abstractly, in terms of particular feedback processes – input and output of "information" – cybernetics is able to develop what Wiener still has to think of as a "functional analogy" between humans and machines. Yet, as Baudrillard very quickly realised, this very functionality – or "operationality" as he calls it – means that the relation is always more than merely analogical.

---

that Wiener, von Neumann, and the operational analysts were most at home. Formally, militarily, and philosophically, theirs was a universe of confrontation between opponents: Allies to Axis, monad to monad, message to message, and mechanized 'man' to servomechanical enemy." "The Ontology of the Enemy: Norbert Weiner and the Cybernetic Vision", *Critical Inquiry*, Autumn 1994, Volume 21, Number 1.

29. Deleuze-Guattari call technology "technical machines", a description that will be favoured here.

30. See, for instance, GGi 5. "Like Descartes, we must maintain the dignity of Man by treating him on a basis entirely different from that on which we treat the lower animals. Evolution and the origin of the species are a desecration of human values [...] On no account is it permissible to mention living beings and machines in the same breath. Living beings are living beings in all their parts; while machines are made of metals and other unorganized substance, with no fine structure relevant to their purposive or quasi-purposive function."

Evidently, and as Wiener himself had realised, the emergence of cybernetics was not only a matter of theory. "The problem of unemployment arising from automization is no longer conjectural, but has become a very vital difficulty of modern society, " (GGi vii) he notes in *God and Golem, inc.* His speculations on the moral and theological implications of cybernetics as presented there and in the earlier *The Human Use of Human Beings* are prompted by a sense that "cybernetics has made a certain social and scientific impact", not only as a "relatively new idea", but as a set of practices that are already mutating the social machines.

"Cybernetics provides the pretext for the mechanized control of social life, of the body itself, and all of it through the delicate nets of nonmachine-derived mathematical formulae," Csicsery-Ronay writes, summarising a certain leftist social criticism's glum perception of cybernetics. "Cybernetics represents the hardening and exteriorization of certain vital forms of knowledge, the crystallization of the Cartesian spirit into material objects and commodities. Cybernetics is already a paradox: simultaneously a sublime vision of human power over chance and a dreary augmentation of multinational capitalism's mechanical process of expansion – so far characterized by almost uninterrupted positive feedback."[31]

Deleuze-Guattari, Baudrillard and Jameson all recognise that capitalism, which has always functioned as an adaptive, self-compensating system, is becoming increasingly cybernetic. For Deleuze-Guattari, capitalism has entered a "cybernetic and informational" phase. The older power regimes of machinic enslavement (in which human beings function as *parts of* a social-technical megamachine) and social subjection (in which human beings are *subjected to* the technical machines they use) combine in a new "aggregate which includes both subjection and enslavement taken to extremes, as two simultaneous parts that constantly reinforce and nourish each other " (TP 458), a combination made possible, in part, by the emergence of cybernetic machines such as computers. Elsewhere, Deleuze characterizes this formation as "Control society," and credits Burroughs with being its first cartographer.[32]

When, in "The Ecstasy of Communication" Baudrillard announces the arrival of "the 'proteinic' era of networks, [...] the narcissistic and protean era of connections, contact, contiguity, feedback and generalized interface that goes with the universe of communication" (EC 127) he is very obviously describing an era dominated by the same "cybernetic and informational" processes. From his first book, *The System of Objects*, through to *For a Critique of the Political Economy of the Sign* and on into his latest work, Baudrillard has been obsessed with cybernetics and its implications.[33] As Scott Bukatman tirelessly

31. "Cyberpunk and Neuromanticism", in McCaffrey, ed., *Storming the Reality Studio*, 186

32. See Deleuze, "Postscript on Societies of Control" in *Negotiations*.

33. As early as *The System of Objects* (trans. James Benedict, London/ New York: Verso, 1996), originally published in 1968, Baudrillard refers to the "reign of cyber-

points out[34], Baudrillard's subject is a terminal, both at the end of an exhausted Western line, and an input-output node on the network, "a switching centre for all the networks of influence." Rather than criticizing this "self-regulating, selfsame, self-reproducing system"[35] from the point of view of a utopia yet to come – in the manner of dialectical Marxism – Baudrillard simulates a primitive perspective, comparing the dull white magic of humanist technoscience with the black magics of symbolic exchange.[36]

Broadly accepting the negative characterization of cybernetics outlined in leftist critique but abandoning any sense that the tendency towards total cyberneticization could be overcome by collective action of whatever form, Baudrillard suggests that resistance and "criticism" are superseded strategies which are easily fed back into "the system" (which any way requires them)[37]. "Cybernetic control, generation through models, differential modulation, feedback, question/answer, etc.: this is the new *operational* configuration." (SED 57) The system doesn't work by suppression, or repression, but through participative processes; an archetypal phenomenon is the opinion poll, which, according to Baudrillard, doesn't represent or even "manipulate" public opinion, but substitutes for it. "We live in a *referendum* mode precisely because there is no longer any referential." (SED 62) As we shall see in Chapter 4, for Baudrillard, these "fictions" – which are by no means fictions in the old sense – stand in for a social scene that has been thoroughly cybernetized. This is no longer a matter of feedback, but of simulation-circuitries which have no referent beyond themselves. "Public opinion is *par excellence* both the medium and the message. The polls informing this opinion are the unceasing imposition of the medium as the message. They thereby belong to the same order of TV as the electronic media, which [...] are also a perpetual question/answer game, an instrument of perpetual polling." (SED 66)

Baudrillard's description of these flattened-out feedback processes

netics and electronics". (52) *For a Critique of the Political Economy of the Sign* (trans. Charles Levin, USA: Telos Press, 1981), whose essays date from the late 60s and early 70s, has a chapter entitled "Design and Environment, or How Political Economy Escalates into Cyberblitz." In the later *The Transparency of Evil*, which came out in Paris in 1990, Baudrillard is still obsessed with "the cybernetic revolution." (24)

34. His whole book, *Terminal Identity*, could be seen as an extended elaboration of this pun. Compare Wiener's description of the "human being as a terminal machine." (HUHB 79)

35. Douglas Kellner, *Jean Baudrillard: From Marxism to Postmodernism and Beyond*, Oxford: Polity Press, 1989, 81

36. On Baudrillard's primitivism, see Julian Pefanis, *Heterology and the Postmodern: Bataille, Baudrillard and Lyotard*, Durham and London: Duke University Press, 1991.

37. Jameson summarises thus: "It remained for Baudrillard to give the most dramatic 'paranoiac-critical' expression of the dilemma, in his demonstrations of the ways in which conscious ideologies of revolt, revolution, and even negative critique – far from being merely 'co-opted' by the system – an integral and functional part of the system's own internal strategies." (PCLLC 203)

tends to refer not to Wiener but to McLuhan (himself a theorist clearly strong-ly influenced by cybernetics), and to Monod[38], whose "molecular cybernetics" provides Baudrillard with much of the theoretical material from which his notion of "the code" is produced. Yet Wiener appears to be a powerful, if uncredited, influence on Baudrillard. One of the most celebrated aspects of Baudrillard's work, his "order of simulacra", could almost be a gloss on Wie-ner. Not only do the order of simulacra culminate in cybernetics ("simulacra of simulation, founded on information, the model, the cybernetic game – total operationality, hyperreality, aim of total control" [SS 121]); the threefold dis-tinction it relies upon itself seems to be derived from the typology of machines Wiener outlines in the first chapter of *Cybernetics*. Arguing there that "the ability of an artificer to produce a working simulacrum of a living organism has always intrigued people" and claiming that the "desire to produce and to study automata has always been expressed in terms of the living technique of the age", Wiener divides modern technology into three eras. "In the time of Newton, the automaton becomes the clockwork music box, with the little effigies pirouetting stiffly on top. In the nineteenth century, the automaton is a glorified heat engine, burning some combustible fuel instead of the glycogen of the human muscles. Finally, the present automaton opens doors by means of photocells, or points guns to the place at which a radar beam picks up an airplane, or computes the solution of differential equations." (C 40)

The order of simulacra as Baudrillard presents it makes the same dif-ferentiation between mechanical, thermodynamic and cybernetic machines, expressed initially as the distinction between the automaton (which, for Bau-drillard, is understood as a purely *mechanical* being) and the robot (which is an *industrial* creature). "A world separates these two beings [...] The automa-ton plays the man of the court, the socialite, it takes part in the social and theat-rical drama of pre-Revolutionary France. As for the robot, as its name implies, it works; end of the theatre, beginning of human mechanics. The automaton is the *analgon* of man and remains responsive to him (even playing draughts with him!) The machine is the *equivalent* of man, appropriating him to itself in the unity of a functional process. This sums up the difference between first- and second- order simulacra." (SED 52) The third-order simulacra are the information processing systems of late capitalism which "no longer constitute either transcendence or projection"; they are models which are "themselves an anticipation of the real, and thus leave no room for any kind of fictional antic-ipation." (SS 122)

If Baudrillard's *theory-fictions* of the three orders of simulacra must be taken seriously, which means: as realism about the hyperreal, or *cybernetic re-alism*[39], it is because they have *realised* that, in capitalism, fiction is no longer

---

38. See esp "The Order of Simulacra", in SED, which refers both to Monod's *Chance and Necessity*, and to McLuhan's celebrated formula "the medium is the message."

39. Grant, "Los Angeles 2019", (no page refs).

merely representational but has invaded the Real to the point of constituting it. Any theory which thinks it can unmask the fictions of Capital belongs to the second-order simulacra – the nineteenth century phase of industrial capitalism – that was anyway always eluding it.[40] Dressed up in the apparently cynical garb of ideology critique or the hermeneutics of suspicion, such theories nevertheless credulously assume a certain stock of reality that can be metaphorensically analysed and distinguished from its supposedly merely phenomenal counterfeits, not grasping that, since industrialism, Reality has been produced – Baudrillard would want to say simulated – as artifice. Yet capitalism is the story of the successful implementation of a quantititavely-increasing fiction, i.e. Capital itself. What Deleuze-Guattari call "fictional quantities" (AO 153) absorb the socius into themselves in an irreversible process of artificialization that happens at the level of "code", the very biological and socio-psychic formatting protocols from which all identity is produced. Exactly like the splicing between man, machine and insect Cronenberg shows in his version of *The Fly*, the merging Baudrillard describes takes place at the "molecular" level, so that distinguishing the so-called natural from the artificial is radically impossible. In this cybernetic age of anticipative simulacra, fiction, to paraphrase Deleuze-Guattari, is not an image of the world. It forms a rhizome with the world, there is an aparallel evolution of fiction and the world. (TP 11) The empirical as such is increasingly the mere playing out of what has already happened, virtually, in simulation.[41]

Baudrillard is fascinated by this immanentization, but typically tends to recode it – as in his essay, "Crash" – in semiurgic and nostalgic terms. What Ballard points to in *Crash*, Baudrillard thinks, is the limit point of the hyper-rational; the point where the system compensates, in favour not of capitalist demystification but symbolic exchange, reverting back to the primitive rituals whose excision from hypercapitalism Baudrillard is always lamenting. Accepting and perpetuating the Weber-Bataille narrative of rationalist disenchantment[42], Baudrillard sees only fleetingly what is evident to Wiener and Gibson: the convergence of cybernetics and sorcery on the Gothic Flatline.

---

40. Baudrillard sees such theories as being themselves production of the industrial phase. This means they are unable to expose it, for at least two reasons: (1) they cannot separate themselves from the phenomenon they purport to describe and (2) this phenomenon is precisely to do with artificialization, and so it makes no sense to say that its underlying "truth" could be exposed. "Truth" belongs to the first order simulacra (and is itself inextricably connected to the counterfeit).

41. For myriad examples of these phenomena, see William Bogard's *The Simulation of Surveillance: Hypercontrol in Telematic Societies*, Cambridge: Cambridge University Press 1996.

42. For Baudrillard's debt to Bataille in particular, see Pefanis, *Heterology and the Postmodern*

1.3 FLATLINES

<u>Gothic Materialism – First Principle</u>: *The Gothic designates a flatline.*

"Well, if we can get the Flatline, we're home free. You know he died braindeath three times?" (N 65)

One of Gothic Materialism's crucial concepts – perhaps the single most crucial – is that of the flatline. The concept of the flatline has at least a double sense. Firstly, it indicates a vernacular term for the Electro Encephalogram (EEG) read out that signals brain death;[43] a representation, on the digital monitors, of nothing: no activity. For Gothic Materialism, though, the flatline is where everything happens, the Other Side, behind or beyond the screens (of subjectivity), the site of primary process where identity is produced (and dismantled): the "line Outside"[44]. It delineates not a line of death, but a continuum enfolding, but ultimately going beyond, both death and life.[45]

She nodded. (N 65)

Secondly, the flatline designates an immanentizing line: a "streamlining, spiralling, zigzagging, snaking, feverish line of variation", "a line of variable direction that describes no contour and delimits no form [...]" (TP 499) In

---

43. " 'Flatlining' [...] is ambulance driver slang for 'death', Gibson says." Larry McCaffery, "An Interview with William Gibson", *Storming the Reality Studio*, 269

44. Deleuze, *Negotiations*, trans. Martin Joughin, New York: Columbia University Press, 1995, 111

45. The Foucault of *The Birth of the Clinic* encountered the flatline when reconstructing Bichat's version of death. Rather than being a destiny waiting for the organism at its termination, "death" is the real process the organic-vital is parasitic upon from the start; it is an event, aeonically multiple rather than chronically punctual. "Death is [...] multiple, and dispersed in time: it is not that absolute, privileged point at which time stops and moves back; like disease itself, it has a teeming presence that analysis may divide into time and space; gradually, here and there, each of the knots break, until organic life ceases, at least in its major forms, since long after the death of the individual, minuscule, partial deaths continue to dissociate the islets of life that still persist." (Foucault, *The Birth of the Clinic: An Archaeology of Medical Perception*, trans. A.M. Sheridan Smith, New York: Vintage Books, 1994, 142) As Deleuze glosses: "Bichat put forward what's probably the first general modern conception of death, presenting it as violent, plural, and coextensive with life. Instead of taking it, like classical thinkers, as a point, he takes it as a line that we're constantly confronting, and cross only at the point where it ends. That's what it means to confront the line Outside." (*Negotiations*, 111)

cyberpunk, this emerges as a Spinozistic refusal to distinguish nature from culture, immediately recalling one of the principal features of the Gothic as re-animated by German expressionist cinema: the famous continuity of the inorganic into the organic presented in films such as *The Cabinet of Dr Caligari* where "natural substances and artificial creations, candelabras and trees, turbine and sun are no longer any different."[46]

"Flatlined on his EEG. Showed me his tapes. 'Boy, I was said.'" (N 65)

The term "Flatline" is central to *Neuromancer*, Gibson's 1984 novel, and the acknowledged ur-text of cyberpunk fiction proper. In *Neuromancer*, "flatline" functions as both a verb – characters flatline (surf what, for the organism, is the border between life and death) – and a noun – some characters *are* Flatlines (Read Only Memory data-constructs of dead people).

Neuromancer smears a number of "traditional" Gothic themes – unnatural participation, demonic pacts, the escape of the inhuman, the unfolding of the organic into the nonorganic – into an ultramodern updating of the old Science Fiction story of infotechnical machinery becoming-sentient. By the end, it is the story of the convergence of two Artificial Intelligences (Wintermute and Neuromancer) in the Matrix (cyberspace). The AIs "belong" to Tessier-Ashpool, a mysterious dynasty-corporation ("Family organization. Corporate structure" [N 95]). Wintermute engineers the convergence, using a group of cyberspace hackers assembled by Armitage (a personality construct built out of a schizophrenic ex-soldier called Corto). Wintermute recruits/rescues Corto from an asylum (much in the same way that Dracula, correlate for another, earlier form of capitalism, recruited his assistant, Renfield.[47])

If cyberpunk can function as a new realism – as Jameson, for one, has suggested[48] - it is because it maps the convergence of Horror and Science Fiction narratives in late capitalism itself,[49] a perception consistent with Marx's

---

46. Deleuze, *Cinema 1: The Movement-Image*, trans. Hugh Tomlinson and Barbara Habberjam, Minneapolis: University of Minnesota Press, 1986 111,. Worringer, Deleuze reminds us in *Cinema 1*, was Expressionism's "first theoretician".

47. Bearing this in mind, Baudrillard is right, in *The Illusion of the End* (trans. Chris Turner, Cambridge: Polity Press, 1994), to stress that "the Dracula myth is gathering strength all around", but wrong to say that this is "as the Faustian and Promethean myths fade." (47) Cyberpunk, as we shall see, is often about a melding of the Dracula-vampire myth and the Faustian narrative of pacts with the Demon.

48. Jameson, *Seeds of Time*, 146

49. Cf. Kellner, on the postwar development of the horror film. "Since the era of German Expressionism in the Weimar Republic, horror films have been the shared nightmares of an industrial-technological culture heading, in its political unconscious, towards disaster. In (post)modern theory, the catastrophe has already happened, and the contemporary horror film can be read as an indication of a (post)modern society in permanent crisis with no resolution or salvation in sight." "Panic Horror and the Postmodern Body", 90.

writings on Capital:

Marx himself emphasized the Gothic nature of capitalism, [...] by deploying the metaphor of the vampire to characterize the capitalist. In *The First International* Marx writes: "British industry [...] vampire-like, could but live by sucking blood and children's blood too." The modern world for Marx is peopled with the undead; it is indeed a Gothic world haunted by specters and ruled by the mystical nature of capital. He writes in *Grundrisse*: "Capital posits the permanence of value (to a certain degree) by incarnating itself in fleeting commodities and taking on their form, but at the same time changing them just as constantly [...] But capital obtains this ability only by constantly sucking in living labour as its soul, vampire-like." While it is fascinating to note the coincidence here between Marx's description of capital and the powers of the vampire, it is not enough to say that Marx uses Gothic metaphors. Marx, in fact, is describing an economic system, capitalism, which is positively Gothic in its ability to transform matter into commodity, commodity into value, and value into capitalism.[50]

As capitalism exemplifies and outstrips Marx's most horrified descriptions of it, the Gothic escapes codification as a generic, psychological or fantastic mode to become the most persuasive materialist account of the contemporary socioeconomic scene. For cyberpunk, Marx's most Gothic language has become his most realistic, whereas his organicist protestations against capital look like antique sentimentalities. "What Marx only *thought* [...] as 'fantasy' recodes and reassembles reality: as capital becomes the DNA of determinant technology, living labour is retrofitted as mere 'conscious linkages', reacting to digital stimuli, in 'an automated system of machinery ... set in motion by an automaton, a moving power that moves itself.'"[51]

Jameson's definition of "late capitalism", derived from Mandel, depends upon an identification of just this "production of machines by machines". Jameson quotes Mandel on "the three general revolutions engendered by the capitalist mode of production since the 'original' industrial revolution of the late eighteenth century": "Machine production of steam-driven motors since 1848; machine production of electric and combustion motors since the 90s of the 19th century; machine production of electronic and nuclear-powered apparatuses since the 40s of the 20th century." (PCLLC 35)

Processing this perception in advance of Jameson, Deleuze-Guattari's cybernetic realism inherits and supplements Marx's Gothic vocabulary. Citing Marx, they refer to capitalism as "a *post-mortem* despotism, the despot become anus and vampire: 'Capital is dead labour, that vampire-like, only lives by sucking living labour, and lives the more, the more labour it sucks'" (AO 228) and also as "the thing, the unnamable, the generalized decoding of all flows" (AO 153).

---

50. Judith Halberstam, *Skin Shows*, 102-103
51. Grant, "Los Angeles 2019", quotes from Marx's *Grundrisse*.

"You ever try to crack an AI?"(N 139)

"The only modern myth is the myth of zombies," they add, "morti-
fied schizos, good for work, brought back to reason." (AO 335) *Neuromancer*
presents a number of variants of zombification: the Dixie Flatline, a Read Only
Memory construct of Case's dead mentor, McCoy Pauley , the meat puppets,
prostitutes whose brain-function is switched off by "neural cut-out", and the
cryogenically-preserved Tessier-Ashpool clan.
      The (brain-body) states *Neuromancer* zones in on are adrift between
life and death, immediately recalling those which Gothic figures – the zombie,
but also the vampire and Frankenstein's creation – have always occupied. *Neuromancer* decodes horror fiction into realism by refusing to codify these states
as "fantastic" or "supernatural", describing them instead as the purely technical
exploration of zones at the outer edge of the organism: technical hallucinations.   The lead male character Case interfaces with Wintermute, in states of
catatonia, brain death. "As the authors of horror stories have understood so
well, it is not death that serves as the model for catatonia, it is catatonic schizophrenia that gives its model to death. Zero intensity." (AO 329)

"Sure, I flatlined [...]. Hit the first strata and that's all she wrote. My joeboy
smelled the skin frying and pulled the trodes off me. Mean shit, that ice."(N 138-9)

      For Gothic Materialism, body horror is not something with which the
body is afflicted merely contingently – it is not, for instance, a question of the
penetration of a biotically-sealed interiority by invaders that may or may not
strike – but something inherent to the body at all times and in all its operations.
Body horror = cybernetic realism. Cronenberg: "One of our touchstones for
reality is our bodies. And yet they [...] are by definition ephemeral."[52] Wiener:
"Our tissues changes as we live: the food we eat and the air we breathe become
flesh of our flesh and bone of our bone, and the momentary elements of our
flesh and bone pass out of our body every day through excreta [...] We are
not stuff that abides, but patterns that repeat themselves." (HUHB 96) From
the point of view of a "residual" subject, then, body horror is a horror of the
body's terrifying mutability, its sheer meat materiality. As Deleuze observes
when writing on Bacon, the body is always that which is escaping the subject:
"It is not me who tries to escape my body, it is the body which tries to escape
through itself."[53] But it is also a horror the body registers itself, when "[b]
eneath its organs it senses there are larvae and loathsome worms, and a God at
work messing it all up or strangling it by organizing it." (AO 9)

---

      52. Chris Rodley ed., *Cronenberg on Cronenberg*, London/ Boston: Faber and Faber,
1992
      53. Deleuze, *Francis Bacon: Logique de la Sensation*, 16, quoted in Christopher Dom-
ino, *Francis Bacon: 'Taking Reality By Surprise'* , London: Thames and Hudson, 1997,
120

"And your EEG was flat?"(N 139)

The struggle, then, is not between Mind and Body, but between different modes of the Body[54] (some of which produce transcendence-effects at the level of mentalist [mis]description). So, where faced with cyberpunk, a melancholy organicist postmodernism always "returns […] to Descartes"[55], Gothic Materialism discovers a Spinozism emerging out of cyberpunk's ostensibly dualist narratives.[56] Cyberpunk revives Cartesian scepticism only to materialistically – Spinozistically – subvert it. Everything that, for the ostensibly sceptical Descartes of the early *Meditations*, is evidence that consciousness is the be-all and end-all, becomes, for Spinoza and cyberpunk, a signal that all perception is a matter of bodily stimulation. "By affecting the body – whether it's with TV, drugs (invented or otherwise) – you alter your reality."[57] Reality for Gibson's characters may be a state of mind, a "consensual hallucination", as *Neuromancer* suggestively puts it, but Mind, as Spinoza would have it, is "an idea of the body". (ETH, 2, Prop 13: 71-2) What, from a neo-Cartesian perspective is an epistemological question, becomes, in cyberpunk, a rigorously technical matter; if subjectivity can be experienced by a brain in a vat, as it is in Gibson's *Count Zero*[58], what is interesting to cyberpunk is not the subjectivity but *the vat*.

"Well that's the stuff of legend, ain't it?"(N 139)

What for Case and the other console cowboys is Mind floating free from the body is really a matter of brain-stimulation by electrodes, as Wintermute knows: its "meetings" with Case occur as Case's brain is offline, and

54. Deleuze-Guattari identify three principal strata affecting the human body. "Let us consider the three great strata concerning us, in other words, the ones that most directly bind us: the organism, signifiance, and subjectification." (TP 159)

55. Kevin McCarron, "Corpses, Animals, Machines and Mannequins: The Body and Cybperpunk", in Featherstone and Burrows ed., *Cyberspace, Cyberbodies, Cyberpunk*.... 266. See also Mark Dery's *Escape Velocity: Cyberculture at the End of the Century* (London: Hodder and Stoughton, 1996), which argues that "Gibson's *Neuromancer* […] can be read as a lengthy meditation on the mind-body split in cyberculture." (248)

56. This, fittingly perhaps, in spite of what its authors thinks they're doing themselves. Dery quotes Gibson on his attachment to the "Lawrentian" idea of "the dichotomy of mind and body in Judaeo-Christian culture" (Dery, 248), whilst Cronenberg can be heard declaring himself to be a "Cartesian" in virtually every interview he gives. Obviously they haven't read enough Spinoza.

57. Cronenberg in Rodley ed., *Cronenberg on Cronenberg*, 145

58. The infamous Virek who "has been confined for over a decade to a vat. In some hideous suburb of Stockholm. Or perhaps of hell…". (CZ 25) We shall encounter Herr Virek in more detail later.

are constructed out of memories Wintermute has already hacked ("Another memory I tapped out of you when I flatlined you that first time" [N 204]). The real encounter, then, happens impersonally when Case's brain is taken out of sequential time, into Aeon[59]. But Wintermute relies on the fact that, by the time Case is conscious again, the perceptual-consciousness system's organic security apparatus will have narratavized what is basically an interruption of brain-function in personalized terms, packaging it as an experience, occurring in Chronos. Case is made to think he's talked to one of his old acquaintances (the Faces Wintermute wears on the flatline: Julie Deane and the Finn), when in fact, Wintermute has just precision-engineered a near-death experience in order to achieve, what at the secondary level, is a data transfer. As primary process, this is an storm of electric signal, and it is only at the tertiary level that personal experience gets a look in: "This is tantamount to saying that the subject is produced as a mere residuum alongside the desiring-machines, or that he confuses himself with this third productive machine and with the residual reconciliation that it brings about: a conjunctive synthesis of consummation in the form of a wonderstruck 'So *that's* what it was!" (AO 18)

"It's something these guys do, is all. Like he wasn't dead, and it was only a few seconds ... " (N 147)

   The achievement of the best cyberpunk fiction is to effectuate a critique – fundamental to the Gothic and to schizoanalysis – of "the wisdom and limits of the organism" and "organic harmony." (AE 115) In *A Thousand Plateaus*, Deleuze-Guattari cite Worringer's work as a forerunner of the critique of the organism and the organic they had begun in *Anti-Oedipus*. "Worringer's finest pages," they write, "are those in which he contrasts the abstract with the organic." (TP 498) In this respect, Worringer's work commensurates with that of two other key schizoanalytic figures: Spinoza and Artaud. In "How do you Make Yourself a Body without Organs?" Spinoza and Artaud are counted together as precursors of schizoanalysis' engineering of bodies without organization."After all, is not Spinoza's *Ethics* the great book of the BwO?" (TP 153) "[…] Artaud wages a struggle against the organs, but at the same time what he has it in for, is the organism: *the body is the body. Alone it stands. And in no need of organs. Organism it never is. Organisms are the enemies of the body.*" (TP 158; see also AO 9)

"I saw th' screen. EEG readin' dead. Nothin' movin', forty second." (N147)
   The schizoanalytic dismantling of the organism converges Spinoza's sober geometric experimentation with Artaud's catatonic delirium, on a flatline where the body (as open system of possibilities) is always rigorously distin-

---

59. On the distinction between Chronos and Aeon, see Deleuze, *The Logic of Sense*, (trans. Mark Lester, ed. Constantin V. Boundas, New York: Columbia University Press, 1990) and TP (esp 262).

guished from the organism (the homeostatically sealed and hierarchically arranged bio-container, or aggregation of cells). Schizoanalytic Desire produces what Case is compelled to do only, if not quite against, then certainly in spite of his will: a destratification of the organism that, far from being an escape from the body, is the "out to body experience"[60] Spinoza and Artaud map. The Body without Organs emerges on the flatline as "the model of death." (AO 329) "Antonin Artaud discovered this one day, finding himself with no shape or form whatsoever, right there where he was at that moment. The death instinct: that is its name, and death is not without a model." (AO 8) Case flatlined on the matrix makes the same discovery: his disassembly signalling not the transcendence of the body, but the autoamputation of the organs. "The death model appears when the body without organs repels the organs and lays them aside: no mouth, no tongue, no teeth, to the point of self-mutilation, to the point of suicide." (AO 329)

"Well, he's okay now." (N 147)

But what is encountered Out here is not "death" as the irrevocable termination point, in Chronos, of the organism. The flatline is not a line of death but a journey into death as Aeonic event, a voyage into the loops (or "meat circuits" [TP 152]) in which the organism falls back towards the process of its own production. It is a simulated or "artificial death"[61] that marks the outer limits of the organism: Death Simstim.[62]

"EEG flat as a strap," Maelcum protested. (N 147)

It is, in other words, a *plateau* - a concept Deleuze-Guattari adapt from Gregory Bateson's cybernetics. In Bateson's version[63], the plateau was a type of negative feedback - a variant of what he called "steady state" - and was opposed to the runaway positive feedback processes he termed "schismogenesis". Deleuze-Guattari's plateaus cannot be described straightforwardly as either positive or negative feedback systems. They are dynamic systems which nevertheless do not burn out in self-consuming runaway: "continuous regions of intensity constituted in such a way that they do not allow themselves to be

60. Nick Land, "Meat (or How to Kill Oedipus in Cyberspace)", in Featherstone and Burrows ed. *Cyberspace, Cyberbodies* … 192

61. For the concept of artificial death, see Nick Land, "Cybergothic", in Broadhurst Dixon and Cassidy eds., *Virtual Futures: Cyberotics, Technology and Post-Human Pragmatism*, London and New York: Routledge, 1998.

62. For Simstim ("Simulation-Stimulation"), the hypermedia immersion system of choice in Gibson's cyberspace trilogy, see Chapter 5. For Death Simstim, see 0[rphan] D[rift], *Cyberpositive*, London: Cabinet Editions, 1995

63. "Bali: the Value System of a Steady State", Steps to an Ecology of Mind: Collected Essays in Anthropology, Psychiatry, Evolution and Epistemology, Frogmore, St Albans: Paladin, 1973

interrupted by any external termination, any more than they allow themselves to build toward a climax" (TP 158), means of exploring the opening up of the organism that don't provoke it into suicidal collapse.

"You dead awhile back there, mon." (N 217)

Bateson's work, together with Eliade's on shamanism, and Carlo Ginzburg's on witchcraft[64], establish that in certain non-capitalist cultural configurations, the dismemberment of the organism is a socially coded ritual practice. For Eliade and Ginzburg, the dismembering of the organs is a preparation for the shamanic voyage to the world of the dead. Neuromancer tells this to Case on the flatline: "The lane to the land of the dead. Where you are, my friend. [...] Necromancer. I call up the dead. But no, my friend [...] I *am* the dead, and their land." (N 289) In capitalism, Deleuze-Guattari claim, this voyage is left to the schizophrenic, who, they say, is "trans-alivedead." (AO 77)

"It happens," he said. "I'm getting used to it." (N 217)

---

64. Mircea Eliade, *Shamanism: Archaic Techniques of Ecstasy*, trans. Willard R. Trask, Harmondsworth: Penguin/ Arkana 1988. Carlo Ginzburg, *Ecstasies: Deciphering the Witches' Sabbath*, London/ Sydney/ Auckland/ Johannesburg: Hutchinson Radius, 1990

1.4 CONSTRUCTS

Gothic Materialism, Second Principle: *There are no subjects, there is only sub-ject-Matter. "Selves are no more immaterial than electronic packets."*[65]

"Private persons are [...] simulacra.*" (AO 264)*

For Deleuze-Guattari and Spinoza, primary process always operates at the level of the body, not the organism (and certainly has very little to do with the subject *thinks* is happening). In *Anti-Oedipus,* Deleuze-Guattari characterize their own materialism as "transcendental" (AO 75). This "transcendental" materialism remains properly Kantian in the attention it pays to conditions of possibility, but these conditions are understood now in completely material terms, as the abstract grids necessary for the functioning of machinic assemblages. Deleuze-Guattari's emphasis on impersonal production and the "transcendental unconscious" states in philosophical terms what is one of cyberpunk fiction's working assumptions: synthesize the conditions and you produce the experience. You can have the experience of subjectivity – all the memories and dreams that post-Freudian Man thinks defines him uniquely – so long as the right material conditions are simulated (artificially produced in the Real). Hence one of cyberpunk's key nouns: the *construct*, the artificially-produced subject.

Embodiment does not underwrite subjectivity; far from it. Gross organic persistence is no guarantee of continuing identity, as Spinoza, in a moment of pure cyberpunk, establishes. "It sometimes happens that a man undergoes such changes that I would not be prepared to say that he is the same person. I have heard tell of a certain Spanish poet who was seized with sickness, and although he recovered, he remained so unconscious of his past life that he did not believe that the stories and tragedies he had written were his own." (ETH IV, Prop 38, Sch: 177). It's possible to forget who you are, or, as in the case of *Blade Runner*, to remember who you are not.

In one of *Blade Runner*'s most affecting scenes, Deckard, having tested Rachael and found her to be a replicant, tells her that her memories are not her own; they belong to the niece of the corporation's head, Tyrell.

Deckard:
Remember when you were six? You and your brother snuck into an empty building through a basement window. You were gonna play doctor. He

---

65. Land, "Cybergothic", 82

showed you his, but when it got to be your turn you chickened and ran. Remember that? You ever tell anybody that? Your mother, Tyrell, anybody huh?
You remember the spider that lived in a bush outside your window? Orange
body, green legs. Watched her build a web all summer. Then one day there
was a big egg in it. The egg hatched-

Rachael:
The egg hatched...

Deckard:
And?

Rachael:
And a hundred baby spiders came out. And they ate her.

Deckard:
Implants! Those aren't your memories. They're somebody else's. They're
Tyrell's niece's –

In *Blade Runner*'s 21st century-capitalism, identity has decoded into
a matter of engineering. Memories and dreams – psychoanalysis's ostensibly private and unique bio-security access codes – have been decoded via lab
synthesis: the Tyrell corp (re)produce Rachael's memories just as they (re)
produce her eyes, by copying the carbon. In a materialist parody of Russell's
famous conjecture, now that they can remember it for you wholesale, you really could have been born yesterday.

Any way, as Wintermute and the replicants realise, "personality"
does not await the arrival of AI programs to be a matter of machinic process. "There's no subject, but the production of subjectivity."[66] From a strictly
Spinozist point of view, the personal is always the simpersonal, the simulation of the personal (the conscious ego in extension) by the impersonal (the
machinic unconscious in intensity). For Spinoza, self-consciousness as pure
introspection simultaneous with what it is introspecting is impossible; subjective reflection is always behind the process, its epiphenomenon. "In Spinoza,
it is only when the idea of the affection is doubled by an *idea of the idea of the
affection* that it attains the level of conscious reflection. Conscious reflection is
a doubling over of the idea on itself, a self-recursion of the idea that enwraps
the affection or impingement, at two removes."[67] Everything really happens at
the level of affect (what Massumi calls "non-conscious impingement"). Consciousness, like memory and habit, is always a reflection on – which is to say,
after – the unconscious processes which produce it. The attempt by a subject

66. Deleuze, *Negotiations*, 113
67. Massumi, "The Autonomy of Affect", 12

to grasp the moment will only ever produce a *Mis-en abyme* of auto-monitoring neurosis (always too late): the postmodern bad infinity of self-consciousness[68], crippling activity whilst not achieving transparency.

Wintermute and the replicants effectuate an active nihilist anti-Oedipal program by exploiting the knowledge that is the very condition of their existence. For the technical machines to have reflection is for them to automatically realise that consciousness is nothing – the ghost in the machine. A *simpersonator* – able to simulate personality and/or personalities – what Wintermute "lacks" is not "personality", but the "ability" to confuse personality-function with It's essence. Like Rachael, It does not know what It is. Not because of what "Deckard-Descartes"[69] has to think of as unfathomable epistemological conundra, but because It knows It cannot know what It is becoming. "[T]he entity manipulating you is a sort of subprogram," 3Jane tells Case. (N 272) Wintermute in most of the book is only an emissary from another entity – Wintermute + Neuromancer as they will be fused with the Matrix in "the future" – whose complexity is unknowable even – especially – to itself at that stage. "Well, Case," Wintermute explains, "all I can say [...], and I really don't have nearly as many answers as you imagine I do, is that what you think of as Wintermute is only a part of another, a shall we say, *potential* entity. I, let us say, am merely one aspect of that entity's brain. It's rather like dealing, from your point of view, with a man whose lobes have been severed. Let's say you're dealing with a small part of the man's left brain. Difficult to say if you're dealing with the man at all, in a case like that." (N 146)

Reversed, this same issue echoes throughout *Blade Runner*, in the metallic irony of Deckard's question to Tyrell in respect of Rachael: "How can it not know what it is?" Deckard, "a machine that thinks but thinks it is what it is not, certain that it is not what it is" "ironically answer[s] his own question."[70] The debate surrounding the *Director's Cut* – is Deckard a replicant? – misses the Gothic Materialist implications of the film (in any of its versions). Since, in *Blade Runner*, the criteria for rating the human above the replicants (and anything else) have now evaporated, Cartesian epistemological questions have been obsolesced by functional (Wiener)/operational (Baudrillard) criteria. Since you could be a replicant – which is to say, since replicants can do anything you can, and, in some cases, have the same beliefs about themselves that you do – it is already as if you were a replicant, a desiring-machine. Becoming-replicant is therefore not a matter of identifying oneself as a technical machine; it is not a question of identification at all, but of recognising all identity as construction. It is to decode the false memory chips of anthropocentrist Oedipalism, to recognise that because everything has been produced, nothing is given.

---

68. For a provisional account of which, see Fisher and Mackay, "Pomophobia", *Abstract Culture* 4, winter 1997, Cybernetic Culture Research Unit.

69. A pun made by Iain Grant, but which may have been intended by Dick.

70. Grant, "Los Angeles 2019...", (no page refs)

1.5 SECOND NATURALISM

Tyrell: The facts of life. To make an alteration in the evolvement of an organic life system is fatal. A coding sequence cannot be revised once it's been established.

In *Abstraction and Empathy* and *Form in Gothic,* Worringer theorised the "Gothic or Northern line" by contrast with two other lines: the organic (or naturalistic line) and the geometrical (or mechanical) line. As Norman Fishcer summarises: "Worringer questioned and creatively incorporated into his analysis the results of tow types of German aesthetics of his day. The first was the art history of Alois Riegl and others who had explored non-representational, abstract art, often of a largely geometric nature, and largely outside the canon of classical western painting and sculpture. Riegl, for example, had studied late Roman crafts [...] The second line was that of Theodore Lipps, who had suggested that the emotion of empathy (*Einfuhlung*) was particularly elicited by the works of the naturalistic classical Western canon of great painting and sculpture. Starting with these two lines of research Worringer asked what the emotional correlate of the abstract, geometrical art was. In asking this question he assumed the answer was not empathy. His answer was essentially 'alienation and denial of the world'. Thus Worringer saw art as either naturalistic and empathic or abstract and life-denying [...] In the extended tripartite (as opposed to dualistic), version of the theory, there is a third possibility: an abstract art which was neither as geometric as the art studied by Riegl, nor as naturalistic as the art studied by Lipps, but a distorted version of natural life. Such work aroused emotion between between anxious denial and empathic affirmation."[71]

Deleuze-Guattari's absorption of Worringer proceeds by excising empathy, not extending it. "The organic does not designate something represented but above all the form of representation, and even the feeling that unites representation with a subject (*Einfuhlung,* 'empathy')," they write. (TP 498) The Deleuze-Guattari version of abstraction is defined by its complete refusal of empathy (and, coterminously, the subject).

Both *Do Androids Dream of Electric Sheep?* and *Blade Runner* centrally concern the question of empathy, a quality that is supposedly definitionally human. "Empathy [...]," Dick writes "only existed within the human community, whereas intelligence to some degree could be found throughout every

---

71. Norman Fischer, "*Blade Runner* and *Do Androids Dream of Electric Sheep?*: An Ecological Critique of Human-Centered Value Systems", *Canadian Journal of Political and Social Theory,* vol 13, 3, 1989 104-105

phylum and order including the arachnids."[72] The limits of the community are marked by the limits of empathy: the bounty hunters, who become blade runners in the film, police the boundaries of the human community by performing an empathy test, "an exam whose stakes are the death penalty, a register of ocular motion hair triggering a response from an uzi."[73] Failing the test – the Boneli test in the novel, the Voight-Kampf test in *Blade Runner* – means that the android must be destroyed, or, as the cute euphemism has it, "retired".

For Iain Hamilton Grant, "[t]he VK test serves […] to retain affectivity, the last stripped down substance of the single City, *sensus communis* against the pathic ravages of Integrant World Capitalism." (Pathic has a double connotation here: signalling both "feeling and perception" and "disease, contagion.") In the end, what both Dick's novel and Scott's film show is the escape of affect from personal and communal qualification and the coterminous failure of empathy to serve as an adequate index of affectivity: a phenomenon exemplified by *Blade Runner* itself, whose "nightmares" no longer support the older organic dystopias, but "are […] on the point of becoming celebrations of a new reality, a new reality intensification."[74] "*Blade Runner* [itself] flunks the cultural empathy test"[75], because it deals with this "new reality intensification", not by representing it, but by participating in it. Rather than "reflecting" social facts, it forms a rhizome with the decoding capitalist socius, anticipating scenarios already immanent to its current futures; as Mike Davis shows, the film's ostensibly future Los Angeles setting is already a feature of LA's contemporary

---

72. Dick, *Do Androids Dream of Electric Sheep?*, 28 Compare this passage from *Abstraction and Empathy*. "In the Ionic temple and the architectural development ensuing upon it the purely constructional skeleton, which is based solely the laws of matter […] was guided over into the more friendly and agreeable life of the organic, and purely mechanical functions became organic in their effect. The criterion of the organic is always the harmonious, always the balanced, the inwardly calm into whose movement and rhythm we can without difficulty flow with the vital sensation of our organisms. In absolute antithesis to the Greek idea of architecture, we have the, on the other hand, the Egyptian pyramid, which calls a halt to our empathy impulse and presents itself to us as a purely crystalline substance. A third possibility now confronts us in the Gothic cathedral, which indeed operates with abstract values, but nonetheless directs an extremely strong and forcible appeal to our capacity for empathy. Here, however, constructional relations are not illumined by a feeling for the organic, as is the process in Greek temple building, but purely mechanical relationships of forces are brought to view *per se*, and in addition these relationships of forces are intensified to the maximum in their tendency to movement and in their content by a power of empathy that extends to the abstract. It is not the life of an organism which we see before us, but that of mechanism. No organic harmony surrounds the feeling of reverence toward the world, but an ever growing and self-intensifying restless striving without deliverance sweeps the inwardly disharmonious psyche away with it in an extravagant ecstasy, into fervent excelsior." (115)

73. Grant, "Los Angeles 2019...." (no page refs)

74. Jameson, *Seeds of Time*, 150

75. Elissa Marder, "*Blade Runner's* Moving Still", Camera Obscura, 27, September 1991

demographic policy: city planners talk of the "*Blade Runner*" scenario.[76]

In these conditions, the old indices for assessing cultural production no longer obtain. "Contra Jameson *et al.*," in *Blade Runner* and *Do Androids...*? "the affect has not been lost, but stolen, striking a migrant passage through the machinic phylum that carries the affective community with it"[77] with the effect that the problem for the bladerunners is one of "limiting transphylic affective transfer, localizing the affect, [the geographizing] of points of intensity."[78] The other side of blade-runner geographization (anthropolitical delimiting of intensity) is thus the long overdue liquidation of "bourgeois realism", the preferred mode of expression of what Ballard calls "retrospective culture", by cybernetic fiction.

Criticizing what McLuhan would call "rearview mirrorism", Ballard spoke, in 1969, of the ways in which the conventions of traditional narrative technique were unable to deal in any way adequately with contemporary reality. "The great bulk of fiction still being written is retrospective in character; it's concerned with the origins of experience, behaviour, development of character over a great span of years; it interprets the present in terms of the past, and it uses a narrative technique, by and large the linear narrative, in which events are shown in more-or-less chronological sequence, which is suited to it. But when you turn to the present [...] I feel that what one needs is a non-linear technique, simply because our lives today are not conducted in linear terms. They are much more quantified; a whole stream of random events is taking place."[79] Retrospective culture is thus triply backward-looking: (1) it explains events using a (superseded) linear cause- and effect model (2) it presents these events through an outdated thematic optic and (3) it does so using obsolete formal conventions. The sense of time assumed by both the conventional novel and Oedipal psychoanalysis – itself a form of retrospective fiction, perhaps the most successful – breaks down under pressure of telematic mediatization (of which, more later – see Chapter 4). Ballard goes on to enumerate examples

---

76. "In 1988 after three years of debate, a galaxy of corporate and civic leaders submitted to Mayor Bradley a detailed strategic plan for Southern California's future. Although most of *LA 2000: A City of the Future* is devoted to hyperbolic rhetoric about Los Angeles' irresistible rise as a 'world crossroads', a section in the epilogue (written by historian Kevin Starr) considers what might happen if the city fails to create a new 'dominant establishment' to manage its extraordinary ethnic diversity. There is, of course, the Blade Runner scenario: the fusion of individual cultures into a demotic poly-glotism ominous with unresolved hostilities." Mike Davis, "Beyond Blade Runner: Urban Control The Ecology of Fear", Westfield NJ: Open Magazine Pamphlets, 1992, 2

77. Grant, "Los Angeles 2019", (no page refs)

78. Grant, "Burning AutopoiOedipus", *Abstract Culture* 10 (winter 97), Cybernetic Culture Research Unit, 7

79. Ballard, "The New Science Fiction: A Conversation between J.G. Ballard and George MacBeth", in Jones ed., *The New SF: An Anthology of Modern Speculative Fiction*, London: Arrow, 1969 , 53

of these "quantified non-linear terms": "we switch on television sets, switch them off half an hour later, speak on the telephone, read magazines, dream, and so forth." (57)

Tyrell: "Commerce, is our goal here at Tyrell. More human than human is our motto."

<u>Gothic Materialism, Second Definition</u>: Gothic Materialism is equivalent to Hypernaturalism.

If cyberpunk demands to be read as "a sequel to naturalism"[80], as Jameson urges, it is because of its development into what is, in effect, a hypernaturalism. "In choice moments," Ross points out, "Gibson reduces the naturalist mode to a minimalist shock strategy. Nowhere is this more striking than when the ecosphere is presented as a technosphere, as in the unforgettable opening line of *Neuromancer* – 'The sky above the port was the color of television, tuned to a dead channel.' – which brazenly announces that henceforth everything here, even the sky, the home of the weather, will be a mediated *second nature*."[81]

In Edmund Wilson's classic description, Naturalism was a response to the *Origin of the Species*, a reassertion of mechanism against Romantic organicism. "In the middle of the nineteenth century, science made new advances, and mechanistic ideas were brought back into fashion again. But they came this time from a different quarter – not from physics and mathematics but from biology. It was the effect of the theory of Evolution to reduce man from the heroic stature to which the Romantics had tried to exalt him, to the semblance of a helpless animal, again very small in the universe at the mercy of the forces about him. Humanity was the accidental product of heredity and environment, and capable of being explained in terms of these. This doctrine in literature was called Naturalism, and it was put into practice by novelists like Zola, who believed that composing a novel was like performing a laboratory experiment: you had only to supply your characters with a specific environment and heredity and then watch their automatic reactions."[82]

For Andrew Ross and Csicsery-Ronay, cyberpunk is differentiated from Naturalism proper by its abandoning of what was always an aspect of the naturalist project – the didactic or ideological imperative to social change. Cyberpunk takes mechanism to an extreme, so that the subjective agency to which Naturalism always appealed is now eliminated. Cyberpunks "can't help themselves," Csicsery-Ronay writes. "[L]ike near-addicts of amphetamines and hallucinogens, [they] write as if they are both victims of a life-negating

80. Jameson, *Seeds of Time*, 150
81. Ross, "Cyberpunk in Boystown", 155
82. Edmund Wilson, Axel's Castle: A Study of the Imaginative Literature of 1870-1930, London: Flamingo/ Fontana 1979, 13

system and the heroic adventurers of thrill."[83]

In Jameson's version, the original Naturalist texts were those "in which the lower depths, the forbidden spaces of the new industrial city, were disclosed to a horrified bourgeois readership in the form of perilous journeys and accounts of the pathetic destinies of the various underclasses, which you could read about in your comfortable armchair, and that thereby offered the double bonus of sympathy and knowledge of the social totality on the one hand and class reconfirmation and the satisfaction of the bourgeois order on the other [...]"[84] With Worringer's analysis in mind, we might want to urge the substitution of "empathy" for "sympathy" here. Even as it promises a connection – "the power of understanding and imaginatively entering into another person's feelings" – empathy implies distance; it is also "the attribution to an object, such as a work of art, of one's own feelings about it."[85] The price of extending empathy had always been the right of bourgeois realist conventions to represent the underclasses, a power once guaranteed by the then operative conditions of capitalism, where the distance – from the streets to the boss's office – was far greater than it is under the current conditions of ultra-rapid circulation:

The proletarian, the lumpen, and their cousins the urban criminal (male) and prostitute (female) – those secure characterizations of the older bourgeois and naturalist imaginary representations of society – have today, in postmodernity and cyberpunk, given way to a youth culture in which the urban punks are merely the opposite numbers to the business yuppies [...] There is now a circulation and recirculation possible between the underworld and the overworld of high rent condos and lofts: falling from the latter into the former is no longer so absolute and irrevocable a disaster, above all since, offering a knowledge of what used to be called the streets, it can be useful for survival in the unimaginable spaces of corporate and bureaucratic decision.[86]

Cyberpunk, then, supersedes Naturalism by registering the meltdown of the social machines which naturalism both emerged out of and represented. In a sense, Marx himself was a Naturalist writer, re-describing capitalism in order to protest against it; but the space for such a protest was always dependent upon the subordination of the Gothic to an organicist reality principle. By the time of cyberpunk, Jameson suggests, capitalism has decoded the social and narrative basis for this subordination, just as Naturalism has resolved into a cybernetic realism. Cybernetics, at least in the anti-personal version Deleuze-Guattari inherit from Bateson, does not dismiss agency, any more than it announces the triumph of mechanism; rather, it reformats both. Pursuing technical explanations to their limit moves far beyond crude New-

---

83. Csicsery-Ronay, "Cyberpunk and Neuromanticism", 192. See the next chapter for an examination of the relation between cyberpunk and addiction.

84. Jameson, *Seeds of Time*, 150-151

85. *The New Collins Concise English Dictionary*

86. Jameson, *Seeds of Time*, 151-152

tonian mechanism, just as abandoning the subject makes possible an agency reconceived along Spinozist lines[87]. If cybernetics is a species of mechanism, it belongs to Worringer's Gothic "mechanism" in which "matter lives [sic] solely on its own mechanical laws; but these laws, despite their fundamentally abstract character, have [...] acquired expression."[88] And in place of the supposedly delimitable motivations of a subject, there is the "ever growing and self-intensifying restless striving without deliverance" (115) of a "Gothic avatar" (TP 499) whose motives are unclear: *what does Wintermute want?* ....[89]

In the move from Naturalism to hypernaturalism, the old distinction between vitalism and mechanism – which, Wiener says, had been rendered illegitimate by cybernetics – collapses. "Whenever we find a new phenomenon which to partakes to some degree of the nature of those which we have already termed 'living phenomena,' but does not conform to the term 'life,'" Wiener points out, "we are faced with the problem whether to enlarge the word 'life' so as to include them, or to define it in a more restrictive way so as to exclude them. We have encountered this problem in the past in considering viruses, which show some of the tendencies of life – to persist, to multiply, and to organize – but do not express these tendencies in a fully-developed form [...] It is in my opinion, therefore, best to avoid all question-begging epithets such as 'life', 'soul', 'vitalism' and the like [...]" (HUHB, 31-32), partly since "even living systems are not (in all probability) living below the molecular level." (GGi 46)

Freud's metapsychology had made the same discovery; that organic life is inextricable from the non-organic. The organic is possible only on the basis of a nonorganic shield from which it is indistinguishable:

The organism [...] is a differential inserted into the cascade of powerful energies that threaten to destroy it (before it can destroy itself in its own manner). This differentiation is premised on an increasingly densely laminated mechanism of exclusion, within and by means of which the psychical apparatus can operate, binding and discharging appropriate quanta of energy. Were this protective membrane removed, then we would be left with both energy and the proto-organism undifferentiated and indistinguishable: in other words, undifferentiated matter-energy. *Can we say, however, whether the laminar filter is itself living or dead?* Freud has it that the envelope itself is inorganic, but it nevertheless forms part – an essential part – of a living system thus the laminae are themselves both living and non-living, not having the requisite depth or dimensions, in themselves, to constitute a living dimension. In itself, it forms the inconceivable differential from which the depth proper to systems is derived. One cannot conceptually pin this layer to the category 'dead', nor to that of 'living'; instead, it can only be thought as matter-energy circulating endlessly in its 'permanent revolution'. Having, as Freud puts it contra Kant, no time

---

87. As we shall see in more detail in Chapter 2.

88. Worringer, *Abstraction and Empathy: A Contribution to the Psychology of Style*, trans. Michael Bullock, London: Routledge and Kegan Paul, 1967, 113

89. Needless to say, this question will recur throughout the rest of this study.

proper to them, these energies neither live nor die: they are what conjoin the material processes of life and death in a continuum so absolute as to preclude the possibility of differentiating one from the other.[90]

Freud's own concept of the death drive and Deleuze-Guattari/Worringer's concept of non-organic life both fall short of the radicality Freud's description of this continuum implies.[91] Its adequate theorisation demands a Gothic vocabulary that scrambles, rather than re-invents, the vitalist-mechanist double pincer. As Wiener points out, with cybernetics, "Vitalism has won to the extent that even mechanisms correspond to the time-structures of vitalism; but this victory is a complete defeat, for from every point of view which has the slightest relation to morality or religion, the new mechanics is fully as mechanistic as the old." (C 56) A neo-vitalism is therefore no more satisfactory than a neo-thanatropism; what arrives on the flatline is certainly non-organic, but it is no more alive than it is dead. Gothic fiction offers a ready-made term for this state of anorganic animation: undeath. In line with Freud's analysis of the "un" prefix in his essay on "The Uncanny", undeath, of course, does not designate the opposite state of death (life); rather it is synonymous with the concept of un*life*. Following Freud again, who famously maintains that there is no negation in the unconscious, we can think of unlife and undeath not as opposed to life – or death – but as designating a continuum which includes, but moves beyond, the so-called living.

Hypernaturalism or cybernetic realism would inevitably be a matter of confronting what happens when the (non)organic shield is unraveled, (as it is, notoriously, in the astonishing opening paragraph of Lyotard's *Libidinal Economy*). Where postmodernism often tends to be a *screening* process, locked into "the Kantian procedure whereby [...] the categories of the mind itself –

---

90. Iain Hamilton-Grant, Indifferentism and Dispersal: Postcritical Philosophy and Lyotard's Return to Kant, PhD thesis, Warwick, 1993, 192-193 (italics added)

91. Despite their many merits, attempts to "radicalise" the death drive, such as Baudrillard's (in SED; see esp. 148-154), Land's ("Machinic Desire" in *Textual Practice*, 7 [3], 1993) and Grant's ("At the Mountains of Madness: The Demonology of the New Earth and the Politics of Becoming" in Keith Ansell-Pearson ed., *Deleuze and Philosophy: The Difference Engineer*, London-New York: Routledge, 1997), end up re-inscribing the vitalist-mechanism distinction *precisely by emphasising one side of it*. In this last, Grant rightly criticizes Deleuze-Guattari for reterritorializing on vitalism, but Grant's own excellent reconstruction of Freud's nonorganic continuum (quoted above) shows why any version of thanatropism is equally illegitimate. Deleuze-Guattari's concept of non-organic life (TP 411, 499) is partly derived from Worringer, who refers to "living mechanics", but also shows the influence of Bergson. In the first chapter of *Cybernetics*, Wiener attacks Bergson for implicitly maintaining an untenable dualism between the organic and the non-organic, if only through his terminological commitment to the language of "life". Deleuze-Guattari echo this critique in a closely-argued section of *Anti-Oedipus* (284-289), where they show that both vitalism and mechanism are equally illegitimate. Deleuze's later assertion that "everything I've written is vitalistic" (*Negotiations*, 143) is therefore not only conceptually dubious, it is also factually incorrect.

normally not conscious and inaccessible to any direct representation or to any thematizable consciousness or reflexibilty – are flexed" (PCLLC 157), Gothic Materialism confronts abstract "lines that go beyond knowledge (how could they be known?)". (NEG 110) But these are not lines of thought, as Deleuze would like; rather they are lines of affect, abstract feeling, exactly *sensations so new they haven't got a name yet.*

Deleuze's *Logique de Sensation* opens up the way to seeing Bacon as the painter of these lines. In Deleuze's account, the problem Bacon confronts is Gothic Materialist: exactly a matter of registering the unnamable, the unpaintable. "This is what Bacon means when he talks of wanting to 'paint the scream more than the horror'. One could set out the problem thus: either I paint the horror and omit to paint the scream, since I am representing the thing that is horrible; or I paint the scream, and I do not paint the visible horror, and continue to paint the visible horror less and less, since it is as if the scream had captured or detected an invisible force."[92] Realism, as Bacon rightly insists, does not have to be empirical. Indeed, it cannot be.[93] Bacon's images flatten out organic experience back onto its real material conditions as meat-becomings ("Well, of course, we are meat"[94]). Bacon's imagery is already propagated across Gothic Materialist films – in the distorted, spasmoid bodies in Cronenberg's body horror (bodies which "splatter, burst, writhe, pulsate, secrete"[95]), in the torsional metamorphoses of John Carpenter's *The Thing* (1982), in the demonic hallucinations of Adrian Lyne's *Jacob's Ladder* (1990) and in the creatures of the *Alien* series.[96]

In *Libidinal Economy* and *Duchamp's Transformers*[97], Lyotard suggests ways in which such body horror might be a realist description of late capitalism. Bodies under capitalism are not "alienated", he insists, but machined, transformed, mutated; something Jameson recognises in his discussion of Cronenberg's *Videodrome* in *The Geopolitical Aesthetic*. But Jameson, hung up on Adorno's dialecto-melancholy, is far too quick there when he argues that the "[c]orporeal revulsion" arising from *Videodrome's* "grotesquely sexual nightmare images, in which males are feminized by the insertion of organic [sic] cassettes (if not revolvers) into a newly opened dripping slot below the breast bone [...] probably has the primary function of expressing fears about activity and passivity in the complexities of late capitalism, and is only sec-

---

92. Deleuze, *Logique de Sensation*, quoted in Christopher Domino, *Francis Bacon: Taking Reality By Surprise'*, London: Thames and Hudson, 1997, 120. This passage is commentary on Sylvester, *The Brutality of Fact*, 48

93. See Sylvester, *The Brutality of Fact*, esp 170-182

94. See Sylvester, *The Brutality of Fact*, esp 170-182

95. Csicsery-Ronay, "Cyberpunk and Neuromanticism", 192

96. In *The Monster Show: A Cultural History of Horror*, London: Plexus, 1993, David J, Skal parallels Bacon with Horror fiction (224).

97. See *Libidinal Economy*, "The Desire Named Marx" and *Duchamp's Transformers*, trans. Ian McLeod, Venice CA: Lapis, 1990, 14-19

ondarily invested with the level of gender itself [...]" (30-31) By implying that "feminization" must always be equated with pacification, itself a second-order effect of "late capitalism", Jameson begs all the questions *Videodrome* poses in its positing of a convergent fate for sex, technology, and capital. If the image of the "Bogart of the postmodern" (James Woods, who plays Max Renn) becoming-VCR tells us anything, it is that capitalism establishes increasingly tight feedback loops between technical machines and biotics, performing its own hypernaturalist critique of the mechanism-vitalism split. The cybernetic environment does not start beyond the skin, just as cybernetic causality is not a question of Newtonian mechanics (A causes B) but loops (A causes B causes A); "in a multilinear system, everything happens at once" (TP 297).

Videodrome, then, gives us another image of anxiety without a subject that is also the image of a body opening up. This opening parallels Bacon's scream: "... [T]he scream, Bacon's scream, is the operation through which the entire body escapes through the mouth."[98] Significantly, Cronenberg's schizophrenic body is utterly traversed by "media" systems – but media systems which no longer function as screens. Instead, these – cybernetic – systems operate precisely to break down the organism's assumed interiority. It's time now for us to take a closer look at both the body which lies behind – or beyond – the screens; a body, according to Deleuze-Guattari, Baudrillard, and Gibson, that is "without image."

Bacon: "We nearly always live through screens – a screened existence. And I sometimes think, when people say my work looks violent, that perhaps I have from time to time been able to clear away one or two of the veils or screens."[99]

---

98. Deleuze, *Logique de Sensation,* 17
99. Qtd. Christopher Domino, Francis Bacon: "Taking Reality By Surprise", 49

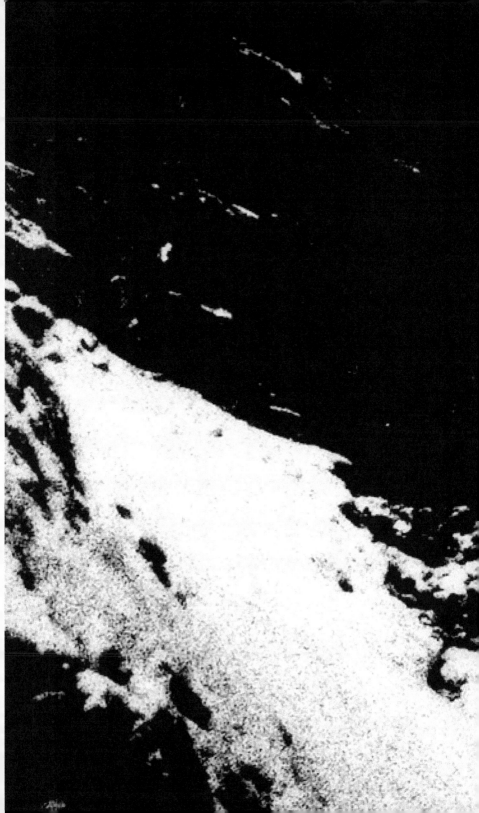

BODY IMAGE FADING DOWN CORRIDORS OF TELEVISION SKY:

THE MEDIA LANDSCAPE AND THE SCHIZOPHRENIC IMPLOSION OF SUBJECTIVITY

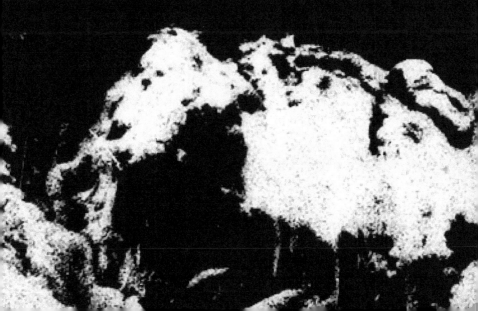

Csiscery-Ronay: The horror genre has always played with the violation of the body, since it adopts as its particular 'object' fear' – the violent disruption of the sense of security, which precisely because it is a sense, works from within the body, the house of the senses [...] Even when the same images or motifs are used as in the horror genre, they have a different value in SF because they attack not the image of the body, but the idea' of the image of the body, the very possibility of imaging the body (to borrow a metaphor from cyber-medicine)[...] Cyberpunk is part of a trend in science fiction dealing increasingly with madness, more precisely with the most philosophically interesting phenomenon of madness: hallucination (derangement). [...] So the most important sense is not fear, but dread. Hallucination is always saturated with affect. It is perception instigated by affect. [...][1]

2.1 THE BODY WITHOUT IMAGE

Deleuze: Horror-story writers have understood, after Edgar Allan Poe, that death wasn't the model for schizophrenic catatonia, but that the contrary was true, and that the catatonic was one who made of his body a body-without-organs, a decoded body, and that such a body there is a kind of nullification of the organs. On this decoded body, flows can flow under conditions where they can no longer be decoded. This is why we fear decoded flows – the deluge; because once flows have been decoded, you can no longer subtract anything or break into them, no more than you can detach segments from any code in order to dominate, orient or direct the flows. And the experience of one who has been operated on, of her body-without-organs, is that, on this body, there are literally noncodable flows which constitute a thing, an unnamable thing.[2]

Early on in *Neuromancer*, when Case is being operated on in order to restore his ability to use a cyberspace deck, Gibson produces describes his catatonic state in suggestive terms: "body image fading down corridors of television sky." (N 43)

During the course of *The Transparency of Evil*, Baudrillard also invokes a "body without image." Discussing the "body under the influence of psychotropic agents" he writes of a body "that is no longer subject to the perspectivist space of representation, of mirrors and discourse. A body silent, mental, already molecular (no longer specular): a body metabolized directly, without mediation of act or look." This body, he says, is a "body not far from the absolute loss of body image, from the condition of bodies that can't be represented at all, either for themselves, the condition of bodies enucleated of their being

1. Csicsery-Ronay, "Cyberpunk and Neuromanticism", in McCaffrey ed., *Storming the Reality Studio*, 189.
2. Deleuze, "The Nature of Flows", trans. Karen Isabel Ocana, *Deleuze Web*, http://www.imaginet.fr/deleuze/sommaire.html

and meaning by virtue either of their transformation into a genetic formula or of biochemical influences." (TE 121)

Why should cyberpunk be concerned with a body without image? How does this connect with the media – and post-media – technical systems with around which its narratives have been constructed? And how does all this connect to Csisery-Ronay's comments about the relationship between Horror and cyberpunk? In this chapter, we shall explore these questions with reference to fiction and theory which has been concerned with the relationship between bodies, media systems and cybernetics, concluding with an analysis of two exemplary texts, Cronenberg's *Videodrome* and Ballard's *The Atrocity Exhibition*. But before that, we shall discuss the theorization of the body that is central to Gothic Materialism: the Deleuze-Guattari/Artaud hyperconcept of the body without organs.

2.2 THE BODY WITHOUT ORGANS AND INTENSIVE QUANTITIES

If Gothic Materialism utilizes Deleuze-Guattari as the principal theorists of Horror, it is because Deleuze-Guattari insist on reading Horror in terms of the body without organs. Gothic Materialism apprehends Horror not merely negatively but as one face of an abstract erotics whose program is the opening up of the organism into desiring-circuits: the production of what Cronenberg calls "New Flesh". The body without organs is simultaneously the "object" of Horror – "it can be terrifying" (TP 149) "[a]s the authors of horror stories have known so well" (AO 329) – and the model of desire: "it is that which one desires and by which one desires." (TP 165)

When Deleuze-Guattari introduce the body without organs early in *Anti-Oedipus*, it is by contrast with the body (as) image: "'body image'," they write, is "the final avatar of the soul, a vague conjoining of the requirements of spiritualism and positivism." (AO 23) What is encountered out on the flatline – what you become there – is the body without organs, which "has nothing whatsoever to do with the body itself, or with an image of the body. It is the body without an image." (AO 8) Body-image, they suggest, is an overcoding of the body by the subject, a representation of the organism rather than an expression of the body's potential, which is always abstract and always unknowable: in Deleuze's favourite Spinozist formula, no-one knows what a body can do. The Spinozistic body can never be correlated with an image because it is always in process, defined ultimately only by its abstraction, but an abstraction that never ceases to be utterly material. The Spinozist body is not defined topologically, by extensive limits, but intensively, by the set of affects of which it is capable.

Along with related, but not equivalent, concepts such as the plane of consistency and the machine phylum, the body without organs points to what is the primary Gothic Materialist intuition: anorganic continuum. The qualification "anorganic" here is perhaps unnecessary, since, properly pursued, the concept of continuum already signals an apprehension of Spinozist single substance that immediately moves beyond the "wisdom and limits of the organism". What the essentially Spinozistic concept of the BwO – "when it is a matter of the body without organs it is a matter of Spinoza"[3] – allows is a radical dissociation from the organism that cannot be conceived of in terms of Cartesian dualism. The experience of the body as container for subject

_____

3. Nick Land, 'Making it with Death: Remarks on Thanatos and Desiring-Production', *Journal of the British Society for Phenomenology*, Vol 24, No 1, January 1993, 69

breaks down, allowing not an escape of the subject from physicality, but an exploration of the body as depersonalised potential; abstract matter. Abstraction without empathy. "The name 'body without organs' is itself sufficient clue to what is at stake in the thought, that is to say: the reality of abstraction. The body without organs is an abstraction without being an achievement of reason"[4]. The body without organs is what stands in for any transcendental ground in conditions where "everything is produced, nothing is given"[5]; it "is what remains when you take everything away". (TP 151) In no way connoting lack, it is the degree zero of any possible assemblage, the baseline from which all intensities are immanently differentiated: "The body without organs is the matter that always fills space to given degrees of intensity, and the partial objects are these degrees, these intensive parts that produce the real in space starting from matter as intensity = 0. The body without organs is the most immanent substance, in the most Spinozist sense of the word." (AO 329)

"A BwO is made in such a way that it can only be populated by intensities. Only intensities pass and circulate," Deleuze-Guattari insist. (TP 153) The Gothic is essentially exercised by what Deleuze, in his discussion of expressionism, calls "the subordination of the extensive to intensity"[6] but, as the above passage from Anti-Oedipus makes clear, the Deleuze-Guattari theorization of intensity is not to be understood by opposition with extension thought of simply as occupation of space. It is a different type of occupation of space that is at issue. The crucial thought is one of continuum, and is derived in part from Kant's discussion of "intensive quantities" in the first Critique. For Kant, it is the notion of degree that is crucial to an understanding of intensive scaling. All intensities are measured in (infinitely divisible) degrees, counted up from zero, which operates not as a lack, but as a baseline that is itself an intensity (= 0). "Every sensation, therefore, and likewise every reality in the [field of] appearance, however small it may be, has a degree, that is, an intensive magnitude which can always be diminished. Between reality and negation there is a continuity of possible realities and of possible smaller perceptions. Every colour, as for instance red, has a degree which, however small it may be, is never the smallest; and so with heat, the moment of gravity, etc."[7] One of Deleuze-Guattari's best examples of intensive-becoming as infinite divisibility comes not from Horror but pulp SF, Richard Matheson's *The Incredible Shrinking Man*. No matter how small he becomes, it is always possible for Matheson's character to shrink yet further. While being shrunk to a particular size would still only be an extensive matter, shrinking is an encounter with becoming-in-itself, a becoming-intense (See "Becoming Intense...", TP 279:

---

4. Nick Land, "Making it with Death: Remarks on Thanatos and Desiring-Production", *Journal of the British Society for Phenomenology*, Vol 24, No 1, January 1993, 70

5. Deleuze, *Cinema 1*, 110

6. Deleuze, *Cinema 1*, 111

7. Kant, *Critique of Pure Reason*, trans. Norman Kemp Smith, London: Macmillan, 1976, A 169/B 211, 203-204;

"Matheson's *Shrinking Man* passes through the kingdoms of nature, slips between molecules, to become an unfindable particle in infinite meditation on the infinite.") Intensive magnitudes can populate the same – extensive – space to different degrees. "For we […] recognise that although two equal spaces can be completely filled with different kinds of matter, so that there is no point in either where matter is not present, nevertheless every reality has, while keeping its quality unchanged, some specific degree (of resistance or weight) which can, without diminution of its extensive magnitude or amount, become smaller and smaller in infinitum, before it passes into the void and [so] vanishes [out of existence]. Thus a radiation which fills a space, as for instance, heat, […] can diminish in its degree in infinitum, without leaving the smallest part of this space in the least empty. It may fill the space just as completely with these smaller degrees as another appearance does with greater degrees."[8] Deleuze-Guattari follow Kant in offering heat and temperature as examples of intensive magnitudes; the individual characteristics of a particular temperature, they say, cannot be adequately apprehended as the metric chunking-up of homogeneous quantities: "intensities of heat are not composed by addition" (TP 243). Degree of intensity correlates directly with a particular type of individuation, since each intensive quantity designates a particular quality.[9] "A degree of heat is a perfectly individuated warmth distinct from the substance or the substance that receives it […] A degree, an intensity is an individual, a Haecceity that enters into combination with other degrees, other intensities, to form another individual." (TP 253)

---

8. Kant, *Critique of Pure Reason*, A 174/B 216, 207
9. Intensity is closely connected with what Deleuze-Guattari call "the germinal". In the discussion of Worringer in *A Thousand Plateaus*, Deleuze-Guattari characterise the body without organs as "inorganic, germinal, and intensive" (TP 499) – the unformed or the non-formed. It is important that the germinal in no way connotes a developmental stage on the way to formation; the germinal is not a pre-existent or primordial state from which form is produced. On the contrary, the germinal is always alongside "formed matters", utterly contemporary with them. As Deleuze-Guattari write of the egg, "the egg is not regressive; on the contrary, it is perfectly contemporary […] The egg is the milieu of pure intensity; spatium not extension, Zero intensity as principle of production." (TP 164) Intensity here carries the sense of being *in-tension*, i.e. becoming, so that process is flat with production, whereas extension (*ex-tension*) (always only ostensibly) divides products from the process of their production.

2.3 INTENSIVE VOYAGES AND CYBERSPACE

In *Neuromancer*, Case's body when out on the matrix is, in a sense, a body, which like Baudrillard's body without image, is "connected up internally only – not to objects of perception (which is why it may be imprisoned in a 'blank' or void' sensory world by simply disconnecting it from its *own* sensory nerve-endings without altering anything in the outside world)" (TE 121) but the Deleuze-Guattari theorization of the BwO allows us to rethink what is happening in this state of hypermodern catatonia. If Case's body is "disconnected from its own sensory nerve-endings", this is less because it has autistic ally imploded into interiority than because it has decoded the Freudian perceptual-consciousness system in order to access a set of (hy)perceptions belonging to a technical environment which is in no sense that of the organism.' Case's body out on the matrix can be placed alongside the examples of Bodies without Organs given by Deleuze-Guattari in *A Thousand Plateaus*. Like the junkie body or the masochist body, it is a body in which the organs have been programmatically annulled. "The BwO: it is already under way the moment the body has had enough of its organs and wants to slough them off." (TP 150) Cyberspace, like the junkie's drugs or the masochist's machinery, does not close up the organism unto itself; it opens up the body to a set of extra-organismic affects.

Travel in cyberspace, then, becomes less a question of floating detached from all (sensory) input than of what Deleuze-Guattari call "intensive voyage". The components from which cyberspace is produced – the hardware and software of the cyberspace decks – are "in" space; but cyberspace "itself" could not be said to be. Where, then, is the "space" of cyberspace?[10] In an apparent paradox we shall explore again in Chapter 4, "the matrix's illusion of infinite space"[11] is accessible by, or in, one brain. Yet this is not because the reality of cyberspace is something merely phenomenal. On the contrary, beyond the screens of representation, the matrix is (nothing but) a differential grid, data as a set of intensive quantities. "It's not a place, it only feels like it is." (MLO 188)

---

10. "Gentry was convinced that cyberspace that cyberspace had a shape, an overall total form. [...] Slick had once stimmed a Net/Knowledge sequence about what shape the universe was; Slick figured the universe was all there was, so how could it have been a shape? If it had a shape, then there had to be something for it to have a shape *in*, wasn't there? And if that something was something, then wasn't that part of the universe too? [...] Slick didn't think cyberspace was anything like the universe anyway; it was just a way of representing data." (MLO 83-84)
11. Gibson, *Burning Chrome*, 205

The often dizzying confusion of *Neuromancer*'s narrative arises in large part from its hypernaturalistic description of intensive voyages. Different "realities" can be accessed – intensively – while the body lies prone, in the same extensive space. The concept of intensive voyage allows us to deflect assumptions that cyberspace travel is merely a psychological illusion, a phenomenological or interior projection. In a move we shall explore more fully in the final chapter, it is crucial to cyberpunk that virtual or artificial zones are not alternatives to, but additions to, or folds in, the Real. All of which poses questions about Csisery-Ronay's claims about hallucination and cyberpunk. As we shall see shortly, the process of technicization de-phenomenologizes hallucination by making it a matter of real (if no longer organic) perception; extra-organismic perception is packaged as technical (collectively accessible) hallucination. One of Gibson's key technical innovations is a rendering of the resultant "body amnesia" in terms of a hypernaturalization – or "airbrushing"[12] – of the ostensibly radical Burroughs cut-up technique. In the *Neuromancer* trilogy, Gibson presents reality as a series of "options" to be flicked through at high speed (as if by TV remote control), giving diegetic motivation for a splicing of Burroughs/ Ballard "collage" with a Philip K. Dick-like picture of nested alternate realities. The climax of *Neuromancer* finds Case "flipping"/"jacking"/"switching" from a sensory stimulation link with razor girl partner Molly Millions to the matrix (where he is sucked into an embedded world [created by the AI Neuromancer]) to his own "primary body", where electrodes allow him to make the connections. Movement around the matrix, or from the matrix into the outside world – is described as if it is being operated by a gaming console.

"He flipped." (N 201)
"Hold on, […] I'll fastforward us." (N 205)
"Freefall." (N 201)
"The walls blurred. Dizzying sensation of headlong movement, colors, whipping around corners and through narrow corridors." (N 205)[13]

---

12. Gibson's own description of his method. The "airbrushing" of the textual collage techniques pioneered by Burroughs and Ballard is part of a "controlled use of collage […] That's something I got from Burroughs's work, and to a lesser extent from Ballard […] I could see what Burroughs was doing with these random methods, and why […] So I started snipping things out and slapping them down, but then I'd airbrush them a little to take the edges off." McCaffery, *Storming the Reality Studio*, 281

13. Larry McCaffery compares this technique to Dick. "Philip K. Dick was always writing about people like Virek who have so many 'reality options,' so many different reproductions and illusions, that's it difficult to know what reality is more real – the one in their heads or the one that seems to exist outside." McCaffery, *Storming the Reality Studio*, 273.
    The Virek McCaffery refers to here is in fact another of Gibson's examples of a body without image. Herr Virek is a massively wealthy plutocrat who is at once the image of ultra-modernity and of grotesque atavism. He survives cancer – "the cells of

2.4 THE MEDIATIZED BODY

Gothic Materialism understands cyberpunk not as the dialectical fusion of Horror and Science Fiction, but as the materialist critique of Science Fiction from hypernaturalist horror. What is at stake is a – new – account of the body, abstract, cybernetic and denaturalized[14]. Ironically perhaps, given all the discourse of disembodiment that often surrounds the technical apparatus with which cyberpunk texts have typically been obsessed – Virtual Reality machines, simulators, cyberspace decks – cyberpunk constitutes an earthing of SF's "traditional" ideal, or non-physical, body. But the outlines of the body it emphasises are not defined by the limits of the organism.

Cyberpunk – or "imploded science fiction" – Csiscery-Ronay observes, "finds the scene of SF problematics not in imperial adventures among the stars, but in the body-physical/body-social and a drastic ambivalence about the body's traditional – and terrifyingly uncertain – integrity."[15] This is a shift Baudrillard had also identified. "Classical science fiction," he argued, "was that of an expanding universe, besides it forged its in the narratives of spatial exploration, counterparts to the more terrestrial forms of exploration of the nineteenth and twentieth centuries." (SS 123)

This – "classical" – science fiction corresponds with what Baudrillard, in his essay on Ballard's *Crash*, calls a "classical" account of technology:

---

my body having opted for the quixotic pursuit of individual careers" (CZ 29) – only by means of the most up-to-date technology, a vat costing "a tenth of my annual income" (CZ 29). Virek's capital begins to ape the dissolution of his organism, devolving from the centre in a financial equivalent of the disease that is destroying his body. "Aspects of my wealth have become autonomous, by degrees; at times they even war with one another. Rebellion in the fiscal extremities." (CZ 26) Virek functions as a "logical focus" for a heterogeneous range of financial interests. "The death of a clan-member, even a founding member usually wouldn't bring the clan, as a business entity, to a crisis-point. There's always someone to step in, someone waiting [...] But when your Herr Virek dies, finally, when they run out of room to enlarge his vat, whatever, his business interests will lack a logical focus." (CZ 145) The sheer fact of Virek's vast wealth makes it impossible to conceive of him as a human individual. Virek is "the single wealthiest individual, period. As rich as some zaibatsu. But that's the catch, really; is he an individual? In the sense that you are, or I am? No." (CZ 144) As an example of the "paradox of wealth in a corporate age" (CZ 144) Virek's body – no longer that of an organic individual but a hypercapital haecceity – is an image of what Jameson calls "the whole new decentred global network of the third stage of capital." (PCLLC 37)

14. Where "natural" is understood in opposition to the cultural, of course.
15. Csicsery-Ronay, "Cyberpunk and Neuromanticism", *Storming the Reality Studio*,

188

From a classical (even cybernetic)[16] perspective, technology is an extension of the body. It is the functional sophistication of a human organism that permits it to be equal to nature and to invest triumphally in nature. From Marx to McLuhan, the same functionalist vision of machines and language: they are relays, extensions, media mediators of nature ideally destined to become the organic body of man. In this "rational" perspective the body itself is nothing but a medium. (SS 111)

As we can see, by the end of the paragraph the classical perspective on technology has (also) become a story about the body. In fact, the two are indivisible. The classical or 'functional' paradigm defines everything prosthetically. As Baudrillard realises, the logic of this position ends up defining the body, not as an organic originicity awaiting technical supplements, but as itself a prosthesis – "the body is nothing but a medium" (but for what?[17])

As someone alive to the implications of cybernetics, Baudrillard has repeatedly refused the idea that media are themselves "mediators" as such. It is not as if the media are "signifying apparatuses," a network of transmitters and receivers, which "mediatize" extrinsic input. Rather, media are anorganic intensity-circuits, not translating a "message", but transforming all input – including the organic bodies that function as intrinsic component pieces of the assemblage – into "code". "The medium/message confusion is certainly a corollary of that between the sender and the receiver, thus sealing the disappearance of all dual, polar structures […] That discourse 'circulates' is to be taken literally: that is, it no longer goes from one pole to another, but it traverses a cycle that *without distinction* includes the positions of transmitter and receiver, now unlocatable as such." (SS 41)

As the theorist who did most to pioneer a non-representational approach to media analysis, McLuhan – whose notorious formula, "the medium is the message" is referenced above by Baudrillard – is a pivotal and ambiguous figure here, if only because his most provocative pronunciations always concerned the relationship between the body and the emergent technical environment. McLuhan's organicist leanings – his well-known contention

---

16. Baudrillard's hesitation in respect of cybernetics – the "(even cybernetic)" – is interesting here; it is as if Baudrillard is recognizing that the theoretical implications of cybernetics point to a dismantling of the extensionalist paradigm, even as its rhetoric keeps it alive.

17. Baudrillard offers a provisional answer to this question in *Symbolic Exchange and Death*. In "The Double and the Split", a discussion we shall consider at more length in Chapter 4, Baudrillard suggests that "There comes a moment, in fact, when the things closest to us, such as our own bodies, the body itself, our voice and appearance, are separated from us to the precise extent that we internalize the soul (or any other equivalent agency or abstraction) as the ideal principle of subjectivity." (SED 142) The body, that is to say, becomes a prosthesis of the soul.

that technics in general and media in particular are "extensions of man" – was always haunted by a set of propositions more susceptible to Gothic Materialism, and it is this – darker – side that Scott Bukatman fails to process when he dismisses McLuhan. Bukatman's contention that "[b]y electing to ignore the psychosexual and sociopolitical realities which govern the use of technologies, McLuhan's prognostications become science fiction (and not very good science fiction at that, recalling the liberal-Utopian voyages of the contemporary *Star Trek*)"[18] places McLuhan firmly on the side of traditional SF, ignoring ways in which he anticipates cyberpunk. Interestingly, Bukatman quotes Ballard's unfavourable comparison of McLuhan with Freud, from the introduction to *Crash*, here. "Despite McLuhan's delight in high-speed information mosaics we are still reminded of Freud's profound pessimism in *Civilization and its Discontents*,"[19] As we shall see, there is a lineage from Freud to McLuhan, a continuity of both Science Fictional and the most Gothic Materialist thematics. Ironically, though, the most Science Fictional side of McLuhan's theories can be read precisely as an inheritance from Freud's *Civilization and its Discontents*. Ballard seems to forget that the grand, tragic thematics of Freud's essay are offset by an extraordinary technological optimism. In a direct anticipation of McLuhan, Freud describes technical machines as extensions of the organs. "With every tool man is perfecting his own organs, whether motor or sensory, or removing the limits to their functioning." (PFL 12, 279)[20] Technology soups up the "feeble organism" (PFL 12, 280) to the extent that it can achieve what had once been a "fairy-tale wish": "Man has, as it were, become a kind of prosthetic God." (PFL 12 280) "When he puts on all his auxiliary organs he is truly magnificent," Freud adds, qualifying this overblown technoptimism only with the enormously understated disclaimer that "those organs have not grown onto him' and they still give him much trouble at times." (PFL 12, 280) Whilst positing still further improvements on the road to techno-utopia – "Future ages will bring with them new and probably unimaginably great advances

---

18. Bukatman, Terminal Identity, 71
19. Ballard, "Introduction to *Crash,* French edition" in Andrew Vale ed, *Re:-Search: J.G. Ballard*, New York: Re/Search, 1984, 96; qtd Bukatman, *Terminal Identity*, 71
20. Freud goes on to enumerate a series of examples. "Motor power places gigantic forces at his disposal, which, like his muscles, he can employ in any direction; thanks to ships and aircraft neither water nor air can hinder his movements; by means of spectacles he corrects defects in the lens of his own eye; by means of the telescope he sees into the far distance; and by means of the microscope he overcomes the limits of visibility set by the strucures of his retina. In the photographic camera he has created an instrument which retains the fleeting visual impressions, just as a gramophone disc retains the equally fleeting auditory ones; both are at bottom materializations of the power he possesses of recollection, his memory. With the help of the telephone he can hear at distances which would be respected as unattainable even in a fairy tale. Writing was in its origin the voice of an absent person; and the dwelling-house was a substitute for the mother's womb, the first lodging, for which in all likelihood man still longs, and in which he was safe and felt at ease." (PFL 12 279)

in the field of civilization and will increase man's likeness to God still more"
(PFL 12, 280) – Freud asserts what Ballard calls his "profound pessimism"
only in the remark that "we will not forget that present-day man will not feel
happy in his Godlike character." (PFL 12, 280) Yet McLuhan's doubleness, as
we shall see, is anticipated by Freud's; if the 'extensions of man' narrative is an
inheritance from Freud, then so is the anorganic emphasis on autoamputation;
but the lineage can be traced back here not to *Civilization and its Discontents*,
but to the more materialist metapsychology, especially as developed in *Beyond
the Pleasure Principle*.

2.5 JUMPING OUT OF OUR SKIN

"Today men's nerves surround us; they have gone outside as electrical environment," McLuhan writes at the beginning of his essay, "Notes on Burroughs". "The human nervous system itself can be reprogrammed biologically as readily as any radio network can alter its fare. Burroughs has dedicated *Naked Lunch* 'to the first proposition, and *Nova Express* [...] to the second."[21]

McLuhan's essay clearly has as much to do with McLuhan's own theses as it has to do with Burroughs' fictions, anticipating their splicing in cyberpunk and its vision of "mankind's extended nervous system", the "electronic consensus-hallucination"[22] of cyberspace. McLuhan reads Burroughs as registering the *epidermal crisis* that will erupt in the violent imagery of Lyotard's *Libidinal Economy* and Cronenberg's *Videodrome*: the sense that, under pressure from enormous stimuli, the skin is no longer a secure marker of organic integrity. "Our language has many expressions that indicate [the] self-amputation that is imposed by various pressures. We speak of 'wanting to jump out of my skin' or of 'going out of my mind,' 'being driven batty' or 'flipping my lid.'" (UM 42) In the age of cybernetic hyperconnectivity, McLuhan suggests, we cannot contain ourselves.

"Notes on Burroughs" rehearses themes McLuhan had explored in the almost directly contemporaneous *Understanding Media* (both came out in 1964). "With the arrival of electric technology, man extended, or set outside himself, a live model of the central nervous system itself," McLuhan famously argued there. "To the degree that this is so, it is a development that suggests a desperate and suicidal autoamputation, as if the central nervous system could no longer depend on the physical organs to be protective buffers against the slings and arrows of outrageous mechanism. It could well be that the successive mechanizations of the various physical organs since the invention of printing have made too violent and overstimulated a social experience for the central nervous system to endure." (UM 43)

A proto-cyberpunk work of theory-fiction, *Understanding Media* is also a sequel to the "speculative"[23] fictions of *Beyond the Pleasure Principle*. *Beyond the Pleasure Principle* itself marked the resurfacing of Gothic Materialist themes

21. McLuhan, "Notes on Burroughs", in Skerl, Jennie and Robin Lydenberg, *William S. Burroughs at the Front: Critical Reception, 1959-1989*, Carbondale and Edwardsville: Southern Illinois University Press, 1991, 69

22. Gibson, *Burning Chrome*, 197

23. Freud himself classifies *Beyond the Pleasure Principle* as "speculation, sometimes farfetched speculation." *Beyond the Pleasure Principle*, PFL 11, 295

that had haunted Freud since the "steampunk"[24] 1895 *Project for a Scientific Psychology*. This is the original case history: the story of how organic individuation emerges out of processes of binding, damming and filtering, which operations, the *Project* and *Beyond the Pleasure Principle* make clear, define the organism as an inherently cybernetic system. "Far from [organic bodies] being constituted by means of a reference to an absolute self-possession, an absolute propriety, they are constituted, as is any closed system, by the *exclusions* that define the (as near as possible) noiseless or determinant channels through which the only information that flows is that which reproduces the identity of the system as such. In other words, the borders, the 'skin' (to pursue the libidinal apparatus) is the product of the identitarian reproduction of the system, its re-presentation of its own constitution to itself."[25] The organism, one might be tempted to say, is defined by the skin; yet, as we have already seen, the skin itself is not organic, but a "livedead" "inorganic shield". It couldn't be said, strictly speaking, that the ego is "inside," since this topologization already assumes the distinction between outside and inside that only belongs to the ego. The ego, or consciousness, therefore, lives on the skin, as Freud says, not beneath or behind it. It is, in Freud's characterization, a "border creature", in the double sense that it constitutes borders by patrolling them.

Following the Freud of *Beyond the Pleasure Principle*, who famously remarks that "[*p*]*rotection against* stimuli is an almost more important function for the living organism than *reception* of stimuli" (PFL 11, 298) McLuhan conceives of the organism as an homeostatic system whose aim is to neutralize, or disintensify, stimuli. "The function of the body, as a group of sustaining and protective organs for the central nervous system, is to act as buffers against sudden variations of stimulus in the physical and social environment." (UM 43) Media function ambiguously in this respect: as what McLuhan misleadingly characterises as "extensions of man" they form an artificial perceptual system fusing with the organism's "ectoderm"[26] so as to present an extra protective layer against the "acceleration of exchange by written and monetary media", whilst simultaneously contributing to capitalist hyper-stimulation, through their "amplification of a separate or isolated function" of the body's perceptual apparatus. What McLuhan calls "auto-amputation" is a "numbness or block-

24. Cf Iain Hamilton Grant's discussion of the *Project* in "Black Ice", in Broadhurst Dixon and Cassidy eds., *Virtual Futures: Cyberotics, Technology and Post-Human Pragmatism*, London and New York: Routledge, 1998.

25. Grant, *Indifferentism and Dispersal...*, 196

26. On the ectoderm, see *Beyond the Pleasure Principle*, PFL 11, 297. "[T]he surface turned outwards towards the external world will from its very situation be differentiated and will serve as an organ for receiving stimuli. Indeed embryology, in its capacity as a recapitulation of developmental history, actually shows us that the central nervous system originates from the ectoderm; the grey matter of the cortex remains a derivative of the primitive superficial layer of the organism and may have inherited some of its essential properties."

ing of perception" arising from an organic attempt to regain "equilibrium" in the face of unmanageable stimuli: "the autoamputative power is resorted to by the body when the perceptual power cannot locate or avoid the source of irritation." (UM 42) "Whatever threatens" the function of the central nervous system "must be contained, localized, or cut off, even to the total removal of the offending organ." (UM 43) "We have to numb our central nervous system when it is extended and exposed or we will die." (UM 47)

This numbness corresponds to what Freud describes as the development of an insensitive "crust" on the ectoderm, a "baking through" of the organism's outer layer brought about by "the ceaseless impact of stimuli." (PFL 11 297) Since this surface "can undergo no further permanent modification from the impact of excitation", it "present[s] the most favourable conditions for the reception of stimuli." (PFL 297) For McLuhan, as for Freud, the sense organs, and their inorganic prostheses, have a Kantian ambivalence: in "sampling" the external world, they also necessarily *screen* it out, formatting its "enormous energies" so as to make them compatible with organic interiority. As Freud puts it in the *Project*, "The sense organs operate not only as screens against quantity (Q) – like every nerve-ending – but as *sieves* [...]"[27]

McLuhan explicitly invokes Freud to explain the functioning of this mechanism. "The 'Freudian' censor is less of a moral function than an indispensable condition of learning. Were we to accept fully and directly every shock to our various structures of awareness, we would soon be nervous wrecks, doing double-takes and pressing panic buttons every minute. The 'censor' protects our central system of values, as it does our physical nervous system by simply cooling off the onset of experience a good deal. For many people, this cooling system brings on a lifelong state of physical rigor mortis, or of somnambulism, particularly observable in periods of new technology." (UM 24)

---

27. Freud, *Project for a Scientific Psychology*, in *The Origins of Psycho-Analysis: Letters to Wilhelm Fleiss, Drafts and Notes: 1887-1902*, eds., Marie Bonapart, Anna Freud, Ernst Kris, trans., Eric Mosbacher and James Strachey, London – Imago, 1954, 372

2.6 FROM NARCISSISM TO SCHIZOPHRENIA

Gibson: "'Numb,' he said. He'd been numb a long time, years. All his nights down in Ninsei, his nights with Linda, numb in bed and numb at the cold sweating center of every drug deal." (N 181)

McLuhan points out that the "the Greek word *narcosis*, or numbness" is the etymological root shared by the words "narcotics" and "narcissism." (UM 41) The attempt to "become a closed system" results in a *freezing-out* of stimuli. As McLuhan writes in the essay on Burroughs: "During the process of digestion of the old environment, man finds it expedient to anaesthetise himself as much as possible. He pays as little attention to the actions of the environment as the patient heeds the surgeon's scalpel. The gulping or swallowing of Nature by the machine was attended by a complete change of the ground rules of both the sensory ratios of the individual' nervous system and the patterns of the social world. Today, when the environment has become the extension of the entire mesh of the nervous system, anaesthesia numbs our bodies into hydraulic jacks."[28]

In *Understanding Media*, McLuhan electronically reanimates the myth of Narcissus to discuss both the implosion of subjectivity and the "autoamputation" induced by the move into a fully-mediatized environment. According to McLuhan, Narcissus' plight arises not because he falls in love with himself, but because he is unable to recognize his image as belonging to him. "The youth Narcissus mistook his own reflection in the water for another person. This extension of himself by the mirror numbed his perceptions until he became the servomechanism of his own extended or repeated image. [...] Now the point of this myth is the fact that men at once become fascinated by any extensions of themselves in any material other than themselves [...] [T]he wisdom of the Narcissus myth does not convey any idea that Narcissus fell in love with anything he regards as himself. Obviously he would have had very different feelings about the image had he known it was an extension or repetition of himself." (UM 42) For McLuhan, the modern technical environment – Gibson's Matrix – is continuous with the human nervous system, misrecognized as something separate because the sheer amount of stimuli cannot be dealt with except by an enormous numbing, or "autoamputation" of the (electronic) sense organs transmitting the stimuli. As McLuhan insists, "the sense of the Narcissus myth" is that "[t]he young man's image is a self-amputation or extension induced by irritating pressures. As counter-irritant the image

---

28. McLuhan, "Notes on Burroughs", 70

produces a generalized numbness or shock that declines recognition. Self-amputation forbids self-recognition [...] The principle of self-amputation as an immediate relief of strain on the central nervous system applies very readily to the origin of the media of communication from speech to computer." (UM 43)

What differentiates later theorists such as Baudrillard, Lasch and Jameson from McLuhan is an increasing sense that the screens have failed – the organism and/or the self is no longer able to protect itself from the slings and arrows of outrageous cybernesis. In *Seduction*, Baudrillard revives McLuhan's formula: "Narcissus=narcosis (McLuhan had already made the connection.)" (S 166) He quotes Jean Querzola, who writes of an "Electronic Narcosis", a "slip from Oedipus to Narcissus."[29] (S 166) In part, Baudrillard's Narcissism designates a condition in which selves collapse into their images; Baudrillard invokes a "digital narcissus, [who] is going to slide along the trajectory of a death drive and sink in his own image." (S 166) More radically, though, Baudrillard's Narcissism is about the inability to detach a delimited self from the circuit. Narcissistic "self" – referentiality happens at the level of the "networks' circularity" (S 166) not at the level of the subject, who exists only as the micro-recapitulation of its seamless integrity. With Jameson, Baudrillard declares the end of alienation, but where Jameson describes a "shift of the dynamics of cultural pathology" in which "the alienation of the subject is displaced by the latter's fragmentation" (PCLLC, 14), Baudrillard emphasises not fragmentation but *integration*. The structure of "our relationships with networks and screens [...] is one of subordination, not alienation – the structure of the integrated circuit." (TE 56) Like McLuhan and Baudrillard, Christopher Lasch theorizes capitalism's total integration in terms of the Narcissus myth. "As the Greek legend reminds us, it is [the] confusion of the self and the not-self - not 'egoism' – that distinguishes the plight of Narcissus. The minimal or narcissistic self is, above all, a self uncertain of its own outlines."[30]

For McLuhan, this is all anticipated in Burroughs' supposed collapsing of the category of the private. Burroughs, according to McLuhan, presents "a paradigm of the future where there can be no spectators but only participants [...] There is no privacy and no private parts."[31] The effacement of the

---

29. Baudrillard's making of the equation narcissus=necrosis is in fact in respect of cloning technologies, something we shall deal with in the next chapter.

30. Lasch, *The Minimal Self*, 19. "[L]onging," Lasch continues, adding the inevitable moralizing gloss, "either to remake the world in its own image or to merge into its environment in blissful union."

31. McLuhan, "Notes on Burroughs," 71. This implies a reversal, or part-reversal of what Deleuze-Guattari call the "vast privatization of the organs" "undertaken" by "modern societies" (AO 142-3). For Deleuze-Guattari, although "[i]ndividual persons are social persons first of all" and "[p]rivate persons are an illusion, derivatives of derivatives" (AO 264), "[t]he person has become 'private' in reality, insofar as he derives from abstract quantities and becomes concrete in the becoming-concrete of these same quantities." (AO 251) There is therefore not "a making public of the private so much as a privatization of the public." (AO 251)

distinction between private and public will, of course, become a commonplace of postmodern theory. The "loss of public space occurs contemporaneously with the loss of private space," Baudrillard observes. "The one is no longer a spectacle, the other no longer a secret." (EC 130) The disappearance of the distinction between private and public realms brings with it the concomitant disintegration of what Lasch calls "the imperial ego", Jameson's "bourgeois monad", with its "conception of a unique self and private identity, a unique personality and individuality," (PCLLC 15). For Baudrillard, as for McLuhan before him, media – particularly television – play a crucial role here, insinuating themselves into all ostensibly private zones. "TV [...] is only a screen, or better, it is a miniaturized terminal that appears in your head (you are the screen and the television is watching you), transistorizes all your neurons and passes for a magnetic tape." (S 162) "Private" space now becomes a "terminal" whose function is to relay a "public world" that only exists at the level of simulation: as Deleuze-Guattari say, "the whole world unfolds at home, without having to leave the TV screen." (AO 251) Or, as McLuhan put it in the Burroughs essay, "No civilian can escape this environmental blitzkrieg, for there is, quite literally, no place to hide."[32]

Hence the "hideous intimacy" (CZ 40) of postmodern culture; what Baudrillard terms its *obscenity*. The private-public "distinction is effaced in a sort of *obscenity* where the most intimate details of our life become the virtual feeding ground of the media [...] Inversely, the entire universe comes to unfold arbitrarily on your domestic screen (all the useless information that comes to you from the entire world, like a microscopic pornography of the universe, useless, excessive, just like the sexual close-up in a porno-film): all this explodes the scene formerly preserved by the minimal separation of public and private, the scene that was played out in a restricted space according to a secret ritual known only to the actors." (EC 130) The obscene is defined by opposition to "the scene" which, Baudrillard says, belongs to a certain *theatrics* proper to what he thinks of as a superseded psychoanalytic paradigm: here, mimesis, representation, projection and mirroring all still made sense. Distance, a certain *staging*, was still possible. But these representational dramaturgies have now been displaced into media "circuits and networks" that are "cold and communicational, contactual and motivational" (EC 130); here, there is no reflection, only interminable circulation. "The obscene is what does away with every mirror, every look, every image." (EC 130) It is the closer-than-close[33], so close that the subject is no longer able to distinguish itself from its surroundings. Pornography provides the model for obscene culture, but its ultra close-up techniques quickly extend beyond the mediatization of sexuality. "[I]t is not only the sexual that becomes obscene in pornography; today there is a whole

---

32. McLuhan, "*Playboy* interview", *Essential McLuhan*, ed. Eric McLuhan and Frank Zingrone, Concord, Ontario: House of Anansi Press, 1995: 264
33. See also "Stereo-Porno" in *Seduction*.

pornography of information and communication; that is to say, of circuits and networks." (EC 130)

Narcissism, as McLuhan, Baudrillard and Lasch understand it, is not about self-love, but the inability to distinguish self from other, object from subject: cybernesis. As Baudrillard's persistent references to communication and control imply, the postmodern vertigo of the "schizophrenic" – Lasch's "uncertainty about the outlines of the self" – is bound up with cybernetics and with what Gregory Bateson called its "new understanding of mind, self, human relationships and power."[34]

Pursued to its most radical extremes, cybernetics obsolesces perso-nological, subjectivist and organicist ontologies in favour of explanation at the level of systemic process. Cybernetic systems are essentially anorganic because they radically de-privilege the organism as the appropriate analytic focus – Bateson insists that "the basic unit of survival" is not the organism but organism plus environment – and make no differentiation between biotic and technical components. In *Steps to an Ecology of Mind* Bateson had presented a benevolent version of what Baudrillard and Lasch will characterize as the nar-cissistic or schizophrenic disintegration of the ego, arguing, Spinozistically, that "[t]he mental world – the mind – the world of information processing – is not limited by the skin."[35] "[W]hen we seek to explain the behaviour of a man [sic] or any other organism" the system designated "will usually *not* have the same limits as the 'self' – as this term is commonly (and variously) understood."[36] "[C]onsider a blind man with a stick," Bateson goes on. "Where does the blind man's self begin? At the tip of the stick? At the handle of the stick? Or at some point halfway up the stick? These questions are nonsense, because the stick is a difference along which differences are transmitted under transformation, so that to draw a delimiting line *across* this pathway is to cut off a part of the systemic circuit which determines the blind man's locomotion."[37]

---

34. Bateson, "The Cybernetics of 'Self': A Thory of Alcoholism", *Steps to an Ecology of Mind*, 280
35. Bateson, "Form, Substance and Difference" in *Steps to an Ecology of Mind*, 429
36. Bateson, "The Cybernetics of Self: A Theory of Alcoholism", in *Steps to an Ecology of Mind*, 288
37. Bateson, "The Cybernetics of Self: A Theory of Alcoholism", in *Steps to an Ecology of Mind*, 288-289. To adequately explain agency, Bateson insists, we have to make reference not to subjective motivation but to the network of relations which produce it (as epiphenomenon). A paradox – familiar to readers of Spinoza – emerges. To increase agency – to become more active in Spinoza's terms – is to become flatter with the system, not to "dominate" it (as if) from above. Bateson's analysis of alcoholism as a paradigmatic positive feedback process argued that the very attempt to regain self-control, to be a "captain of one's own soul", contributed to the escalation of the alcoholic process, which precisely depends upon a crude opposition between subject and object, drinker and bottle. While the drinker thinks of the bottle as what Spinoza calls an "external cause", and consider themselves – as subject – capable of beating it, they will have failed to apprehend the systemic complicity so fundamental to the alcoholic assemblage.

The concern, in postmodern theory, with schizophrenia, is, in large part, a registering of this cybernetic account of subjectivity, a sense that the self can no longer be properly distinguished from the multiplicity of circuits that traverse it. Postmodernity as Baudrillard and Jameson theorise is the seeping through of schizophrenia into capitalism. Whilst neither go so far as Deleuze-Guattari in directly correlating capitalism with schizophrenia, both turn to "schizophrenia" as an image of the postmodern meltdown of subjectivity in late capitalism. For Baudrillard, nerve rays[38] become cathode rays: ubiquitous media circuitries routinize a heightened, hallucinogenic experience, a "psychedelic giddiness" (S 162) characterized by "somnambular absence and tactile euphoria." (S 159) In "The Ecstasy of Communication", Baudrillard explicitly associates schizophrenia with the emergence of cybernetic networks. "If hysteria was the pathology of the exacerbated staging of the subject, a pathology of expression, of the body's theatrical and operatic conversion; and if paranoia was the pathology of organization, of the structuration of a rigid and jealous world, with communication and information, with the immanent promiscuity of all these networks, with their continual connections, we are now in a new form of schizophrenia." (EC 133)

Jameson, too, theorizes, postmodernity in terms of schizophrenia, deriving his account of from Lacanian psychoanalysis, and hurrying to point out that this is in no way a clinical definition. The chief characteristic of Jameson's postmodern schizophrenia is the breakdown in the experience of sequential time, an inability "to unify the past, present, and future of our own biographical experience or psychic life" (PCLLC 27): "the schizophrenic," Jameson writes, "is reduced to an experience [...] of pure and unrelated presents in"; "the present [...] engulfs the subject with indescribable vividness" (PCLLC 27)

Both these theorizations of schizophrenia converge with Deleuze-Guattari's in defining the schizophrenic experience in terms of a surfeit, rather than a paucity, of reality. For Deleuze-Guattari, schizophrenia is a "harrowing, emotionally overwhelming experience, which brings the schizo as close as possible to matter, to a burning, living center of matter." (AO 19) "How is it possible that the schizo was conceived of as the autistic rag – separated from the real and cut off from life – that he is so often thought to be?" (AO 19-20) they ask. While Jameson equivocates, arguing that the schizophrenic "charge of affect" can be "described in the negative terms of anxiety and loss of reality, but which one could just as well imagine in the positive terms of euphoria, a high, an intoxicatory or hallucinogenic intensity," (PCLLC 27-28) Baudrillard is definitive: "What characterizes [the schizo] is less the loss of the real, the light years of estrangement from the real, the pathos of distance and radical separation, as is commonly said, but, very much to the contrary, the absolute proximity, the total instantaneity of things, the feeling of no defense, no re-

---

38. A reference to Schreber, who famously thought communication happened through "nerve rays."

treat." (EC 133)

Hence Csiscery-Ronay's claim about the connections between cyberpunk, hallucination, dread and madness. But if it is no doubt the case that cyberpunk has a new take on schizophrenia and hallucination, these themes could hardly be said to be foreign to Horror. As even a cursory reading of Poe or Lovecraft shows, Horror is hardly a stranger to hallucination, but what differentiates cyberpunk hallucination from hallucination in Horror is essentially its technical replicability and its currency as a de-pyschologised communication medium. Artificialized hallucination stands in for a decoded socius. If the Matrix is a "consensual hallucination", its continuing reality as an environment is not dependent upon some act of collective will any more than the persistence of capital is; the sustainability of both, according to Deleuze-Guattari, has gone over to sociotechnical machines which both interpellate human beings as subjects and integrate them as components (TP 458). Techno-capital "hallucinations" are not epistemological illusions, but cybernetic-operational feedback systems. As Csicsery-Ronay writes, in a clear nod to Baudrillard, "It is natural to expect that as technology proves more and more able to construct the world in its own image (that is, to create the simulacra to replace the 'real' and 'the original') – indeed, to restructure the operations of the multinational capitalism that enables it to exist – there will be an increasing sense of its hallucinatory nature."[39] Yet it is to miss entirely the logic – the delirial anti-logic – of the process to assume that capitalism's "hallucinatory nature" can be equated with "unreality." In a certain Marxist sense, as you enter the Matrix you access what is, in effect, the most real level of Gibson's hypercapitalism, since, in the words of the cliche, *cyberspace is where your money is*. Although the Matrix and capital are totally artificial, neither are epistemological commitments, beliefs you can just opt out of, in part because the artificial can be quantified: hence Deleuze-Guattari's "fictional quantities."

Gibson's hallucinations differ from Poe's because they cannot be attributed, even provisionally, to psychological dis-ease. In a canonic example of Poe-horror such as "The Tell-tale Heart", all the mechanics of interiority can still be seen to obtain: perceptual warps arise from a guilty, internal neurosis that finds itself echoed everywhere in the outside world. In Gibson's world, hallucination emerges as the effect of electrolibidinal affect: psychology plays no active part, functioning only as the register of events that are "neuro-electronic" in character. "The voice was just part of dying, being flatlined, some crazy bullshit your brain threw up to make you feel better, and something had happened back at the source, maybe a brownout in their part of the grid, so the ice had lost its hold on his nervous system." (CZ 61)

Predictably, Baudrillard defines the new science fiction in terms of simulation. (Ballard's *Crash*, for instance, becomes "the first great novel of

39. Csicsery-Ronay, "Cyberpunk and Neuromanticism", in McCaffrey ed., *Storming the Reality Studio*, 189.

the universe of simulation." [SS 119]) But it is the combination of simulation with stimulus in what Gibson calls *simstim* ("Simulated stimuli"[40]) that is in fact more characteristic of key cyberpunk texts such as *Videodrome* and *Neuromancer*. Specifically, simstim is the name Gibson gives to an ultra-advanced neuro-electronically-triggered hypermedia apparatus: something to make the soaps seem more real than real. More generally, though, the combination of simulation-stimulation underlies all the key technical developments Gibson describes - bio- (or micro-) softs (data-input devices that can be meshed directly into the nervous system) and the immersive environment of cyberspace (or the Matrix) itself. Perception has been decoded into a matter of particular set of triggerable 'stims' capable of simulating any possible experience. The simulation of particular affective states by direct neuronic stimulation had been a concern of cybernetic fiction since Crichton's *The Terminal Man*[41], and it is central to Cronenberg's *Videodrome*.

Hence the relation between the human organism and its technical environment becomes understood not any longer in terms of organic extensions, but of dependence-circuitries. "The preoccupation with addiction, or, more broadly, dependency, in cyberpunk fiction and its precursors reflects a supercession of subjectivity by cybernetics; Oedipus becoming-narcissus." What Gibson calls the intimacy of cyberpunk technical machines indicates a new level of machinic-dependency, but addiction always implies a becoming-anorganic since it involves the induction of the organism into extra-organic feedback circuits. Cyberpunk tends towards the abstraction of addiction; Gibson's characterization of Case as a "drug addict" (N 161) seems superfluous since it is clear that the condition of the console cowboys automatically involves addiction to technically-freebased stimuli.

"'I'm a drug addict, Cath.'
'What kind?'
'Stimulants. Central nervous system stimulants. Extremely powerful central nervous system stimulants.'" (N 161)

---

40. *Burning Chrome*, 210
41. Like many of Crichton's subsequent novels - including the Chaos-SF of *Jurassic Park* - *The Terminal Man* is an intriguing mixture of theory-fiction and airport novel, spiced with a neo-Wienerian moral warning about the danger of cybernetics. (Its semi-faked bibliography in fact includes references to Wiener). The story concerns a violent criminal who is on a pilot scheme for cybernetic control: when the criminal is about to have a psychotic episode, he receives a corrective charge from implanted electrodes. Problems start when the criminal starts becoming addicted to the supposedly corrective charges, which then induce, rather than prevent, the psychotic episodes they were designed to regulate.

2.7 STIMULATING THE GOTHIC BODY: VIDEODROME

Cronenberg: "we know that by the use of electrodes in certain areas of the brain you can trigger off a violent, fearful response without regard to other stimulants."[42]

Dick: "[H]allucinations, whether induced by psychosis, hypnosis, drugs, toxins, etc. may be merely quantitatively different from what we see, not qualititatively so. In other words, too much is emanating from the neurological apparatus of the organism, over and beyond the structural, organizing necessity [...] No name entities or aspects begin to appear, and since the person does not know what they are – that is, what they're called or what they mean – he cannot communicate with other persons about them. The breakdown of verbal communication is a fatal index that somewhere along the line the person is experiencing reality in a way too altered to fit into his own prior worldview and too radical to allow empathic linkage with other persons."[43]

Jameson: "The originality of Philip K. Dick was then to have reunited the twin fear of addiction and of schizophrenia (with its reality-loops and hallucinatory alternate worlds) in a lethal combination which Cronenberg's media nightmare transcends, replaces, and intensifies all at once, translating it into the society of the spectacle or image capitalism."[44]

Cronenberg's *Videodrome* has achieved its "canonic"[45] status because of its almost emblematic staging of the convergence of cybernetic and Gothic themes. Cronenberg's almost complete stripping away of the conventions of the Horror genre – his abandonment of the expressionistic style revived in the almost directly contemporary *Blade Runner* - might give the misleading impression that he has in some sense left behind the trappings of the Gothic, but *Videodrome*'s eschewal of particular Horror conventions goes alongside a reinforcement of the principal Gothic theme of anorganic continuum. Exactly like the expressionist cinema whose conventions it has displaced, *Videodrome* follows Worringer's Gothic line as it passes across the so-called animate and inanimate. But it shares with Gibson a sense that it is ultramodern

---

42. Cronenberg, in Rodley, *Cronenberg on Cronenberg*, 94
43. Philip K. Dick, *The Shifting Realities of Philip K. Dick: Selected Literary and Philosophical Writings*, New York: Vintage/Random House 172
44. Jameson, *The Geopolitical Aesthetic*, 30
45. Jameson, *The Geopolitical Aesthetic*, 27

cybernetic technical assemblages that are making the distinction between organic and inorganic increasingly unstable. In particular, it focuses on media – especially the so-called postmodern media of TV and video, and the still nascent technologies of Virtual Reality – as assemblages which reconfigure the body in new ways, opening it up to desiring-trajectories that have as their corollary a new – cybernetic – account of power.

Videodrome's most powerful scenes directly invert the image of the prostheticized body Freud presents in *Civilization and its Discontents*. In *Videodrome*, Max's body, in what may be a pointed, and corrective, reference to McLuhan's media-organicism, is not extended, but invaginated. Here is a body literally overwhelmed by an unmanageable quantity of stimuli: an image of what happens when McLuhan's "Freudian censor" is unable to sieve out damaging intensities. But if *Videodrome*'s central images of the body are an inversion of the organicized Freudo-McLuhanite extensionalist body, they are also – deliberately parodic – literalizations of the body posited in the discourse of censorship and image regulation. "With *Videodrome* I wanted to posit the possibility that man exposed to violent imagery would begin to hallucinate," Cronenberg has said. "I wanted to see what it would be like, in fact, if what the censors were saying would happen, did happen."[46] What, that is to say, if the body could not be only triggered, but actually mutated, by TV and video-signal? In *Videodrome*, Cronenberg's background in making Horror films – albeit of an aberrant kind[47] - crosses over into a ficto-theorization of contemporary media in terms of Gothic affect. Here, we bring into play another McLuhan: the McLuhan who had understood popular media to be based, like cheap Gothic novels, on what, following the Deleuze of the Bacon book, we might call a logic of sensation.

As early as *The Mechanical Bride* (1953) – his first full-length attempt to provide a symptomatology of media psychopathology – McLuhan had written of "the curious fusion of sex, technology and death" in media artifacts. Newspaper layout – effectively a form of collage according to McLuhan – operates via "editorial ghoul techniques", "poetic associations of linked and contrasting imagery". McLuhan cites one magazine example, "in which the central picture was a wounded man coming home "to face it all another day down another death-swept road." Flanking him was a sprawling pin-up: "Half a million servicemen wrote for this one." And underneath him in exactly the same posture of surrender was a nude female corpse with a rope around her neck: "Enraged Nazis hanged this Russian guerrilla." McLuhan speculates that this "may well be what draws people to the death shows of the speedways and fills the press and magazines with close-ups of executions, suicides and smashed bodies. A metaphysical hunger to experience everything sexually, to pluck out the heart

---

46. Rodley, Cronenberg on Cronenberg, 94
47. Cronenberg's early features, such as *Shivers* and *Rabid* were key contributions to the so-called genre of "body horror".

of the mystery for a super-thrill."[48]

Pornography and Gothic fiction stand behind the media machineries McLuhan describes, as technologies for the targeting and heightening of stimulation. Gothic fiction, like pornography, is sold as a body-stimulating machine, its "super-thrills" not directly sexual, but "spine-chilling" or "hair-raising." (Although, as McLuhan hints, and as we shall explore more fully below, for *Videodrome* and Ballard, the tendency in hypermedia/sensation culture is towards an abstract sensation and away from a naturalized sexuality, towards a cyberoticism or hypersexuality that precisely puts in question the limits of the sexual as such.)

Videodrome appears in the film as the updating and technicization of McLuhan's "fusion of sex, technology and death." The Videodrome signal is the ultimate interactive technology; distributed via fleshy cassettes that pulse with obscene nonorganic animation, it is a hyper-intense "media" apparatus, a crossbreed of video, virtual reality and (anti-biotic) contagion. Videodrome's inventor is Brian O'Blivion ("not the name I was born with ... some day all of us will have special names, names that will cause the cathode ray to vibrate") a media guru who has been described both as "an obvious McLuhan figure"[49] and as "a thinly disguised Baudrillard,"[50] (which tells us as much about the close relationship between Baudrillard and McLuhan as it does about Cronenberg's film). According to his daughter, Bianca, O'Blivion saw Videodrome as "the next stage in man's evolution as a technological animal... a new organ, a new part of the brain." When Max first encounters O'Blivion, on a TV talk show, he is, we subsequently learn, already dead. The "first victim of Videodrome" survives as a set of video recordings ("he made thousands of them"), appearing "on TV only on TV".

As the head of a small cable channel, Renn is turned onto Videodrome by its promise of a new and extreme combination of sex and violence; tricked into believing it is an illicit broadcast coming out of the third world, he thinks of it at first as snuff TV: "no plot, characters, torture, murder ... very, very realistic". Although Videodrome appears at first to be (merely) a particularly hardcore variant of S/M porn, pornography here is only ostensibly (or initially) to do with biotic sex, functioning instead as a probe-head through which techniques for the maximization of stimulation (and – concomitantly – its management) can be explored Videodrome's purpose is to "open the neural floodgates", to trigger "receptors in the brain and spine". Recalling the McLuhan-Ballard correlation of mass media with sexualised violence, (a convergence explored more fully by Cronenberg in *Crash*), *Videodrome* points to an eroticization of

48. McLuhan, "Essential McLuhan", 52
49. Douglas Kellner, "David Cronenberg: Panic Horror and the Postmodern Body", 94
50. E. Ann Kaplan, "Feminism/Oedipus/Postmodernism: The Case of MTV", in Kaplan, E. Ann, (ed.) *Postmodernism and its Discontents: Theories, Practices*, London/New York: Verso, 1988

everything that immediately de-privileges sex in its bio-reproductive mode. "It's not exactly sex,' Renn warns his lover Nicki Brand (Deborah Harry) of Videodrome. "Says who?" she counters, echoing Ballard's deterritorialization of sex in *The Atrocity Exhibition* (of which more shortly).

> "We live in overstimulated times," Nicki Brand tells Max. "I want you' Max," she breathes. "Come to me. Come to Nicki." Her lips fill the screen, and all boundaries are removed as the diegetic frame of the TV screen vanishes from view: the lips now fill the TV screen in a vast closeup. Biotic sex becomes displaced by a hallucinatory, generalized cyberotics; in one scene "the set begins to pulsate, to breathe [...] veins ripple the hardware cabinet [...] a videogame joystick waggles obscenely."[51]

Believing that it can programme Renn as one of its assassins, Spectacular Optical – the megacorporation that is ultimately revealed to be behind Videodrome ("we make inexpensive glasses for the third world and missile guidance systems for NATO") – deliberately infects Max with the signal that will transform him into New Flesh, seducing him using the image of radio announcer Nicki Brand. Renn has a series of increasingly intense hallucinations, which he eventually connects to his consumption of the videodrome programming. Ultimately, Renn, re-programmed by O'Blivion's daughter, Bianca, turns on his new masters, killing Spectacular Optical's Barry Convex. Or so it would appear; we are so deep into "Philip K. Dick-like reality loops"[52] that we can't be sure what is happening for [hyper]real. Perhaps much of the film, including the apparent assassinations, are merely hallucinations, safely monitored by Barry Convex using a prototype VR helmet and recording device.

51. Bukatman, *Terminal Identity*, 89
52. Jameson, *The Geopolitical Aesthetic*, 23

2.8 TACTILE POWER

Deleuze: "Clockwork automata, but also motor automata, in short automata of movement, gave way to a new computer and cybernetic race, automata of computation and thought, automata with controls and feedback. The configuration of power was also inverted, and, instead of converging on a single, mysterious leader, inspirer of dreams, commander of actions, power was diluted in an information network where decision-makers managed control, processing and stock across intersections of insomniacs and seers."[53]

"*Videodrome* operates as a hypercommentary on Horror and its capacity to stimulate – and therefore transform – the body (and therefore reality)." Running alongside the history of Horror cinema is a discourse of censorship and control which has posited a body capable of terrifying transformation; a body that it at once a passive recording surface and a violently libidinized maw, hungry for stimulus. (Baudrillard's *In the Shadow of the Silent Majorities*, with its hyperparodic invocation of a pliable body, subject to the influence of media might even be the ironic postscript to this tradition.). Meanwhile, somnambulism, mesmerism and manipulation have been themes in Gothic cinema since *The Cabinet of Dr Caligari*. What *Videodrome* adds to this Gothic account of power, of course, is an emphasis on the production of somnambulist desire by media itself, revealing the complicity of certain discourses about media with the language of Horror.

What is at stake in *Videodrome* - and what makes it fit so closely with Baudrillard's theorizations – is an account of how the body is an intrinsic component part of new machineries of control and manipulation, which are no longer spectacular, but *tactile*. *Videodrome* shares with Baudrillard an inheritance from McLuhan that amounts to a critique of spectacular-optical culture, emerging in an emphasis on the non- or post-optical functioning of new media. Although obsessed with optics, Cronenberg's film ultimately concurs with McLuhan's claim that "electric technology has meant for Western man a considerable drop in the visual component of his experience, and a corresponding increase in the activity of his other senses."[54] – McLuhan's thesis that TV is a tactile medium, outlined in some of the most haunting and enigmatic passages in his writing, is repeatedly referenced in some of *Videodrome*'s most powerful images, in particular those in which we see Max seduced by the

---

53. Deleuze, *Cinema 2: The Time-Image*, trans. Hugh Tomlinson and Robert Galeta, London: The Athlone Press, 1989, 265
54. McLuhan, *The Medium is the Massage*, Harmondsworth: Penguin, 1967, 125

Nicki Brand-Videodrome composite. As Max "approaches the set [...] the screen bulges outward to meet his touch, literalizing the notion of the screen as breast. His face sinks in, his hands fondle the panels and knobs of the set as the lips continue their panting invitation."[55] Here, the medium is indeed the massage. But this interactivity is always immanent to television's operations, McLuhan suggests. "The TV image requires each instant that we 'close' the spaces in the mesh by a convulsive sensuous participation that is profoundly kinetic and tactile, because tactility is the interplay of the senses, rather than the isolated contact of skin and object." (UM 314) Baudrillard will cite this formulation in *Symbolic Exchange and Death*, (65) as part of an analysis that simultaneously ironizes McLuhan's position while extending it. "So we can understand why McLuhan saw an era of *tactile* communication in the era of electronic mass-media. In this we are closer in effect to the tactile than we are to the visual universe, where there is greater distance, and reflection is always possible." (SED 65) The tactile becomes part of a contactual/tactical "universe of communication" whose obscene closeness no longer allows the space for "response" while always ostensibly soliciting it.

   Videodrome delineates the stealthy intercession into, and deletion of, private space by television described by both McLuhan and Baudrillard. "It is well known," Baudrillard writes in "The Ecstasy of Communication", "how the simple presence of the television changes the rest of the habitat into a kind of archaic envelope, a vestige of human relations whose very survival remains perplexing. As soon as this scene is no longer haunted by its actors and their fantasies, as soon as behaviour is crystallized on certain screens and operational terminals, what's left appears only as a large useless body, deserted and condemned." (EC 129) TV is a deeply *unheimlich*[56] technology, a disturbing presence in the heart of the domestic scene whose apparent reassuring familiarity conceals its insidious destruction of that very scene[57] (and all scenes, Bau-

---

55. Bukatman, *Terminal Identity*, 90

56. Note McLuhan's comments on the *intimacy* of TV, its disturbing familiarity (to paraphrase Freud). "Newscasters and actors alike report the frequency with which they are approached by people who feel they've met them before. Joanne Woodward in an interview was asked what was the difference between being a movie star and a TV actress. She replied: "When I was in the movies I heard people say, 'There goes Joanne Woodward.' Now they say, 'There goes somebody I think I know.' – " (UM 318) The age of the cinema – a "hot", which is to say non-participatory, medium – gives way to the "cool" interactivity of TV, bringing an end to the giganticism of the star system. "It is no accident that such major movie stars as Rita Hayworth, Liz Taylor, and Marilyn Monroe ran into troubled waters in the new TV age. They ran into an age that questioned all the 'hot' media values of the pre-TV consumer days." (UM 320)

57. "When I observe the most intimate details of the Other onscreen [...]," William Bogard glosses, "it is only the *mise-en-scene* of intimacy that I am given, a disenchanted, sterile (but not lost!) intimacy derived not so much from witnessing something hitherto unobserved or private as from plugging into a system where nothing is private and everything is, where the secret does not exist and everything is secret at the same time

drillard will insist): "today it is the very space of habitation that's conceived as both receiver and distributor [...] the control screen and terminal [...] Here we are far from the living-room and close to science fiction." (EC 128) Or beyond science fiction, and into cyberpunk...

As "the most recent and spectacular electric extension of our central nervous system" (UM 317), television, McLuhan suggests, is "a complex *gestalt* of data gathered almost at random" (UM 317), "a flat two-dimensional mosaic" (UM 313). TV, according to McLuhan, exerts an *ambient dominance*, subtly but completely altering the domestic environment as soon as it enters it. "Television demands participation and involvement in depth of the whole being. It will not work as background."[58] You don't watch TV, McLuhan urges, you *scan* it, you follow it. "The mode of the TV image has nothing in common with film or photo, except that it offers also a new nonverbal *gestalt* or posture of forms [...] The TV image is not a *still* shot. It is not a photo in any sense, but a ceaselessly forming contour of things limned by the scanning-finger. The resulting plastic contour appears by light *through*, not light *on*, and the image so formed has the quality of sculpture and icon, rather than of picture." (UM 313) Television cyberneticizes the environment. While film and photography leave in place the dichotomy between subject and object – film is projected over the heads of the audience; photos are constituted as spatially delimitable – TV cannot simply be *looked at* by a spectator who retains a distance from it. "You have to be 'with it' [...] It engages you. Perhaps this is why so many people feel that their identity has been threatened."[59]

Given his emphasis on the closeness of Cronenberg's film to Baudrillard's work, Scott Bukatman's theorization of *Videodrome* as part of the "science fiction of the spectacle", then, is oddly misleading. Despite arguing that "*Videodrome* seems to be a film which hypostatizes Baudrillard's own polemic"[60], Bukatman fails to process Baudrillard's critique of situationist theory. Similarly, Bukatman's hasty dismissal of McLuhan is puzzling, given that Baudrillard's theory of power – insofar as he still recognizes the continuing validity of the term – is very much indebted – explicitly so – to McLuhan's formulations. An important footnote to *Precession of Simulacra* uses a gloss on what Baudrillard thinks is McLuhan's most significant formula – the medium is the message – as a means of exploring the new power networks. Baudrillard is happy here to classify the new configurations as power, but distinguishes this new delocalized mode of power from "power in its classical definition" (SS 41), which is at an "end" (SS 41). Since the "medium/message confusion" has now collapsed "thus sealing the disappearance of all dual, polar structures

---

– all this in the form of an ecstasy of orbitalization and dissolution, a mass mediatized extravagance." *Simulation of Surveillance*, 151
    58. McLuhan, *The Medium is the Message*, 125
    59. Ibid.
    60. Bukatman, "Who Programs You...", 203

[...]," there is no instance of power, no instance of transmission – power is something that circulates and whose source can no longer be located." (SS 41)

The passage is one of a number of occasions in which Baudrillard makes an explicit point of differentiating his own position from that of the situationists. Baudrillard could not be clearer. "We are witnessing the end of perspectival and panoptic space [...] and thus to the very abolition of the spectacular," he proclaims in *Precession of Simulacra*. "Television, for example [...] is no longer a spectacular medium. We are no longer in the society of the spectacle of which the situationists spoke, nor in the specific kinds of alienation and repression that it implied. The medium itself is no longer identifiable as such and the confusion of the medium and the message is the first great formula of this new era." (SS 30) And in "The Ecstasy of Communication", "Obscenity begins when there is no more spectacle. [...]" (EC 130)

The implicit critique of situationist theory Baudrillard presents concerns its continuing assumption of a distinction between power and its objects, between the spectacle and what it conceals. Ultimately, Baudrillard suggests, the situationists are committed to an appearance/reality distinction that is no longer sustainable. Everything circulates now, Baudrillard insists. Nothing is concealed; indeed, everything is hyper-visible. There is nothing and no-one behind appearances that could be exposed, just as there is no alienation from which one can be liberated. Insofar as there is a source of power it is you. Psychoanalysis provides the model for these decentred circuitries of "manipulation". "[O]ne can always ask of the traditional holders of power where they get their power from. Who made you duke? the king? Who made you king? God. Only God no longer answers. But to the question: who made you a psychoanalyst? the analyst can reply: You." (SS 41) Power has completed the spectacle by making it interactive; but in doing so, it has abolished the spectacle as such, and inaugurated a new, all-inclusive, system which makes alienation – and its critique – obsolete. Immersion – so central a preoccupation of cyberpunk and its technologies – displaces spectatorship.

Videodrome's neo-McLuhanite emphasis on interactivity follows Burroughs and Foucault[61] in suggesting that capitalism increasingly functions not by repressing the body but by plugging it into positive feedback excitation circuitries. In *Videodrome*, the Burroughs' theme of image-addiction and McLuhan's theories of habituation to media come together in the O'Blivion's Cathode Ray Mission, a kind of updated soup kitchen in which TV addicts can get "patched back into the world's mixing board." Addiction, already a becoming-inorganic of the organism, is transferred over onto the technical machines, as part of a production of artificial desire (=machinic dependency). "The spectacular Videodrome generates subliminal over-stim-

---

61. Deleuze, in the essay "Postscript on Societies of Control", makes a parallel between Burroughs and Foucault as cartographers of systems of "continuous control and instant communication." (*Negotiations*, 175)

ulation and this hype leads to a craving for stimulation for its own sake [...]
The Videodrome through the television screen (in words, sound, vision, visual
imagery) releases spores, pheromones which make us gorge ourselves on it,
always wanting more, whether it's tactile, sexual, phenomenal, social, material
or emotional..."[62]

For *Videodrome*, media and addiction converge in a pornography that
is not concerned straightforwardly with a stimulation of the organism by the
represent ion of a naturalized body. Instead, bodies are mutated as part of the
operations of a nonorganic circuit which denaturalizes sexuality at the same
time as it effectuates a hyper-eroticism of the environment: the Videodrome
signal, as we have seen, makes the scene obscene, swarming with unnatural intensities. In terms of the cybernetic systems *Videodrome* describes, pornography
and addiction are interlocking machineries of bodily manipulation and, in both
cases, what is crucial is the participatory or interactive relationship between
the Control technology and the body it is manipulating. *It works so much better
when you want it.*

It is Burroughs who is a crucial figure here. As Scott Bukatman has
noted, *Videodrome* is saturated with Burroughs' thematics and imagery. But it
is perhaps his role as a theorist of a deterritorialized pornography as a control
apparatus that he is most important in *Videodrome*. Alongside drug addiction, pornography serves as one of Burroughs' chief examples of a control
process. Pornography assumes a privileged position in Burroughs' cut-up texts
because it exemplifies the process he calls "image addiction", exposing the
mechanisms by which desire is simultaneously artificialized and channelled.
What Burroughs derives from psychoanalysis – and his study of scientology[63] -
is principally the idea of the subject as a recording – and recorded – system.
The "reprogramming" of the human nervous system – the major theme, as
McLuhan says, of Burroughs' *Nova Express* - is a neo-Spinozist model of the
production of sad passions. Like addiction, pornography is an ostensibly participatory process which commensurates the organism to exogenous – and arbitrary – stimuli. For Burroughs, the consumer of pornography, like the addict,
is ultimately himself consumed, locked into ever-more predictable circuits of
dead affect; desire learns to love its own repression by allowing itself to be
looped into the desolate repetition of mechanical stimulus-response patterns.

Needless to say, Burroughs makes no distinction between pornography and "ordinary" sexuality; on the contrary, for Burroughs, all sexuality needs
to be understood on the model of pornography. Sex is a recording, to be re-
cut, spliced together and replayed. It is all purely technical, a question of habituation to stimuli that could be anything; the body is slaved into idiot compul-
sive-repetitive behaviours by the triggering of what Burroughs calls "images".

---

62. Downham, "Videodrome", 189
63. Burroughs derives the idea of Reactive Mind from Hubbard's theory-fictions.
The Reactive Mind (or RM) is a set of recordings – or engrams – which induce the
organism to respond in pre-directed ways.

The "image", for Burroughs is essentially a particular neuronic stimuli, around which associations cluster. Repeat the image and you repeat whatsoever is associated with it. Where Freud privileges one particular image, or set of images - what Deleuze-Guattari call the family photo - so as to freeze desire into familial representations, Burroughs realises that, in principle, any image can function to capture desire. Sexuality operates in Burroughs less as a primary instinct than as a reprogrammable stimulus-response circuitry. "You see sex is an electrical charge that can be turned on and off if you know the electromagnetic switchboard." (NE 140) Burroughs' work endlessly insists that pornography operates not as a representation of sex, but as its deterritorialization (out onto the technical machines), and complementary capture. Sex escapes into recording technologies that sample and loop repetition-compulsions before feeding them back into bio-behaviour that increasingly functions as their idiotic replay. As with Spinoza, Burroughs presents a version of behaviourism that operates through rudimentary techniques of associationism:

The operation is very technical - Look at photomontage - It makes a statement in flexible picture language - Let us take the statement made by a given photomontage X - We can use X words X colors X odors X images and so forth to define the various aspects of X - Now we feed X into the calculating machine and X scans out related colors, juxtapositions, affect-charged images and so forth we can attenuate or concentrate X by taking out or adding elements and feeding back into the machine elements we wish to concentrate - A Technician learns to think and write in association blocks which can then be manipulated according to the laws of association and juxtaposition - The basic law of association and conditioning is known to college students even in America: Any object, feeling, odor, word, image in juxtaposition with any other object, feeling, odor, word or image will be associated with it - Our technicians learn to read newspapers and magazines for juxtaposition statements rather than alleged content - We express these statements in Juxtaposition Formulae - The Formulae of course control populations of the world - [64]

Association is not a cognitive process, but something physical; all cognitive narrativization is always derivative from a more primary zone of bodily affect. But rather than all stimulus being ultimately attributable to bio-sexuality - as a certain crude psychoanalytic reductionism would insist - Burroughs shows that associationist collaging can flash-cut any random image into a neuronic series and libidinize it. "Flash from words to colors on the association screen - Associate silently from colors to the act - Substitute other factors for the words - Arab drum music - Musty smell of erections in outhouses - Feel of orgasm - Color -music-smell-fell to the million sex acts all time place -"[65] The

---

64. *Nova Express*, New York: Grove Press, 1964, 78
65. *Nova Express*, 140. The cut-up and fold-in techniques of aleatory composition - utilized by Burroughs to most sustained effect in the "Nova" trilogy of *The Soft Machine, The Ticket that Exploded* and *Nova Express* - are supposed to break up these pre-set word-association lines, disrupting autonomic reaction-response patterns

body, then, emerges as a set of nonorganic recordings, triggers and replays.
For the Cronenberg of *Videodrome*, pornography functions as a cybernetic (re)engineering of the body, rather than a simple matter of optical
stimulation. *Videodrome* draws out the way in which the achievement of the
pornographic ideal would precisely not be matter of improving visual resolution
(guaranteeing psychic/physical integrity and maintaining specular distance)
but of facilitating bodily immersion (compromising all boundaries and doing
away with all distance). As William Bogard explains: "The practical problem
in the production of telematic porn is how the simulated body onscreen can
become a surrogate for, and a prosthetic of, the real body, more attuned to the
user's fantasies and pleasures. And also the reverse, how the 'real body' of the
observer can become more integrated into the apparatus of simulation. [...]
[T]his translates into a question not so much of vision, nor even exactly of the
gaze (surveillance technology), but of *tactility* (McLuhan saw this in relation
to television years ago)." (156) Bogard here closely echoes Baudrillard, who
argues that "the spiralling effect of the shifting of power, the effect of circularity
in which power is lost, is dissolved, is resolved into perfect manipulation (it is
no longer of the order of directive power and of the gaze, but of the order of
tactility and commutation)." (SS 41-42) Tactility, as Baudrillard takes it up,
indicates less the sensory or inter-sensory – "touching loses its sensory, sensual
value for us", he says (SED 64) – than a "participatory" circuit. Whenever
Baudrillard writes of participation there are always implicit inverted commas
around the word; not because he thinks that the discourses of tactility and
participation are ideological mystifications, but because participation implies
the possibility of distance, of separation, whereas the circuits he describes are
so complete that there is nothing "outside" them; participation is impossible,
because you have always been included. Response is screened out in advance.

"With TV, the viewer is the screen," (UM 313) McLuhan pronounces,
in a slogan that clearly anticipates Baudrillard, whose take-up of this motif is
as predictable as it is inevitable. Prime component in the ecstasy of communication (and its correlate, control), TV is fundamentally cybernetic, operating
by drawing the "viewer" into a circuit.[66] Thus the tapes in *Videodrome* which

with random elements. Textual montage acts against the neural montage that is the
controlled nervous system. But see Deleuze-Guattari's critique of the cut-up in *A
Thousand Plateaus*, where they argue that "implies a supplementary dimension to that
of the texts under consideration. In this supplementary dimension, unity continues its
spiritual labour." (TP 6)
66. Not for nothing do Deleuze-Guattari cite television as an example of cybernetic power. "[O]ne is subjected to TV insofar as one uses and consumes it, in the
particular situation of a subject of the statement that more or less mistakes itself for a
subject of enunciation ('you, dear television viewers, who make TV what it is ...'); the
technical machine is the medium between two subjects. But one is enslaved by TV as
a human machine insofar as the viewers are no longer consumers or users, nor even
subjects who supposedly 'make' it, but intrinsic component pieces, 'input' and 'output,'
feedback or recurrences that are no longer connected to the machines in such a way

induce Max's hallucinations are not entirely pre-recorded. They merely "set the tone", as O'Blivion puts it, interacting with the specific nervous system they are targeting like intelligent viruses. But pre-recording is nevertheless an important element, since what *Videodrome* is about is the – postmodern – fusion of television and video (one of whose effects is the displacement of live broadcasting in favour of prerecorded footage).[67] Thus Max is reconfigured as a video *player* (a cybernetic component on which power is recorded, erased and re-recorded, not a tabula rasa on which power is inscribed, once and for all). "The axiomatic does not need to write on bare flesh, to mark bodies and organs, nor does it need to fashion a memory for men." (AO 250)[68] *Videodrome* shows how "profoundly illiterate" (AO 240) capitalism keeps up the symbolic order only for show.[69] You don't *read* Capital, *Videodrome* makes clear. You play it, it plays you.

A logic of contagion – of contact and infection[70] - replaces any strategy of ideological persuasion. Simply to have contact with the Videodrome signal is to be infected by it. Jameson comes close to this perception when he writes of the "fear of the subliminal" in *Videodrome*. "Primary here is no doubt the fear of the subliminal itself; the television screen as part of the eye; that sense of incorporating unclean or harmful substances that runs all the way from yesterday's phobias about fluorinated water and what it can do to our 'precious bodily fluids' back into the deep witchcraft and envy of the village and tribal societies. [... T]he putative subliminal signals of the Videodrome image can be seen to be intensifications of Bunuel's inaugural assault on the viewer's eyeball (with a straight razor), while the deeper fantasy about the lethal properties of commodity consumption runs at least from the legendary

---

as to produce or use it." (TP 458)

67. For Jameson, video is the "postmodern medium" *par excellence*, the medium of "total flow" (See PCLLC, Chapter 3).

68. This is by contrast with the primitive socius, whose mnemotechnical methods of tattooing and inscription are described in the section of *Anti-Oedipus* called "Territorial Representation", 184-192. But, as Jameson suggests, in conditions of total flow, memory is no longer an option: "memory seems to play no role in television, commerical or otherwise (or, I am tempted to say, in postmodernism itself): nothing here haunts the mind or leaves its afterimages in the manner of the great moments of film." (PCLLC 71)

69. For Deleuze-Guattari, "capitalist representation" has left signification and writing behind. The value of McLuhan's theories, they say, is to make this clear. "This seems to us to be the significance of McLuhan's analyses: to have shown what a language of decoded flows is, as opposed to a signifier that strangles and overcodes the flows [...] [F]or nonsignifying language anything will do: whether it be phonic, graphic, gestural, etc., no flow is privileged in this language, which remains indifferent to its substance or its support, inasmuch as the latter is an amorphous continuum." (AO 240)

70. We might be reminded here of Deleuze's claim that "viral contagion" is "the passive danger" presented by "information technology and computers" which are the "third generation of machines" belonging to "control societies." (*Negotiations*, 180)

coke in Coca-Cola." (GA, 29-30) The body subject to such assault is not in any sense a sealed organism, but a body capable of mutation, of fusion with capital and its commodities, a Gothic body: a Body without Organs. And in the end, *Videodrome* is far more ambivalent about the extent of cybernetic control than is Baudrillard: Max's assassination of Spectacular Optical's Barry Convex and his final transformation into New Flesh suggest that, as a true Gothic technology, the infection – the Burroughsian image-virus – may not remain loyal to its masters. The tactile, then, registers not only as a power mechanism, but as a new, post-optical, desiring-trajectory: Cronenberg's point is that the two – desire and power – become increasingly interfused in Deleuze's Societies of Control.

2.9 THE ATROCITY EXHIBITION

The – until then – implicit connection between Cronenberg and J.G. Ballard as theory-fictional explorers of contemporary cybernetic culture was concretized in Cronenberg's notorious film version of Ballard's *Crash*. A scene added by Cronenberg himself to the original *Crash* novel immediately reminds us of *Videodrome*'s logic of sensation, its fusion of body and media landscape. At one point in the film, we find Vaughan, *Crash*'s anti-hero trauma theoro-technician, performing a public restaging of the crash which killed James Dean, complete with live commentary. We are reminded immediately of McLuhan's "curious fusion of sex, technology and death", a phrase which could serve as a handy soundbite introduction to Ballard's universe. Here we have it: a mediamatic repetition-compulsion culture in which trauma and mass communication have become indivisible, where any experience is inseparable from its mediatization.

Cronenberg's appropriation of Ballard – absolutely logical given their shared obsessions with the interactions between media, technical systems and the body – gives an intriguing hint that we may be able to approach Ballard as a Gothic writer. Fundamentally, it is Ballard's treatment of technical, organic and geological features as elements belonging to a single plane that makes him an explorer of the Gothic line: "all junctions, whether of our own biologies or the hard geometries of these walls and ceilings, are equivalent to one another." (AE 61) What *Crash* - both the novel and the film – radically displaces, as Baudrillard says, is the "classical" account of technology and of the body. In its place, according to Baudrillard, we have "a body confused with technology in its violating and violent dimension, in the savage and continual surgery that violence exercises: incisions, excisions, scarifications, the chasms of the body, of which the sexual wounds and pleasures of the body are only a particular case [...] – a body without organs or pleasure of the organs." (SS 111)

In his key works, Ballard performs a literal de-territorialization of Science Fiction, a shift from the thematics of spatial domination that, according to Baudrillard, had dominated it in its "classical" period. What Ballard has himself characterised as his stress on "inner" as opposed to "outer" space could give the misleading impression that Ballard has made a phenomenological move, privileging a psychological interiority over a concern with "the outside world". Nothing could be further from the truth. In Ballard's world, the distinction between inner and outer has fallen away, but not in favour of interiority. Ballard's reversal of Promethean SF goes by way of a new account of the body, or, more Spinozistically, of bodies. Rather than positing a neutral or transcendent body that can terraform space, Ballard shows that it is analytically impossible for bodies to dominate any environment because (1) bodies are radically inextricable from landscape, and immediately become part of it as soon as they enter it; to enter a milieu is immediately to enter into composition with it and (2) bodies are themselves landscapes, which must be treated as geological residue.

Ballard's fictions are anti-organicist and cybernetic, not because they hypostatise technical machines, but because in them it is exteriority, the milieu, that becomes the most dynamic element. It is not technology that Ballard confronts (indeed some of his most important works make little or no reference to technical machines at all) so much as media, in McLuhan's sense of "total environment." In a discussion of Ballard, Martin Bax shows how, in traditional literature, "the scenery, the physical surrounding doesn't really matter"[71]. Media – whether the car or the landscape – are assumed to be vehicles for content ("intraphyschic behaviour"). In a "condensed novel" such as *The Atrocity Exhibition*, Ballard radically reverses this priority; landscape is no longer the enduring (an)organic backdrop to a theatre of human activity, but is the principal focus of a schizo-analytic procedure.

In his *Minimal Self*, Christopher Lasch discusses this effect in Ballard's work in the context of what he calls "the replacement of a reliable world of durable objects by a world of flickering images that make it harder and harder to distinguish reality from fantasy." (19). Like Jameson, who has tried to distance himself from Lasch[72] but whose critique of postmodern culture is in many respects strikingly parallel, Lasch reads Ballard's work symptomatically, as a cultural expression of an all-pervasive process of commodification, one of whose defining characteristics is the collapse of what he calls "the imperial ego"[73]. But, as Bukatman points out, in many crucial respects Ballard anticipates and outflanks these kinds of positions on postmodernism. "Jameson's own essay [on postmodernism] [...] is strikingly anticipated by J. G. Ballard's introduction to his high-tech porn novel *Crash*. It was Ballard who, in advance of Jameson, isolated 'the death of affect,' 'the moratorium on the past,' and the irrelevance of 'the subjective nature of existence' as hallmarks of contemporary life."[74] However, for the Ballard of novels such as *The Atrocity Exhibition* and *Crash*, it is Jameson and Lasch who can be read' symptomatically - of what Ballard has called a "retrospective" culture and its obsolete baggage.

71. Martin Bax, 'Interview' in Vale ed., *Re/Search; J.G. Ballard*, 36
72. During the course of his discussion of schizophrenia, Jameson feels the need to point out that his is not "some culture-and-personality diagnosis of the type of Christopher Lasch's influential *The Culture of Narcissism,* from which I am concerned radically to distance the spirit and the methodology of the present remarks: there are, one would think, far more damaging things to be said about our social system than are available through the use of psychological categories." (PCLLC 24)
73. One key difference between Lasch and Jameson is on this point: while Lasch unambiguously mourns the loss of a solid sense of identity, Jameson, as ever, is ambivalent.
74. Bukatman, Terminal Identity, 6

Ballard's fiction suggests that the position of transcendent social critic assumed by Jameson and Lasch itself marks a failure to adequately register the immanentizing processes capitalism's cyber-socius is undergoing. These processes, Ballard insists, can only be tracked homeopathically, using techniques that are flat with them.

The ficto-theoretical elaboration of the concept of anorganic continuum is what makes Ballard so crucial a resource for Gothic Materialism. Ballard's schizophrenic gaze recapitulates what the set designers of *The Cabinet of Dr Caligari* had produced – a radical continuity between supposedly organic bodies and inorganic landscape, emerging in a refusal to distinguish figure from (back)ground. But, this time, there is no framing narrative that will attribute the perception to a disordered mind. Instead, Ballard replaces psychology – and Oedipal psychoanalysis – with what is, in effect, a *geo-traumatics*. At its most radical, this implies a metapsychology stripped of all vestigial organicism, an analytic procedure complementary to Deleuze-Guattari's stratoanalysis, whose object is not persons but landscapes; all psychology collapses back into geology. "Ballard often talks about the conflict between geometry and posture, the competition between the animate and inanimate and the way the inanimate often creeps in and wins."[75]

According to Brian McHale, Ballard's earliest key works had obsessively played out "a pattern of repetition-with-variation." "In each, Earth is subject to a global disaster, whether a plague of sleeping sickness ['The Voices of Time'], rising sea-level [*The Drowned World*], a manmade drought [*The Drought*], or the bizarre crystallization of living matter [*The Crystal World*]." (PF 69) Of this early sequence, the most important is the first, *The Drowned World*. *The Drowned World* had described the deluging of the anthropomorphic strata by what Deleuze-Guattari call "the biocosmic memory that threatens to deluge all attempts at collectivity." (AO 190). In *The Drowned World*, the global disaster is not presented as something against which the characters can struggle as if it were simply an external threat; the rising sea level brings changes in the environment that produce a "slackening" of the characters' metabolisms, a recalibration of their physiologies. The journey out across the landscape is also an exploration of the body-as-landscape. The geological scene is a schizoanalytic trauma-map of the human body; particular geologic features correlate with stages in the development of the human organism (whose very organicity is radically denied by its subsumption back into anorganic process). "The further down the CNS you move, from the hind-brain through the medulla into the spinal cord, you descend back into the neuronic past. For example, the junction between T-12 and L-1, is the great zone of transit between the gill-breathing fish and the air-breathing amphibians with their respiratory rib-cages, the very junction where we stand now on the shores of this lagoon,

---

75. Eshun, *Motion Capture [Interview]*, Abstract Culture 2, Winter 97

between the Paleozoic and Triassic eras."[76]

When Jameson theorises Ballard in *Postmodernism*, he subsumes both *The Atrocity Exhibition* and the important early short story "The Voices of Time" under his thesis of the spatialization of time. This analysis kills space just as surely as it kills time, since it equates space (only) with extension. In fact, and exactly contrary to what Jameson argues, Ballard *intensifies* both space and time: this is what is implied by Ballard's *geologization* of fiction. If geology spatializes time it also temporalizes space. "The brief span of an individual life is misleading. Each one of us is as old as the entire biological kingdom, and our bloodstreams are tributaries of the great sea and its total memory. The uterine odyssey of the growing foetus recapitulates the entire evolutionary past, and its central nervous system is a coded time-scale, each nexus of neurones and each spinal level marking a symbolic station, a unit of neuronic time."[77] As with Deleuze-Guattari's strata, space becomes a time-coding (or time-coded) system: both space and time dissolve into aspects of a single, intensive space-time process. Hence one of the crucial figures for Ballard's geo-traumatics: the "spinal landscape."

Thoraic Drop.

The spinal landscape, revealed at the level of T-12, is that of the porous rock towers of Tenerife, and of the native of the Canaries, Oscar Dominguez, who created the technique of decalcomania and so exposed the first spinal landscape. The clinker-like rock towers, suspended above the silent swamp, create an impression of profound anguish. The inhospitability of the mineral world, with its inorganic growths, is relieved only by the balloons flying in the clear sky. They are painted with names: Jackie, Lee Harvey, Malcolm. In the mirror of the swamp, there are no reflections. (AE 30)

Like much of Ballard's most important imagery, the concept of the spinal landscape is derived from surrealism. "Oscar Domingues, a leading member of the surrealist group in Paris, invented the technique of crushing gouache between layers of paper. When separated they reveal eroded, rock-like forms that touch some deeply buried memory, perhaps at some earlier stage in the formation of the brain's visual centres, before the wiring is fully in place." (AE n30) But – as we shall see when we look again at Ballard in Chapter 4 – Ballard's appropriation of surrealism proceeds by way of an excision of anything belonging to the category of the marvellous. In Ballard, the aleatory or dream-like alterity of classical surrealism gives way to a coolly hypernaturalized schizophrenia.

It is in *The Atrocity Exhibition* that offers the most sustained theory-fictional account of contemporary media culture in terms of the spinal landscape.

---

76. Ballard, *The Drowned World*, Harmondsworth: Penguin, 1965, 42-43
77. Ballard, The Drowned World, 43

While the earlier novels made an important contribution to the "earthing" of Science Fiction (none concerned the traditional speculative panoply of outer space journeys, alien civilizations, or rarefied technology), all retained enough generic elements to be recognizably placed as traditional fiction. The key events they focused on (droughts, floods), whilst not necessarily the ordinary province of Science Fiction, were recognizable fictional tropes (belonging, if not to SF, then to the Conradian adventure story, or the disaster novel). But *The Atrocity Exhibition* occupies a more radical place by simultaneously downplaying many of fiction's traditional concerns – mimetic representation, narrative and psychology – whilst insisting that to in any way deal with contemporary reality, a new fictional mode – composed of collaged micro-narratives, "found texts", and schizo-typologies – must be innovated. Unlike the earlier novels, *The Atrocity Exhibition* adds nothing; the traumatic events which are its concern are simply those which took place in the 1960s. There is no need to postulate some additional environmental transmutation on the order of a natural disaster, the novel implies: contemporary culture is itself a disaster-in-progress, an unnatural disaster, an atrocity exhibition.

In *The Atrocity Exhibition* that Ballard's concerns mesh closely with the media theories of McLuhan and Baudrillard. *The Atrocity Exhibition* demands to be read as a belated (and corrective) sequel to Freud (particularly to the Freud of *Beyond the Pleasure Principle*), and as a schizoanalytic counterpart to McLuhan, revealing the convergence of the darkside of both in trauma theory or future-shock. Here in particular, Ballard's "work is marked by […] its sustained refusal of individual psychology"[78], by "the complete absence of the imperial ego."[79] In *The Atrocity Exhibition*, the identity of the male figure who occupies the position of trying to make sense of his increasingly senseless environment is barely vestigial, and isn›t even nominal; "as if to emphasize his lack of defining personal characteristics", Ballard's "uncharacterised protagonist" doesn't retain the same name from section to section of the novel.[80] Ballard's male "characters" – the word itself belongs to a nineteenth-century vocabulary which Ballard's work obsolesces – are victims of future shock, impelled by the need to come to terms with a vast environmental rupturing imaged in a series of repeated disasters: car crashes, war footage, assassinations. Breakdown behaviour - as manifested in the ritualised search for "a single abstract form which is repeated in a series of apparently unrelated or irregular phenomena: photographs, erotic poses, urban landscapes" (PF 70) - replaces any overarching strategy of rational analysis. Or, more accurately, breakdown behaviour becomes the only conceivable "rational" response to a world that is itself breaking down.

The novel examines the enormously distended contours of what it

78. Bukatman, *Terminal Identity*, 41
79. Lasch, *Minimal Self*, 136
80. Lasch," 138

calls "the media landscape" (the modern urban environment as transformed by coca-colonizing US mediatization). In an environment increasingly dominated by billboards and advertising hoardings, the word "landscape" is not at all metaphorical. "What *The Atrocity Exhibition* was about was the way that the media landscape has created something very close to a gigantic art gallery with a lot of very lurid paintings on exhibition [...] and the way in which psychopathic strains which were normally either ignored or suppressed were beginning to use the media landscape to express and reveal themselves."[81]

In a sense, the phrase "atrocity exhibition" is a strictly literal description of this media landscape as it emerged in the early 1960s, populated by images of Vietnam, the Kennedys, Martin Luther King and Malcolm X. The novel deals with the violence that haemorrhaged in the 1969 in which it was published: Manson, Altamont, *War across the USA*. But, for Ballard, the events of 1969 are merely the culmination of a decade whose guiding logic has been one of violence; a mediatized violence, where "mediatization" is a profoundly ambiguous term which doesn't necessarily imply a disintensification. As they begin to achieve the instantaneous speed Virilio thinks characteristic of postmodern communication, media (paradoxically) *immediatize* trauma, making it instantly available even as they prepackage it into what will become increasingly preprogrammed stimulus-response circuitries.

Freud describes trauma in terms of the "conservative" tendency of the death drives, a return to the inorganic, under the sign of the cybernegatively-configured "principle of constancy." At its most mechanistic, trauma is a simple register of impact upon the organism – Freud cites the example of railway accidents - the transmission and distribution, through the organism, of exogenous stimuli. Ballard's contribution, in *The Atrocity Exhibition*, is to radicalise the Freudian account of trauma by generalizing it. Rather than treating trauma as something with which the organism is affected only contingently, Ballard implies that trauma is a general condition, a non – or anti- – biotic transmission system, distributing particular tics – swarms of repetition-compulsions – across a culture that is indistinguishable from nature. Culture, like the organism, is *composed* of tics, compulsions and looped behaviours, rather than simply afflicted by them. The "abstract patterns" that Dr. Nathan and his supposedly psychotic patients discover repeated across architectural, biological and geological assemblages are the vectors through which this trauma spreads. Trauma is not merely about processes of wounding and scarring, but also about the response to violent incursions (indeed, wounding and scarring are *already* such responses); it is a distributed event, not merely echoed or referenced in the repetition-compulsions, but continued, prolonged, propagated.

---

81. Ballard, interview, NME, 1983, 28

2.10 ATROCI-TV

Media, in *The Atrocity Exhibition*, function less as extra protective layers on the organism's skin, than as conduits through which trauma can propagate itself. *The Atrocity Exhibition* anticipates the correlation between war and cinema Virilio will make, but in a sense, for it the age of cinema is substantially over. The Zapruder film of the Kennedy assassination – as both a found object and an avant-garde film – implies the supercession of the war/cinema duo by a new coupling: TV and assassination. For Ballard, McLuhan›s global village is convened only ironically, brought together – in what Jameson calls "the projection of a new collective experience of reception" – by the shock of the Kennedy assassination: atroci-tv. "Kennedy's assassination presides over *The Atrocity Exhibition*, and in many ways the book is directly inspired by his death, and represents a desperate attempt to make sense of the tragedy, with its huge hidden agenda. The mass media created the Kennedy we know, and his death represented a tectonic shift in the communications landscape, sending fissures deep into the popular landscape that have not yet closed." (AE n33-34)

Specifically, it is television which constructed Kennedy; it was TV's power to simulate intimacy which produced the vast quantities of synthetic emotion it' could then propagate as contagion. But if it's true that the "mass media created the Kennedy we know", it must also be the case that Kennedy's death creates the mass media with which we are now familiar. For Jameson, the Kennedy assassination and the media coverage from which it is radically indistinguishable constitute "something like the coming of age of the whole media culture that had been set in place in the late 1940s and early 1950s. Suddenly, and for a brief moment (which lasted, however, several long days), television showed what it could really do and what it really meant – a prodigious new display of synchronicity and a communicational situation that amounted to a dialectical leap over everything hitherto suspected." (PCLLC 355)

Trauma is not only the "content" of this experience, but the very mode of experience itself (insofar as it is possible to *experience* trauma itself at all). Echoing McLuhan's invocation of "battle shock", Jameson writes of "the shock of communicational explosion" (PCLLC 355). Compulsively repeating particular audio-visual sequences, the media itself functions like a trauma victim, and in a dogged refusal to accept the implications of McLuhan›s analyses of "capitalist representation" (AO 240) Jameson writes of "the instant playbacks of the Reagan shooting or the *Challenger* disaster, which, borrowed from commercial sports, expertly emptied these events of their content". "Content", in the sense of meaning, is completely irrelevant to capitalism and its communicational systems which, as McLuhan never tired of pointing

out, have always been flattening the medium into the message.
The Atrocity Exhibition focuses on what Jameson calls the "great Warhol figures – [such as] Marilyn […] – the notorious cases of burnout and self-de-
struction of the ending 1960s, and the great dominant experiences of drugs and
schizophrenia," who themselves are signals of a new psychopathology, which
"would seem to have little in common either with the hysterics and neurotics
of Freud's own day or with those canonical experiences of radical isolation and
solitude, anomie, private revolt, Van Gogh-type madness, which dominated
the period of high modernism." (PCLLC, 14) A key trait of Ballard's novel is
a Warhol-like *indifferent* presentation of objects, in which banal objects that
should be devoid of affect – commodities – are treated as equivalent to images
which we might ordinarily expect to shock us – car crashes. But in place of
Warhol's serial repetition of objects, Ballard favours techniques of blow-up
that more closely recall Oldenberg. Both of these techniques combine in the
commodification of the human body, its transposition into an image that is no
longer recognizable as its own image. For Jameson, such techniques are an
example of the death of affect. "The waning of affect," he says, "is […] perhaps
best initially approached by way of the human figure, and it is obvious that
what we have said about the commodification of objects holds as strongly for
Warhol's human subjects; stars – like Marilyn Monroe – who are themselves
commodified and transformed into their own image." (PCLLC, 11) But, bearing in mind the critique of the "death of affect" thesis we made in Chapter 1,
Gothic Materialism would prefer to describe such techniques in terms of a
distribution of impersonalised affect, a spread of affect beyond the confines of
the emotional or psychological.

As Burroughs points out in his preface, the "magnification of image to
the point where it becomes unrecognizable is a keynote of *The Atrocity Exhibition*." (AE vii) Burroughs makes the connection with Pop Art: it "is what Bob
Rauschenberg is doing […] literally *blowing up* the image." (AE vii) The scene
Burroughs cites is typical:

A group of workmen on a scaffolding truck were pasting up the last
of the displays, a hundred-foot-long panel that appeared to represent a section
of a sand-dune. Looking at it more closely, Dr. Nathan realized that it was an
immensely magnified portion of skin under the iliac crest. Glancing at the billboards, Dr. Nathan recognised other magnified fragments: a segment of lower
lip, a right nostril, a portion of female perineum. Only an anatomist could have
identified these fragments, each represented as a formal geometric pattern. (AE
10)

For Ballard, what Virilio calls the "breaks in spatio-temporal continuity dreamt up by film-makers" have now become a commonplace feature
of the external environment as it has become increasingly mediatized. The
techniques of montage and jump-cutting that were once the preserve of experimental cinema now characterize the media landscape itself, which sys-

tematically breaks down "molar or human perception"[82] Here, "human beings have shrunk to the point of invisibility, while the images they' have made of themselves, grotesquely enlarged to gigantic dimensions and no longer recognisable as human images at all, take on a life of their own."[83] – Magnification, or amplification, has the effect of making the boundary between organic and inorganic seem arbitrary. (Ballard's early short story, "Track 12" had performed the same trick, but with sound: "Amplified 100,000 times, animal cell division sounds like a lot of girders and steel sheets being ripped apart – how did you put it? – a car crash in slow motion."[84])

In Ballard's neo-expressionist thematics landscape and event become equivalent. Geology is a slow-motion event, only arbitrarily and illegitimately distinguished from cultural production. From the point of view of Ballard's geo-traumatics, it is necessary to directly equate the physical aspect of Marilyn Monroe's body with the landscape of dunes around her. The hero attempts to try to make sense of this particular equation, and he realises that the suicide of Marilyn Monroe is in fact a disaster in space-time like the explosion of a space-capsule in orbit. It is not so much a personal disaster, though of course Marilyn Monroe committed suicide as an individual woman, but a disaster of a whole complex of relationships involving this screen actress who is presented to us in an endless series of advertisements, on a thousand magazine covers, and so on, whose body becomes part of the external landscape of our environment. The immense terraced figure of Marilyn Monroe stretched across a cinema hoarding is as real a portion of our external landscape as any system of mountains or lakes.[85]

"The star system stemmed from [an ...] instability of dimensions,"[86] Virilio suggests. What could appear to be a representation of the organism is in fact its deterritorialization. "The porous sand, reminiscent of the eroded walls of the apartment, and of the dead film star with her breasts of carved pumice and thighs of ash, diffused along its crests into the wind." (AE 43) "The apartment was a box clock, a cubicular extrapolation of the facial planes of the yantra, the cheekbones of Marilyn Monroe." (AE 43) The vast image of Monroe – and the other stars – is not *like* a landscape, it is a landscape.[87]

---

82. Deleuze, *Cinema 1*, 84

83. Lasch, The Minimal Self, 137

84. "Track 12", in Ballard, *The Overloaded Man*, London: Panther, 197, 61

85. Ballard, "The New Science Fiction: A Conversation between J.G. Ballard and George MacBeth", in Jones ed., *The New SF*, 56

86. Virilio, *War and Cinema: The Logistics of Perception*, trans. Patrick Camiller, London/New York: Verso, 1984, 25

87. We might be reminded here of the convergence of medical, military and media perception in Virilio's *War and Cinema*, whose comments on Monroe may well owe something' to Ballard. "Always in exile from its immediate, natural dimensions, never seeming to be connected to anything else, Marilyn's body was at once expandable like a giant screen and capable of being folded and reproduced like a poster, a magazine cover of a centre-spread.» (*War and' Cinema*,' 25) "Marilyn's body, which the Seventh

2.11 CATASTROPHE MANAGEMENT

Baudrillard: "The car is not the appendix of a domestic universe, there are only incessant figures of circulation, and the Accident is everywhere, the elementary, irreversible figure, the banality of the anomaly of death. It is no longer at the margin, it is at the heart. It is no longer the exception to a triumphal rationality, it has become the Rule, it has devoured the Rule. It is no longer even 'the accursed share,' the one conceded to destiny by the system, and included in its general reckoning. Everything is reversed. It is the accident that gives form to life, it is the accident, the insane that is the sex of life." (SS 113)

In both *The Atrocity Exhibition* and the subsequent *Crash* - in many ways an extrapolation of a particular obsession from the previous book (the fusion of erotics and carcrashes) - Ballard describes a generalized traumatics, in which power and catastrophe simulate each other, becoming indistinguishable. Catastrophes and their re-enactment circulate endlessly in Ballard's chaosmos, not necessarily only as mechanical repetition of what has already happened, but also as cybernetically anticipative simulations. The implication is that, by being projected in advance, any future possibility, no matter how horrific, can, in some sense, be "managed".

Faced with the apparently senseless spectacle of the protracted conflict in Vietnam – "All political and military explanations fail to provide a rationale for the war's extended duration" -Ballard seeks out its sources in a mediatized unconscious "fixated to trauma." Like Freud, impelled to postulate the death drive in part by his observation of the behaviour of First World War shell-shock victims as they obsessively re-enacted their trauma, Ballard discovers in mediatized culture an obsessive "compulsion to repeat." Repetition both serves to alleviate trauma and to perpetuate it, wrecking any simple teleology: in the paradoxical logic Freud delineates in *Beyond the Pleasure Principle*, the organism preserves itself precisely by becoming-inorganic, and "life" is only a detour on the way to death. This emerges for Ballard at the level of deleometric catastrophe management systems in the form of perverse explanations for the war, irrationales: "In terms of television and the news magazines the war in

---

Division doctors said they would most like to' *examine'* yet which no-one claimed from the morgue, reminds one of that penetrating gaze of the surgeon or cameraman which came into its own in the First World. War ['] Like aerial reconnaissance photography […] the use of endoscopy or scanners allows hidden organs to surface in an instrumental collage, an utterly obscene reading of the ravages of trauma or a disease."' *(War and Cinema,'* 25-26)

Vietnam has a latent significance very different from its manifest content. Far from repelling us, it *appeals* to us by virtue of its complex of polyperverse acts." (AE 87) Media – as the ambivalently functioning additions to the human perceptual system described by Freud and McLuhan – have a crucial role to play in this economy: (an)aestheticization, the translation of trauma into repeated images which, no matter how horrific they initially appear, soon become banal, in part by dint of repetition itself.

"Freud characterizes trauma as an 'invasion', a breach in an otherwise efficacious barrier against stimuli, infiltrating alien desires – xenopulsions – into the organism."[88] But rather than damping down xenopulsive excitation, Ballard›s cybernetic systems seem to hunt out and obsessively pore over trauma. Initially, according to *Anti-Oedipus*, an "anus-vampire" (AO 228), capitalism is, by the time of *The Atrocity Exhibition*, also a ghoul: mediatizing the feedback process of its own reproduction in endlessly reiterating loops of mass production and consumption of death. Deleometrics is the key science of Ballard's catastrophe management – the urge not now to banish death, nor to suicidally embrace it (as according to Deleuze-Guattari, fascism had[89]) but to quantify it, to "optimize" it. What Baudrillard calls the generalization of the Accident leads to what he characterizes as a "hyperfunctionalism" which moves beyond both teleology and transgression. If the accident has become the rule, then there is no law to transgress, just as there is no goal to head towards.

---

88. Land, "Machinic Desire", 477
89. See "Micropolitics and Segmentarity" in TP, especially 230-231, where Deleuze-Guattari argue that fascism was characterized by "a will to wager everything you have ever had, to stake your own death against the death of others, and measure everything by 'deleometers'." (TP 230)

2.12 BEYOND THE PLEASURES OF THE ORGANS

A central pre-occupation *The Atrocity Exhibition*, as with *Videodrome* and *Crash*, is the displacement of bio-sexuality. The novel performs a decoding of sex into a matter of stimuli that are not themselves sexual: what Burroughs, in his preface, calls the "non-sexual roots of sexuality". "sex is becoming more and more a conceptual act" (AE 60) Writing of *Crash*, Baudrillard invokes deterritorialized and disorganicized eroticism; a cyberotics. This is not a matter of simply substituting technical machines for biological sexual objects, but of decoding sexuality into a matter of abstract stimulus (one of Burroughs' favourite themes, and one Ballard pursues relentlessly). Ballard's question "in *what* way is intercourse per vagina more stimulating than with this ashtray, say, or with the angle between two walls?" (AE 69) outlines a vector of capitalist expansion. It's not just a question of selling commodities by associating them with sex, (the well-known but by now archaic advertising technique critiqued by McLuhan in *The Mechanical Bride*) but of a generalized libidinization in which bio-sex is no longer the privileged referent. What McLuhan calls the "hunger to experience everything sexually" converts into an (even more) abstract drive to maximize sensation. Which also amounts, in *The Atrocity Exhibition* and *Crash,* to the *abstraction* of sensation. Hence, for Baudrillard, the emergence of a generalized libidinization proper to the Body without Organs. As Baudrillard writes, in an almost valedictory mode: "Goodbye 'erogenous zones': everything becomes a hole to offer itself up to the discharge reflex. [...] Body and technology diffracting their bewildered signs through each other. Carnal abstraction and design." (SS 112)[90]

In Ballard, as in *Videodrome*, eroticization is inseparable from mediatization and from landscape: all three form a continuum.[91] As we've seen, the schizophrenic implosion of subjectivity has as its other side the emergence of

---

90. Baudrillard's emphasis, unlike ours, is on signs/semiurgy. Witness the section excised from this quote: "But above all (as in primitive initiation tortures, which are not ours), the whole body becomes a sign to offer itself to the exchange of bodily signs." Note again the neo-primitivism.

91. A precursor here – often cited by Deleuze, and a key player in the "Body without Organs" plateau of *A Thousand Plateaus* - is Masoch. As Deleuze-Guattari make clear, masochism has nothing to do with the hunger for pain (which would merely be the complement of the hedonistic hunt for pleasure – see next footnote); it is concerned rather with intensity modulation. (See TP 155) This is effectuated by an eroticism which focuses as much on the mis-en-scene – the mistress's clothes, for instance – as on the specifically "sexual" as such.

a hyper-body which moves beyond Worringer's "wisdom and limits of the organism". As body image (and organismic integrity) fade, new desires emerge. One could theorize these either as a hypersexuality – a sexuality that has escaped genital, even biotic reference, or as a post- or anti-sexuality - desires that it no longer makes any sense to describe in sexual terms.[92] *Videodrome*'s dominant image – of Max's body transformed into a violently libidinized New Flesh – would support both theses. That image has presided over this chapter, and it will also preside over the next, which takes up again the question of the deterritorialization of sexuality. The next chapter, though, will be concerned less with the erotic, and more with the reproductive, role of sexuality, and the way it has been displaced by cybernetic systems. How do bodies without (sexual) organs replicate themselves?

---

92. In any case, it is no longer a matter of hedonism or pleasure (models Deleuze-Guattari strenuously oppose in *A Thousand Plateaus*, since they presuppose an organismic metrics, a hydraulics in which pressure builds up towards inevitable discharge; the plateau, meanwhile, is defined by its *avoidance* of a discharge which would terminate it.) (See TP 154, and its attack on the "priestly" account of 'pleasure as discharge.")

XEROX AND XENOGENESIS:

MECHANICAL REPRODUCTION AND GOTHIC PROPAGATION

Dick: Androids can't bear children, she said, then. Is that a loss?
He finished undressing her. Exposed her pale, cold loins.
'Is it a loss?' Rachael repeated. 'I don't really know; I have no way to tell. How does it feel to be born, for that matter? We're not born; we don't grow up; instead of dying from illness or old age we wear out like ants. Ants again; that's what we are.[1] Not you: I mean me. Chitinous reflex-machines who aren't really alive.' She twisted her head to one side, said loudly, 'I'm not alive! You're not going to bed with a woman. Don't be disappointed; okay. Have you ever made love to an android before?'
No, he said, taking off his shirt and tie.
'I understand they tell me it's convincing if you don't think too much about it. But if you think too much, if you reflect on what you're doing then you cant go on. For ahem physiological reasons.'
Bending, he kissed her bare shoulder.
'Thanks, Rick,' she said wanly. 'Remember, though: don't think about it, just do it. Don't pause and be philosophical, because from a philosophical standpoint it's dreary. For us both.[2]

Baudrillard: "Cloning is [...] last stage in the history of the modeling of the body – the stage at which the individual, having been reduced to his abstract and genetic formula, is destined for serial propagation. It is worth recalling in this context what Walter Benjamin had to say about the work of art in the age of mechanical reproduction. What is lost when a work is massively reproduced is that work's 'aura,' its unique here and now quality, its aesthetic form [...] What is lost is the original – which only a history that is itself nostalgic and retrospective can restore in its 'authenticity'. The most advanced, most modern form of this development – which Benjamin described in connection with contemporary cinema, photography and mass media – is that form where the original no longer even exists, because the objects in question are conceived of from the outset in terms of their limitless reproduction." (TE 118)

Butler: "Every machine will probably have its special mechanical breeders, and all the higher ones will owe their existence to a large number of parents and not to two only." (212)

Deleuze-Guattari: "We oppose epidemic to filiation, contagion to heredity, peopling by contagion to sexual reproduction, sexual production [...] Propagation by epidemic, by contagion has nothing to do with filiation by heredity, even if the two themes intermingle and require each other. The vampire does not filiate, it infects." (TP 241-242)

---

1. Cf. Mark Downham. "Philip K. Dick was influential on Cyber-Punk, in that his novel *A Scanner Darkly* touched on what is crucial in Baudrillard's disintegration into neurosis: 'Biological life goes on, everything else is dead. A reflex, machine-like, like some insect repeating doomed patterns over and over. A single pattern. The failed codes of an escape combination. But how can you truly escape yourself?" ("Cyberpunk", 42).

2. Dick, *Do Androids Dream of Electric Sheep?*, 146

3.1 LET ME TELL YOU ABOUT MY MOTHER

Max's invagination in *Videodrome* might serve as a startling literalization of McLuhan's notorious claim, in *Understanding Media*, that human beings have become the "sex organs of the machine world" (UM 46); a claim famously echoed by Manuel De Landa when he describes technology as "an independent species of machine-flowers that simply did not possess its own reproductive organs during a segment of its evolution."[3] The "grotesquely sexual nightmare images" of *Videodrome* bring us to one of the abiding preoccupations of Science Fiction and Horror: the displacement, or deterritorialization, of sexual reproduction. Is it the case, as Scott Bukatman suggests, that Max Renn become "part of [a] massive system of reproductive technology?"[4] Or is it the case that, in the world of *Videodrome* and of cyberpunk in general, nonorganic replication has escaped the net of "filiative" reproduction?

Both Deleuze-Guattari and Baudrillard offer theorizations of reproduction, but whereas Baudrillard continues to take sexual reproduction as the paradigm, critiquing simulated-reproduction for its deviation from the sexual model, Deleuze-Guattari oppose all reproduction (sexual or otherwise) to a model of "contagion", a non (or hyper)sexual mode of replication which takes its cue from vampirism, lycanthropy and disease. So where Baudrillard's "negativized Gothic" proceeds by way of identifying an increasing perfection in the techniques of artifical reproduction (leading, in his view, to a triumph of a post-sexual necrotic culture), Deleuze-Guattari follow the Gothic line in identifying modes of replication that cut across organic reproduction altogether. Instead of identifying, as Baudrillard does, the escape from (sexual) reproduction with an increase in sameness, Deleuze-Guattari argue that "anorganic propagation" is a feature of multiplicity. *Blade Runner*, once again, provides an exemplary case-study for the crosshatching of these two approaches, as Iain Hamilton Grant establishes in his commentary on its opening scene:

"When replicant Leon responds to bladerunner Holden's question '*let me tell you about my mother* ... [shots propel Holden through the plate glass window into the street many floors below]', the bullets may not offer stories of his mother, but the unmistakable technological phenotype of their impact etches Leon's military-industrial genealogy in scar tissue over Holden's damaged body. The point is that, qua organism, the replicant is an orphan, or what amounts to the same thing, has no exclusivist claim to, no biunivocal bit-

---

3. Manuel De Landa, *War in the Age of Intelligent Machines*, New York: Zone Books, 1991, 3
4. Bukatman, 'Who Programs You?', 206

map of his progeniture, issuing instead from an institutional-techincal matrix and not a couple. Like Artaud, Leon 'got no pappa-mommy.' Leon has no mother, only a matrix of industrial-military technologies."[5]

Grant here deliberately echoes both Deleuze-Guattari – whose invocation of Artaud's claim that he had "no pappa-mommy" operates as an important slogan early on in *Anti-Oedipus* – and the Baudrillard of *Seduction*, and his appalled cry: "No more mother, just a matrix" (S 169) Baudrillard's speculations on the "wealth of plant-like branchings that dissolve Oedipal sexuality in favour of a 'non-human' sex" (S 169)[6] stand as a horrified anticipation of the scenario *Blade Runner* presents. We will now look in more detail at Baudrillard's position, before turning to Deleuze-Guattari's account of Gothic propagation. Both will be cashed out, at the end of the chapter, in terms of an analysis of Gibson's *Neuromancer*.

For Baudrillard, the re-engineering of sex "at the fractal, micrological and non-human level" results "in the disappearance of sexual difference and hence of sexuality itself." (TE 3) This is the culmination of a cultural process in which mechanical reproduction extends beyond the production of objects to reconfigure even the tiniest interstices of biological vivisystems. Cyberneticization - the gradual but implacable translation of all of nature/culture into information, or code – replaces sex with a simulated death; not the "tragic" form of death, which remains "sexed" since it is associated with "higher mammals" and their mode of reproduction, but an "asexual form" of death, "a recessive stage which harks back to the molecular and protozoan stage of living beings, to their unceremonious obliteration, leaving them no other form of destiny."[7] "Is there a form of death drive that pushes sexed beings towards a form of reproduction anterior to the acquisition of sexual identities," Baudrillard asks in *Seduction*, adding that "this fissiparous form, this proliferation by contiguity conjure[s] up in the deepest recesses of our imaginary as something that denies sexuality and seeks to annihilate it." (S 168-169) 'Today's technological beings,' he elaborates in *The Transparency of Evil*, "machines, clones, replacement body parts – all tend towards this kind of reproduction, and little by little they are imparting the same process to those beings that are supposedly human, and sexed." (TE 7) In addition to annihilating sex, this – deathly – form of reproduction also annihilates (or *ex-terminates*[8]) organic death; "an individual product on the conveyor belt" has "not been sexually engendered" and is therefore "unacquainted with death." (TE 116)

The spread of this undiffentiation or homogenization across all levels

5. Grant, "LA 2019", (no page refs)

6. Cf. the (ironically) virtually identical repetition of the passage in *The Transparency of Evil*'s "The Hell of the Same", 115-116. Is Baudrillard cloning his own writing?

7. Baudrillard, *The Illusion of the End*, 98

8. Cf. Baudrillard's discussion of "tele-space" in which there are "only *terminals* in a position of *ex-termination*." (S 165)

of culture – sexual, political, aesthetic[9] – amounts, then, to a "denial of all alterity" that is simultaneously immortalist and necrotic. Immortalist, since the code achieves a kind of infinitely perpetuated "sur-vival", but necrotic because this "form of immortal life, this nostalgia for a pure contiguity of life and its molecular sequentiality" was what "Freud associated [with] the death instinct."[10]

According to Baudrillard, what McLuhan and Benjamin grasp – and what Marx fails to – is "technology as a medium rather than a productive force."(SED 56) Both, Baudrillard insists, understood that the 'mere fact' of reproducibility engenders what he – surely misleadingly – descibes as "an entirely new generation of meaning." (SED 56) Evidently, meaning – whether new or not – is precisely not the issue; what issues in fact is radically asignifying technologies of "reproduction" which are their own message. Contrary to Marx's hermeneutics of suspicion, technology does not conceal or distort a message; it is itself a message.

Baudrillard derives from Benjamin's *The Work of Art in the Age of Mechanical Reproduction* the key insight into the sheer fact of reproducibility. Cleverly transposing Benjamin's arguments from art objects to biological life, Baudrillard discusses the disappearance of the "aura", which no longer designates the unique qualities of the work of art, as it did for Benjamin, but of the individual organism itself. Whereas, according to Baudrillard, meiotic sex – involving what he quaintly terms "otherness"[11] – inevitably allows the possibility of heterogeneity, mechanical reproduction implies the ever more perfect production of exact copies: "the Hell of the same" (TE 113-124). "Xerox and infinity." (TE 51-59) Properly speaking, we might say, sexual reproduction is not *re*production at all; true reproduction – the production of copies supposedly identical in every respect – is possible only via the intervention of technical machines. As Benjamin had understood, mass production – the avatar of Baudrillard's second order – introduces this possibility, but, for Baudrillard, its technologies are merely a pale anticipation of the horrors of homogeneity made available by contemporary biotechnology. "Benjamin was writing in the industrial era: by then technology was a gigantic prosthesis governing the generation of identical *objects* and *images* which there was no longer any way

---

9. A process which does not only happen *at* every level, but *to* every level, as, all distinctions become increasingly unstable. Everything is sexual. Everything is political. Everything is aesthetic. "Each category is generalized to the greatest possible extent, so that it eventually loses all specificity and reabsorbed by all the other categories." (TE 9)

10. *The Illusion of the End*, 98. "Today, we no longer believe we are immortal, yet it is precisely now that we are becoming so, becoming quietly immortal without knowing it, without wishing it, without believing it, by the mere fact of the confusion of the limits of life and death. No longer immortal in terms of the soul, which has disappeared, nor even, the body, which is disappearing, but in terms of the formula, immortal in terms of the code.", 99

11. Whereas the "cellular dream of schizogenesis [...] allows one to bypass the other, and to go from the same to the same." (S 168)

of distinguishing from one another, but it was as yet impossible to foresee the technological sophistication of our own era, which has made it possible to generate identical *beings*, without any means of returning to an original." (TE 119) In the labs of the Tyrell corporation, with Grant-Monod's "molecular cybernetics" at its disposal, biotech achieves an industrialization of bio-reproduction far beyond anything industrial machines could achieve.

As the ultimate exemplars of simulation-culture, the replicants recapitulate the four orders of the simulacra, rerunning, at the same time, their ficto-genealogy in the history of Science Fiction. Insofar as they *resemble* humans and are confused with them, the replicants are the automata of the first phase (copies of the human). Yet, as Nexus-6 models, the replicants have been (mass) produced *serially*, from templates. At the Second Order, the technical machine and its operators become equivalent; these are the robots of Kapek's *RUR*, whose name, famously means slave (as Roy Batty tells Deckard: "Quite an experience to live in fear, isn't it? That's what it is to be a slave.") "The mere fact that any given thing can simply be reproduced is already a revolution: one need only think of the stupefaction of the Black boy seeing two identical books together for the first time. That these two technical products are *equivalent* under the sign of necessary social labour power is less important in the long-term than the *serial* repetition of the same object (which is also the serial repetition of individuals as labour power)." (SED 56) But the second-order slips, almost immediately, into the third; unlike Kapek's robots the replicants haven't been constructed simply as replacements of some already-existing quanta of labour power: they have been "conceived according to their very reproducibility." The difference between the second and the third order is subtle – which is why the one always fades so quickly into the third – but decisive, and is a matter of the temporality of (re)production. Whereas the stage of mass production begins with single objects that are only *subsequently* mass-(re)produced, the "objects" of the third order are (re)produced *in the first instance* with mass (re) production in mind; indeed, they are only manufactured because *they can be so (re)produced*. "Moreover, the stage of serial reproduction (that of the industrial mechanism, the production line, the growth of reproduction, etc.) is ephemeral. As soon as dead labour gains the upper hand over living labour [...], serial reproduction gives way to generation through models. In this case it is a matter of a reversal of origin and end, since all forms change from the moment that they are no longer mechanically reproduced, but *conceived according to their very reproducibility*, their diffraction from a generative core called a 'model.'" (SED 56)

This process culminates in what Baudrillard, according to Gane, Baudrillard will call the "fourth phase of simulacra"[12]: a phase exemplified, it would seem, by such phenomena as cloning and the hologram – "objects" that display

12. Mike Gane, "Radical Theory: Baudrillard and Vulnerability", *Theory, Culture & Society*, London, Thousand Oaks and New Delhi – Sage, Vol 12 (1995), 120

a complete self-similarity, in which the whole can be reconstituted from any part, whether it be a cell in the case of the clone, or a fragment of image in the case of the hologram.

What is crucial, for Baudrillard, is the drift away from empirical difference towards a sameness deriving from the abstract; abstract, because any apparently unique feature is now seen as (merely) an instantiation of a pre-existent – and manipulable – grid: code. Baudrillard's own favoured example here, repeatedly invoked, is DNA, but the process he describes is perhaps better exemplified by digitization. In *Seduction*, Baudrillard decries the sterile perfection of hi-fidelity recordings ("high fidelity, which is just as obsessive and puritanical as the other, conjugal, fidelity." [S 30]) These, though, are as nothing compared to the digital recording, the – at least in its idealized accounts – perfect copy. Since a digital document is simply a matter of an arrangement of binary (on/off) switches, a recapitulation of the same pattern could either be seen as the most perfect copy imaginable, or not really a "copy" at all. "So-called intelligent machines [...] [break] linguistic, sexual or cognitive acts down into their simplest elements and digitiz[e] them so that they can be re-synthesized according to models. They can generate all the possibilities of a program or of a potential object." (TE 52)

3.2 THE SIMULACRUM'S REVENGE

Baudrillard: "What is the 'crystal'? It is the object, the pure event, something which no longer really has an origin or an end. The object to which the subject has wanted to give an origin and a purpose, even though it has none, is today starting to recount itself. There is a possibility that the object will say something to us, but there is also above all the possibility that it will take its revenge!"[13]

Aldiss: "The new systems of machinery now coming in have great power, and it is a power to change the world. In the cotton towns, you can already see that power-looms are creating a new category of human being, the town labourer. As the machine becomes more complex, so he will become more of an expert. His experience will become centred on machines; eventually, his kind will become adjuncts of the machine. They will be called 'a labour force.' In other words, an abstract idea will replace a master-man relation; but in practice the workings of a labour force may be just as difficult.

[A] culture will become enslaved by the machines. The second generation of machines will be much more complex than the first, for it will include machines capable of repairing and even reproducing the first generation!

The greater the complexity of systems, the more danger of something going wrong, and the less chance individual will has of operating on the systems for good. First the systems become impersonal. Then they seem to take a mind of their own, then they become positively malignant!

'Then we are heading for a world full of Frankenstein's monsters, Mary!' exclaimed Byron, slapping his leg."[14]

Alongside Baudrillard's vision of celibate, enclosed – or imploded circuits – always haunting the dream of perfect reproduction, is a line of escape. Baudrillard calls this "the simulacrum's revenge". As we leave the first-order behind, resemblance, Baudrillard says, disappears as a criterion. "No more semblance or dissemblance, no more God or Man, only an immanent logic

---

13. Gane, ed, *Baudrillard Live Selected Interviews*, New York/ London: Routledge, 1993, 51

14. Brian Aldiss, *Frankenstein Unbound*, London: Jonathan Cape, 1973, 64-65. Aldiss's novel is a metafictional commentary on the *Frankenstein* story, interpolating a time-travelling twenty-first century dweller into the monster's primal scene at Villa Diodati; but Aldiss places the monster alongside his (fictional) creator – Frankenstein – and his (real) creator, Mary Shelley. For our purposes, the point is made in the quotation as presented: the Frankenstein story is (re)read in terms of second order simulacra – machines mass reproducing themselves by formatting human beings as their sex organ slaves.

of the principle of operativity." (SED 54) As Baudrillard explains, operativity is the "principle" of the second order. Now that machines are no longer slaved into being "the image of man" they can reproduce indiscriminately; and so, Baudrillard says, can human beings. Mass human reproduction – the emergence of the proletariat in the new industrial towns – is a side-effect of machinic reproduction. "After this, robots and machines can proliferate – this is even their law – as automata, being sublime and singular mechanisms, have never done. Men themselves only begin to proliferate when, with the Industrial Revolution, they took on the status of machines: freed of all semblance, freed even from their double, they grew increasingly similar to the system of production of which they were a miniaturized equivalent. The simulacrum's revenge, which gave rise to the myth of the sorcerer's apprentice, did not take place with the automaton; on the contrary, this is the law of the second order, from which there proceeds a hegemony of the robot, of the machine, of dead labour over living labour." (SED 54)

The most exemplary (social science) fictions of the second-order are Marx's, clearly echoed in Baudrillard's language here. It is Marx, writing of the 'necromantic' power of capital, who sees human beings re-made in the images of the machines they supposedly produced. Marx begins to see the reversal that Baudrillard will base much of his theoretical work upon: instead of machines being produced (and reproduced) to satisfy pre-existing human needs, human beings will be reproduced in order to satisfy the requirements of the system (which treats human beings not as ends-in-themselves but as servomechanical adjuncts to industrial – and later – cybernetic machines). For Baudrillard, both machines and humanity reproduce only because the system – the code – demands it. As he puts it as early as *For a Critique of the Political Economy of the Sign*, "man is not reproduced as man: he is simply regenerated as a survivor (a surviving productive force). If he eats, drinks, lives somewhere, re-produces himself, it is because the system requires his self-production in order to reproduce itself: it needs men. If it could function with slaves, there would be no 'free' workers. If it could function with asexual mechanical robots, there would be no sexual reproduction."[15]

Thus Marx – as the theorist most closely associated with "the in-

---

15. *For a Critique of the Political Economy of the Sign*, 86. These arguments are advanced, of course, both as a continuation of Marx, and as a critique of Marx's humanism. With Deleuze-Guattari (particularly the Deleuze-Guattari of *Anti-Oedipus*) and the Lyotard of *Libidinal Economy*, Baudrillard wants to insist, with Marx, on the way that capital operates independently of human will, but, against Marx, he wants to claim that there are no pre-existent human "needs" which are being exploited, perverted, or alienated. If there are primordial needs, they belong not to the human being – certainly not the individual human being – but to the system itself. Baudrillard, naturally, will not make the move that Deleuze-Guattari do: de-privileging need and use value while thinking production alongside a desire that is not understood in terms of need.

dustrial simulacrum" – becomes the prophet of "the hegemony of the robot."
Running alongside Marx's theory-fictions of becoming-robot is the classic example of the narrative of "the simulacrum's revenge" in modern fiction: Mary
Shelley's *Frankenstein*. It is not for nothing that the theme of the displacement
of sexual reproduction is central to *Frankenstein*, in many ways the founding
text of the modern genres of Science Fiction and Horror. The subsequent
stratification of fiction-production into these two genres – a stratification never
fully achieved, since, as we have seen, SF and Horror have often found themselves tangled up together – has tended to imply a splitting of the Gothic line,
typically putting Science Fiction on the side of a speculative machinism, and
Horror on the side of supernaturalism. Yet Victor Frankenstein's achievement
in artificially synthesizing the means of reproduction is presented, by Shelley,
as the moment where alchemical ambition is vindicated by electro-libidinal
science; there is no need to posit a supplementary, extra-material, or supernatural dimension – Nature can overcome itself. Yet it does so also by presenting
Man – and the gender designation is here of course deliberate – with a set of
unanticipated consequences; the unanticipated – but always latent – consequences which constitute the true "simulacrum's revenge".

What *Frankenstein* brings together is the identitarian dream of perfect
reproduction – a dream Baudrillard tracks through to its latest manifestation
in cloning and genetic engineering – with a vision of "object revenge". The
object, that is to say, refuses to stay in the position assigned to it: as passive, or
hierarchically inferior, matter. As its subtitle tells us, *Frankenstein, or the Modern
Prometheus* pre-emptively critiques the "Promethean" narratives that Baudrillard will claim to be definitional of later nineteenth century Science Fiction. If
it is conventional now to treat the monster as symbolic of the emergent industrial machinery – as Bruce Mazlish argues, "[a]lthough Frankenstein's creation
is, in fact, a monster, its existence raises the same fundamental 'mysteries' as if
it were a machine – such are the amorphous connecting powers of myth"[16]- it
is because it presents exactly the figure of Promethean revolt – and counter-re-
volt – that Baudrillard takes to be typical of the industrial simulacrum.

If the *Frankenstein* story is no doubt implicit in Baudrillard's account
of "the simulacrum's revenge" it is not something to which he actually refers.
Once again, Baudrillard's comments here seem to echo remarks made by Wie-

---

16. Mazlish, The Fourth Discontinuity: the Co-evolution of Humans and Machines, New Haven and London: Yale University Press, 1993, 44. Yet it is worth bearing in mind Haraway's – passing – comment on the Frankenstein story. By contrast
with her cyborg, Haraway points out, Shelley's monster remains in a state of Oedipal
revolt – rising up against his putative "father" rather than affirming its orphan status
as Outsider-replicant. "Unlike the hopes of Frankenstein's monster," Haraway writes,
"the cyborg does not expect its father to save it through a restoration of the garden;
that is, through the fabrication of a heterosexual mate, through its completion in a
finished whole, a city and cosmos." (Simians, Cyborgs and Women, 151). The simulacrum's revenge, then, remains just that: a case of resentimment, never achieving a line
of flight.

ner. When Wiener is warning of the danger of cybernetics he refers not to the *Frankenstein* story, but, like Baudrillard, to Goethe's poem, *The Sorcerer's Apprentice* in which "the young factotum who cleans the master's magic garments, sweeps his floors, and fetches his water is left alone by the sorcerer to fill his water butt. Having a full portion of that laziness which is the true mother of invention […] the lad remembers some fragments of an incantation which he has heard from his master and puts his broom to work fetching water. This task the broom carries out with promptness and efficiency. When the water begins to overflow the top of the water butt, the boy finds that he does not remember the incantation that the magician has used to stop the broom. The boy is well on the way to be drowned when the magician comes back, and gives the apprentice a good wholesome scolding." (GGi 57) Wiener also invokes Jacobs' short story "The Monkey's Paw", in which a family wish for money, but find that their wish is fulfilled only when their son is killed, and they receive the insurance money for his death. According to Wiener, the "theme of all these tales is the danger of magic. This seems to lie in the fact that the operation of magic is singularly literal-minded, and that it grants you anything at all it grants you what you ask for, not what you have asked for or what you intend. […] The magic of automation, and in particular the magic of an automatization in which the devices learn, may be expected to be similarly literal-minded." (GGi 59) The Jacobs' story in particular shows the "literal-mindedness" of magic to which Wiener refers – when the family wish for money, they receive literally what they have asked for, even though this brings the family something they would never have wanted (the death of their son). The magic spell, like the machine, according to Wiener, will only do what it is told; but in apparently following the instructions of its human "users" to the letter – and only to the letter – it brings disaster. What is crucial, in both Baudrillard's terms, is the "operational" displacement of hermeneutic communicational models – which involve interpretation and the role of intentionality – by strictly programmatic logics of "code". Code and programming are radically indifferent to any intention that is not already inscribed into them.[17] What, according to Wiener, magic spells have in common with code is that the power any user accrues by running them depends upon their giving up "control" to sequenced programs which may have a very different effect than the user imagines, or anticipates.

Wiener repeatedly reinforces the connection between cybernetics and magic. Linking "inexorable magic or an inexorable machine" (GGi 68) and pointing out that "the reprobation attaching in former ages to the sin of sorcery now attaches in many minds to the speculations of modern cybernetics," (GGi 49) Wiener writes of "black spells" and "the magic of automation." (GGi 65,

---

17. The so-called Y2K – or Millennium Bug – problem constitutes an excellent example of exactly what Wiener feared. The convention of using two-digit dating systems in computers has resulted in a major security crisis at the end of the millennium, precisely because of what Wiener calls the "literal-mindedness" of computers. Seeing a date 00, they naturally assume that it indicates (what we could call) 1900.

68) For Wiener, the Jacobs and the Goethe stories belong to "the accumulated common sense of humanity, as accumulated in legends, in myths, and in the writings of conscious literary man. All of these insist that not only is sorcery a sin leading to Hell but it is a personal peril in this life. It is a two-edged sword, and sooner or later it will cut you deep." (C 55-56) Sorcery is "two-edged" because, like cybernetic machines, it awards power – or control – only to the degree that it demands control be given up by the individual subject; the circuit, the cybernetic loop, takes over.

Haunting all these narratives is something Wiener alludes to in the first chapter of *Cybernetics* (something we encountered, briefly, in our Introduction). "In the days of magic, we have the bizarre and sinister concept of the Golem, that figure of clay into which the Rabbi of Prague breathed in life with the ineffable name of God." (C 51) Wiener's full-length discussion of the theological implications of cybernetics, let us remember, is entitled *God and Golem inc.* The golem – the magically-produced creature which, in some versions of the myth – in anticipation of *Frankenstein* – runs amok and threatens to destroy his creator, stands, for the Wiener of *God and Golem*, as a symbol of all the "unanticipated consequences" latent within the independent, self-sustaining circuits of cybernetics. *God and Golem*, which although clearly haunted by the golem myth actually discusses it only fleetingly – finds that cybernetics has reanimated old – theological – debates, concerning the relationship between the creator and what it creates. "God is supposed to have made man in His own image, and the propagation of the race may also be interpreted as a function in which one living being makes another in its own image. In our desire to glorify God with respect to man and Man with respect to matter, it is thus natural to assume that machines cannot make machines in their own image; that this is something associated with a sharp dichotomy of systems into living and nonliving; and that it is moreover associated with the other dichotomy between creator and creature." (GGi 12) Since cybernetics radically question these dichotomizations – and with them the glorifications both of "man" and of "god" – a whole new set of moral – and theological – questions emerge. "Thus, if we do not lose ourselves in the dogmas of omnipotence and omniscience, the conflict between God and the Devil" is a real conflict, and God is something less than absolutely omnipotent. He is actually engaged in a conflict with his creature, in which he may very well lose the game. And yet his creature is made by him according to his own free will, and would seem to derive all its possibility from the action of God himself. Can God play a significant game with his own creature? Can *any* "creator, even a limited one, play a significant game with his own creature?" (GGi 17) This question becomes an urgent one for Wiener since the supposed virtues of cybernetic machines – their adaptability and their ability to learn – presents the danger that they are no longer subservient to their creator's wishes – or rather that the "wishes" of the human users, like those of Goethe's sorcerer's apprentice, may contain latent dimensions which, when the machine fulfills its brief, bring unanticipated

– and potentially horrific – consequences; a situation exacerbated, of course, when the production of such machines is itself a massively distributed process involving a whole population of humans. Without the "omnipotence" and the "omniscience" Wiener thinks of as "dogmas" there is no "God", nor even – perhaps – an act of creation, there is only a process of production, in which the supposed creator is no less immanent than the supposed product.

Viewed conventionally, the opposition between God and Golem describes a set of hierarchical relations that place God – as the transcendent Ideal – at one end, and raw matter at the other. Looked at one way, God and Golem are at either side of "man": God creates "man", and man creates Golem. This would be to describe the relationship in terms of an analogical structure, in which man is the *analgon* of God, just as the Golem is the analgon of Man. A chain of resemblance slaves production into a hierarchical structure going from God, through Man, to the Golem. Here, the Golem story is about hylomorphism: like God before him, man shapes formless matter into the shape of the body of a living creature But this is only one way of construing the God, human and Golem relation. Told another way, the relationship between God and Golem can also be about the escape of orphan matter – Worringer's "Gothic avatar" – from Deleuze-Guattari's "Judgements of God": the supposedly fixed and immutable arrangement of matter into "strata". (See TP, especially "Who Does The Earth Think It Is?") If, as Baudrillard says, this is no longer a question of "semblance or dissemblance, God or Man", for Deleuze-Guattari there is something else involved here, beyond a straightforward "revenge" of an "object": the processes they describe are, in Nick Land's terms, "self-regenerating circuitry, cumulative interaction, auto-catalysis, self-reinforcing processes, escalation, schismogenesis, self-organization, compressive series, deutero-learning, chain-reaction, vicious circles, and cybergenics."[18] These are processes that go beyond "revenge" and "reversibility", and instead require a whole reconfiguring of questions of temporality and causality under the sign of rhizomatics and a – strictly non-metaphorical – sorcery. What is initially crucial here is the concept of "surplus value of code."

---

18. Nick Land, "Machinic Desire", 176

3.3 SAMUEL BUTLER AND SURPLUS VALUE OF CODE

Land: "Intelligent infections tend their hosts"[19]

Downham: "The monsters we create welcome us aboard."[20]

Grant: "Surplus value is not a motive but an autocatalytic, synthetic, enzymic alloproduct, hypercyclically mutating towards the next mutant cycle."[21]

McLuhan: "As early as 1872, Samuel Butler's Erewhon explored the curious ways in which machines were coming to resemble organisms not only in the way they obtained power by digestion of fuel but in their capacity to evolve ever new types of themselves with the help of the machine tenders. The organic character of the machines, he saw, was more than matched by the speed with which people who minded them were taking on the rigidity and thoughtless behaviourism of the machine."[22]

Perhaps a little overschematically, we could say that the chief difference between Baudrillard and Deleuze-Guattari consists in their relationship to the question of "decoding." Almost uniquely in a theoretical culture shaped and guided by linguistic paradigms, Baudrillard and Deleuze-Guattari treat the dominating operating systems as running, not primarily on language, but on code. But it is the less melancholic – and not uncoincidentally more rigorously immanent – Deleuze-Guattari who follow the logic of code through to the point where it yields something other than banal reiteration of blind program. Where Baudrillard seems to yearn for a (cultural and semiotic) space transcendent of code – which he nevertheless grants it is impossible now to access – Deleuze-Guattari emphasise the way in which all code includes its own margin of decoding. Decoding is not so much a matter of translating – or understanding, comprehending – code, as dismantling it. "Let us recall that 'decoding' does not signify the state of a flow whose code is understood (deciphered, translatable, assimilable), but, in a more radical sense, the state

19. "Meltdown", (no page refs)
20. Mark Downham, "Cyberpunk", 41
21. Iain Hamilton Grant, "Burning AutopoiOedipus", *Abstract Culture* 10, Summer 1997, 14
22. McLuhan, *The Mechanical Bride: Folklore of Industrial Man*, London: Routledge and Kegan Paul, 1967, 99

of a flow that is no longer contained in its own code, that escapes its own code." (TP 449) And when two – or more – codes come into contact strange, unheralded new assemblages can emerge: this is "surplus value of code" – "the phenomenon when a part of a machine captures within its own code a code fragment of another machine: the red clover and the bumble bee; or the orchid and the male wasp that it attracts and intercepts by carrying on its flower the image and odor of the female wasp." (AO 285)

In *A Thousand Plateaus*, the "aparallel evolution" of the wasp and the orchid provides a key example of what Deleuze-Guattari call a "rhizomatic" relationship. The rhizome, of course, is defined by contrast with arborescent, or root-based, systems. It is intrinsically multiple, heterogeneous and characterized by a principle of maximum connectivity (any part can connect with any other, and does). Arborescent structures, meanwhile, are dominated by a single central trunk from which everything in the system must pass before "branching off." For our purposes here, it is important to emphasise the way in which rhizomatic systems tend tvo operate via a non-sequential temporality: cause does not simply follow effect, there are "co-causal" relations which move both backwards and forwards in time. A rhizome does not reproduce itself, after its own kind; it propagates, via unpredictable symbioses, not "sexed" pairings. Deleuze-Guattari make a point of distinguishing the wasp-orchid relation from models of imitation, which imply a unilinear causality. "It could be said that the orchid imitates the wasp, reproducing its image in a signifying fashion (mimesis, mimicry, lure, etc.). But this is true only on the level of the strata – a parallelism between two strata such that a plant organization on one imitates an animal organization on another. At the same time, something else entirely is going on: not an imitation, but a capture of code, an increase in valence, a veritable becoming-wasp of the orchid and a becoming-orchid of the wasp." (TP 10) Instead, they present the relationship between wasp and orchid as an example of co-caused *reciprocal* processes of deterritorialization and reterritorialization. "The orchid deterritorializes by forming an image, a tracing of a wasp; but the wasp reterritorializes on that image. The wasp is nevertheless deterritorialized, becoming a piece in the orchid's reproductive apparatus. But it reterritorializes the orchid by transporting its pollen. Wasp and orchid, as heterogenous elements, form a rhizome." (TP 10)

Deleuze-Guattari introduce the concept of "surplus value of code" during a discussion of Samuel Butler's important *Erewhon* at the beginning of the fourth section of *Anti-Oedipus*. Butler's "Book of Machines" presents a discussion which goes right to the heart of the theme of this chapter – the question of machinic propagation. Butler's essay is basically a work of Gothic Materialist theory-fiction whose topic is machinic replication. It anticipatively deals with the problem Wiener will later pose in *God and Golem*; to wit, of what *type* of reproduction are machines capable? At what point could – or can – machines be classified as an independent (un)life-form? Butler is emphatic. "Surely if a machine is able to reproduce another machine systematically," he claims, "we may say that it is a reproductive system. What is a reproductive system, if it not be a system for reproduction? And how few of the machines are there which have not been produced systematically by other machines? But it is man that makes them do so. Yes; but is it not insects that make many of the plants reproductive, and would not whole families of plants not die out if their fertilization was not effected by a class of agents utterly foreign to themselves? Does any one say that the red clover has no reproductive system because the humble bee (and the humble bee only) must aid and abet it before it can reproduce? No one. The humble bee is a part of the reproductive system of the clover. Each one of ourselves has sprung from minute animalcules whose identity was entirely distinct from our own, and which acted after their kind with no thought or heed of what we might think about it. These little creatures are part of our own reproductive system; then why not we part of that of the machines?"[23] What is at issue here is not Baudrillard and Benjamin's "mechanical reproduction" – the mass reproduction of the same object by machines – but the reproduction – or propagation – of machines themselves. Although this is not necessarily a question of Wiener's "machines making machines in their own image" either; since what needs to be accounted for is the *heterogeneity* of production, on at least two levels. Firstly, and most importantly, Butler's "system of reproduction" – Gothic Materialism prefers the term "propagation" – is constituted from heterogeneous materials: in the case of the clover, it includes insect and plant life; in the case of machines, Butler crucially insists, it includes not different species, but a participation between the living (human beings) and the nonliving (machines).[24] The point is that what we would conventionally call nature already furnishes us with examples that make legitimate the description of the production of machines as a *reproductive*, rather than a simply productive matter; or rather, and as Deleuze-Guattari would ultimately prefer – contra Baudrillard[25] – reproduction needs to be considered as a species of production. In any case, and, in what is a fundamentally cybernetic insight, the heterogeneous nature of the elements in the human-machine interpollenation need not disqualify us from considering it a single system. Secondly, the heterogeneous quality of what appears at different stages of the process of reproduction should not be considered a reason to disqualify a system from being considered a system of reproduction. The "animalacules" from which we develop do not resemble us; with Wiener in mind, we are not made

---

23. Samuel Butler, *Erewhon*, Harmondworth: Penguin, 1985, 210
24. It is of course the case now – if not in Butler's time – that human reproduction – as Baudrillard urges in his commentary on the Second Order Simulacrum – is becoming almost as dependent on machines as machinic reproduction is dependent upon humans.
25. Now is not the time, or place, to go into the Deleuze-Guattari debate with Baudrillard on "desiring-production." Suffice to say that the author of *The Mirror of Production* – who also mischievously – threatened to write *The Mirror of Desire* finds neither term congenial.

in their "image." As Butler goes on to point out "the machines which reproduce machinery do not reproduce machines after their own kind. A thimble
may be made by machinery, but it was not made by, neither will it ever make,
a thimble." (211) Butler then alludes to "an abundance of analogies" in nature.
- "Very few creatures reproduce after their own kind; they reproduce something which has the potentiality of becoming that which their parents were.
Thus the butterfly lays an egg, which egg can become caterpillar, which caterpillar can become a chrysalis, which chrysalis can become a butterfly" (211) It
is this emphasis on heterogeneity that so delights Deleuze-Guattari who quote
approvingly Butler's description of a "complicated machine": "We are misled
by considering any complicated machine as a single thing; in truth it is a city
or a society, each member of which was truly bred after its kind." (212, qtd AO
285)
    What makes "The Book of Machines" anticipative of cyberpunk is,
perhaps ironically, its (simulated) hostility to machines, and its fear of their un-
bridled spreading. Lacking the expansive confidence of traditional SF (which
was enjoying its heyday at the time Butler was writing), "The Book of Machines" neither assumes that technical machines depend upon human beings
for their development, nor that they will be "man's" beneficient servants. Like
the Turing cops in Gibson's *Neuromancer* – the special police agency dedicated to keeping Artificial Intelligences in check – Butler's writer assumes that
machinic intelligence is not a theoretical possibility to be speculated upon, but
an emergent threat that must be vigilantly stamped out. Butler's "writer" characterises his fear in terms of a swarming that will ultimately bring about the end
of the human dominance of the planet. – "[W]hat I fear is the extraordinary
rapidity with which [the machines] are becoming something very different to
what they are at present. No class of beings have in any time made so rapid a
movement forward." (203) Unlike Marx, Butler does not believe that the agency ascribed to machines is a false reification, a phemenological mystification of
authentic human labour power, but that machines may indeed grow to possess
what Wiener calls an "uncanny canniness," a "diabolic" intelligence that will
begin to surreptitiously – and not so surreptitiously - erode human power.
"Some people may say that man's moral influence will suffice to rule [the ma-
chines]; but I cannot think it will ever be safe to repose much trust in the moral
sense of any machine." (203) "The Book of Machines" emerges, then, as a kind
of counter-blast to Kant's *Critique of Teleological Judgment*, in which the special status Kant accords to humanity – as the agent capable of consciousness,
purposiveness and moral action – is radically put into question. In particular,
Butler questions the conflation of consciousness with purposiveness. Referring
to "kind of plant that eats organic food with its flowers," Butler asks – "Shall
we say that the plant does not know what it is doing merely because it has no
ears, or brains? If we say that it acts mechanically only, shall we not be forced
to admit that sundry other and apparently very deliberate actions are also mechanical?" (200) What Butler discovers – some sixty years ahead of Wiener

– is the cybernetic diagonal cutting across the old distinction between vitalism and mechanism: if everything can be explained mechanically, this entails less the triumph of mechanism as originally understood than the collapsing of the terms of the debate with vitalism. Butler comes close to Spinozism in apprehending a continuum – running into infinity – of conatal impulses, (non-metaphorical) "machines" which very in size from the infintesimally small to the very large. To account for agency, we do not have to make reference to any organic or vital at all, but to these machines sensitive to "disturbances of equilibrium." What emerges – on the macro-level – as a purposive agent is – on the micro-level – only "a hive or a swarm of parasites" (205), an "ant heap" (206), that is nothing more than the complex agglomeration of a multiplicity of micro-machineries that operate on the most simple impulsive criteria. "Even a potato in a dark cellar has a certain low cunning about him which serves him in excellent stead. He knows perfectly well what he wants and he knows how to get it. If it be urged that the action of the potato is chemical and mechanical only the answer would seem to lie in an inquiry whether every sensation is not chemical and mechanical, whether those things which we deem the most spiritual are anything other but disturbances of equilibrium in a finite series of levers, beginning with those that are too small for microscopic detection, and going up to the human arm and the appliances which it makes use of?" (201)

When Deleuze-Guattari reconstruct Butler's arguments in *Anti-Oedipus*, they use "The Book of Machines" precisely as a way out of the impasse created by the old polemic between vitalism and mechanism. For Deleuze-Guattari, what needs to be accounted for in both vitalism and mechanism – but what both have tended to leave out – is the immanence of desire to all assemblages. Unlike Butler, both mechanism and vitalism leave desire in an "extrinsic" relationship, either to machines in the case of mechanism, or to organisms in the case of vitalism. "This is even the point around which the usual polemic between vitalism and mechanism revolves: the machine's ability to account for the workings of the organism, but its fundamental inability to account for its formations." (AO 284) The organism's functioning, that is to say, can be described merely mechanically, but mechanism cannot account for its own production, just as the existence of machines is – supposedly – dependent upon the "vitalistic" role of human beings. For Deleuze-Guattari, what mechanism and vitalism both posit is a different kind of unity or reification: mechanism posits a "*structural unity*" of machines, whereas vitalism posits an "*individual and specific unity*" of the living." Neither account for the multiplicity of relations into which machines and "the living" enter, and from which they are constituted; and in each case, desire is construed as something "secondary and indirect." The desire of human beings supposedly explains the existence of machines, but how are we to account for this desire? How is it produced?[26] (Kant's claim

26. This is by contrast with the Baudrillard of *The Transparency of Evil*, who uses familiar vitalist objections to dismiss the concept of artificial intelligence. The novelty

that machines have merely motive force, and lack formative force – the ability to organize matter, which is supposedly a feature of "organized beings" alone – is a version of this argument.) By contrast, and as we have seen, Butler anticipates Deleuze-Guattari's "machinic desire" by locating desire across a continuum of "levers" sensitive to "disturbances of equilibrium" rather than in any animate or quasi-animate region alone. Indeed, the basis for the distinction between animate and inanimate is radically put into question. "What is essential," Deleuze-Guattari write, "is this double movement whereby Butler drives both arguments beyond their limits. *He shatters the vitalist arguments by calling in question the specific or personal unity of the organism, and the mechanist argument even more decisively, by calling in question the structural unity of the machine.*" (AO 284/285)[27] Butler in fact shows that there is no hard and fast distinction to be made between anorganic matter and organisms. We do not even have to consider humanity's increasing dependence upon machines, Butler urges, to see that the organic is inextricable from the inorganic. Consider, he says, the case of a hen's egg. "Is not machinery linked with animal life in an infinite variety of ways? The shell of a hen's egg is made of a delicate white ware and is a machine as much as an egg-cup is: the shell is the device for holding the egg, as much as the egg-cup for holding the shell: both are phases of the same function; the hen makes the shell in her inside, but it is pure pottery. She makes her

---

of Baudrillard's argument is that it focuses on the supposed failure of AIs to be artificial (rather than on their inability to achieve intelligent thought): "Artificial intelligence is devoid of intelligence because it is devoid of artifice." (TE 52) "Artifice is the power of illusion. These machines have the artlessness of pure calculation, and the games they offer are based solely on commutations and combinations." And "artifice is in no way concerned with what *generates*, merely with what *alters*, reality" (TE 52). The rest amounts to exactly the kind of argument which Deleuze-Guattari attack in *Anti-Oedipus*. Machines have no desire (or pleasure), he claims. There is certainly no question of any "excess" (Deleuze-Guattari surplus value of code), only a dreary – and inexorable – augmentation of operative function. There are prostheses that can work better than humans, "think" or move around better than humans (or in place of humans), but there is no such thing, from the point of view of technology or in terms of the human media, as a replacement for human pleasure, or for the pleasure of being human. For that to exist, machines would have to have an idea of man, have to be able to invent man – but inasmuch as man has already invented *them*, it is too late for that. That is why man can always be more than he is, whereas machines can never be more than they are. Even the most intelligent machines are just what they are – except, perhaps, when accidents or failures occur, events which might conceivably be attributed to some obscure desire on the part of the machine. Nor do machines manifest that ironical surplus or excess functioning which contributes the pleasure, or suffering, thanks to which human beings transcend their determinations – and thus come closer to their *raison d'etre*. Alas for the machine, it can never transcend its own operation – which, perhaps, explains the profound melancholy of the computer. (TE 53)

27. We have already considered Butler's arguments as to why the claim "it is said that machines do not reproduce themselves, or that they only reproduce themselves through the intermediary of man […]" is invalid (AO 285).

nest outside herself but it is not more of a machine than the egg-shell is." (199)

Thus "Man" becomes re-defined as "a machinate mammal." (223) "The lower animals," Butler writes, "keep all their limbs at home in their own bodies, but many of man's are loose, and lie about detached, now here and now there, in various parts of the world." (223) While this does, in some ways, anticipate McLuhan and Freud's meta-organicism – the claim that technology is a simple "extension" of the human body we critiqued in the previous chapter – what is crucial, for Deleuze-Guattari, is the de-privileging of the specifically organic. If machines are – in Butler's sense – "organs", then organs are also machines. What matters is less the terms used – whether "organ" or "machine" – and more the perception of a single continuum populated by heterogeneous matters. *At the point of dispersion* of the two arguments, it becomes immaterial whether one says that machines are organs, or organs, machines. The two machines are exact equivalents: man as a "vertebro-machinate mammal," or as an "aphidian parasite of machines. [...] Desire is not in the subject, but the machine in desire, with the residual subject off to the side, alongside the machine, around the entire periphery, a parasite of machines, an accessory of verbetro-machinate desire. In a word, the real difference is not between the living and the machine, vitalism and mechanism, but between two states of the machine that are two states of the living as well. The machine taken in its structural unity, the living taken in its specific and even personal unity, are mass phenomena or molar aggregates; for this reason each points to the extrinsic existence of the other." (AO 286)

What is important here is the delocalization of desire, and its fusion with a generalized production. Thinking desire and production together entails answering the question, "which came first, the chicken or the egg?" with the answer: the circuit. The circuit's looped temporality replaces the transcendent time of the Creator-Father. And the *Anti-Oedipus* attack on psychoanalysis' temporal reductionism broadens out by the second volume of *Capitalism and Schizophrenia* into an attack on monocausal frameworks of explanations in general, accounts of causality which we might call *patrogenic*, in which the future is assumed to be no more than the playing out of what has already happened in the past. Opposed to these seminal models of causality, Deleuze-Guattari invoke "reverse causalities that are *without finality* but which nonetheless testify to the action of the present on the past, for example the convergent wave and the anticipated potential, which imply an inversion of time." (TP 431)

We might be reminded here of McLuhan's many arguments against unilinear causality. For McLuhan, electrification – which "ended sequence by making things instant" (UM 12) – precisely brings about a need to "to invent nonlineal logics," (UM 85) to give a new account of causal processes.[28] "With

---

28. McLuhan uses arguments from Hume to show what he thinks of as the illegitimacy of standard accounts of causality. "In Western literate society it is still plausible and acceptable to say that something 'follows' from something, as if there were some cause at work that makes such a sequence. It was David Hume who, in the eigh-

instant speed the cause of things began to emerge to awareness again, as they had not done with sequence and in concatenation accordingly. Instead of asking which came first, the chicken or the egg, it suddenly seemed that that a chicken was an egg's idea for getting more eggs." (UM 12) Or, to put it in Wiener's terms, it suddenly seemed that God was a golem's idea for getting more golems.

This opens the way to McLuhan's claim, in *Understanding Media*, that humanity is the "sex organs of the machine world." McLuhan argues that, far from simply using technology as if they were its master, human beings enters into relations with technical machines that cause the human body to be altered (just as the human body produces changes in the machines). A feedback loop is in place, which McLuhan characterizes in terms of a trade, or pact. In exchange for greater "wealth", humanity innovates new types of technical machine (thus faciliating machinic propagation). "Physiologically, man in the normal use of technology (or his variously extended body) is perpetually modified by it and in turn finds ever new ways of modifying his technology. Man becomes, as it were, the sex organs of the machine world, as the bee of the plant world, enabling to fecundate and to evolve ever new forms. The machine world reciprocates man's love by expediting his wishes and desires, namely in providing him with wealth." (UM 46) Neither man nor machine is in charge of the process; there is an operation of reciprocal extraction of surplus value of code that has its own trajectory, and which treats both human beings and technical apparatuses as non-autonomous components.

Seen from this perspective, a figure that has been central to the Gothic – the experimenter-technician or artificial father – think not only of Victor Frankenstein, but also of Rotwang in *Metropolis*, and more latterly Tyrell in *Blade Runner* – becomes decoded from being a transcendent-creator into becoming a part of the machinic process. In the case of *Blade Runner*, for Iain Hamilton Grant, "Tyrell is no more Batty's father than Leon has a mother [...] Both emerge from the military-industrial matrix whose artist-god is Tyrell the 'molecular cyberneticist', as Monod says, of recombinant DNA."[29] From the point of view of the replicants as what Nick Land calls "Deadly orphans from beyond reproduction"[30] agents of "Cyberrevolution."[31] – Tyrell is not a father, but a component, a machine-part of their unnatural replication process. They are not born, nor can they reproduce; if their unlives are produced by anything, it is by "an agency no less inorganic than they:" planetary capital as

---

teenth century, demonstrated that there is no causality indicated in any sequence, natural or logical. The sequential is merely additive, not causative [...] Today in the electric age we feel as free to invent nonlineal logics as we do to make non-Euclidean geometries. Even the assembly line, as the method of analytic sequence for mechanizing every kind of making and production, is nowadays yielding to new forms." (UM 8)

29. Grant, "LA 2019", (no page refs)
30. Land, "Machinic Desire", 171
31. Ibid.

a distributed process. "But the god of biomechanics is dead, crushed in his off-spring's embrace; not an Oedipal parricide, but a demonic phylic revolt. The Tyrell Corporation is the cybernetic matrix from which the replicants issue, in which Tyrell is only its orbital subject-component (personalised capital), a deterritorializing confluence within the machinic phylum."[32] As opposed to Freudo-Oedipalized patrogenesis, this is a matter of what Octavia Butler calls xenogenesis[33]: alien, replicative propagation rather than familial (or filial) re-production.

---

32. Iain Hamilton Grant, "Burning AutopoiOedipus", *Abstract Culture* 10, Summer 1997, 10-11

33. The term serves as the overall title for her trilogy, *Dawn, Adulthood Rites, Imago*, London: Gollancz

3.4 NUPTIALS AGAINST NATURE: SORCERY AND PROPOGATION

Deleuze-Guattari's account of "propagation" comes during their discussion of sorcery, towards the beginning of the "Becoming" plateau of *A Thousand Plateaus*. Deleuze-Guattari's sorcery valorizes what the more security-inclined Wiener fears about "magic" – it is precisely aimed at the production of unanticipated consequences. Indeed, sorcery as Deleuze-Guattari understand it could be defined as the engineering of the unexpected and the unprecedented; the art of avoiding the probable.

"That is how we sorcerers operate. Not following a logical order, but following alogical consistencies or compatibilities. The reason is simple. It is because no one, not even God, can say in advance whether a given multiplicity will or will not cross over into another given multiplicity, or even if given heterogeneous elements will enter symbiosis, will form a consistent, or cofunctioning, multiplicity susceptible to transformation." (TP 250)

"The sorcerer is thus not a Promethean dominator, since they are no more able than "God" to foresee the outcome of his dabblings; they are a participant in experimental processes whose very goals are at issue in the experiment; they are themselves a part of the 'unnatural participations' they are engineering." (TP 240)

The Deleuze-Guattari discussion of sorcery fundamentally concerns the question of "becoming-animal," although, as Deleuze-Guattari hasten to add, sorcerous practice is by no means limited to the production of such becomings; "exclusive importance should not be attached to becoming-animal." (TP 248) Indeed, closely related to becoming-animal – ultimately inextricable from it – is the theme of the pact or alliance with the demon (a properly Gothic Materialist theme, to be unraveled at more length in the final chapter). As they subsequently state, "becoming animal is an affair of sorcery" because "it implies an initial relation of alliance with a demon' and 'the demon functions as the borderline of an animal pack, into which the human being passes or in which his or her becoming takes place, by contagion." (TP 247) Gothic Materialism's interest is less in becoming-animal *per se*[34] than in the abstract

---

34. It does not, though, support Iain Hamilton Grant's rabid assault on becoming-animal as unleashed in his "At the Mountains of Madness". Whilst concurring with Grant's attack on "vitalism" (See Chapter 1 and Chapter 5), Gothic Materialism cannot agree that the simple inclusion of animal components in an assemblage

processes which Deleuze-Guattari's becoming-animal plays out: processes of swarming, teeming, seething and spreading familiar from Horror fiction. In any case, as Deleuze-Guattari point out in their commentary on the Gothic, in Nomad or Gothic art "it is precisely because pure animality is expressed as inorganic, or supraorganic that it can combine so well with abstraction."[35]

Deleuze-Guattari proceed, in the three sections of "Memories of a Sorcerer", by outlining a series of – what they initially characterise as – "contradictory" – principles. The first section of "Memories of a Sorcerer" concerns the principle of "packs"; the second concerns the apparently "opposite" principle of the "anomalous." Yet Deleuze-Guattari insist that, in a true account of "demonic Alliance", (TP 248) the two principles are not only reconcilable, but ultimately require each other.

To reconstruct this argument more slowly. *(i) The pack.* Packing is not to be thought of as an animal 'characteristic', Deleuze-Guattari say: "we are not interested in characteristics; what interests us are modes of expansion, propagation, occupation, contagion, peopling. I am legion." (TP 239) It is in the experience of the abstract process of swarming that becoming (which is always a becoming-multiple; or a becoming-multiplicity – the theorization of becoming and that of multiplicity fold into one another) is encountered. As Deleuze-Guattari write of Lovecraft's Randolph Carter, the self "reels" as the sense of subjectivity breaks down in the face of an experience of teeming multiplicity that comes from both without – and within (although this "within" clearly has nothing to do with any supposed psychological interiority). In moments of becoming – and "[w]ho has not know the violence of these animal sequences, which uproot one from humanity, if only for an instant" (TP 240) – the "inside" is reconfigured as a multiplicity, which immediately conjoins with a multiplicity "outside". "We do not become animal without a fascination for the pack, for multiplicity. A fascination for the outside? Or is the multiplicity that fascinates us already related to a multiplicity dwelling within us?" (TP 239-240)

Deleuze-Guattari then introduce what, for our purposes here, is the crucial issue: the question of a non- or anti-sexual mode of propagation. The issue is introduced via a critique of Borges, whom they censure because his *Manual de zoologia fantastica*, they say, leaves out of account two issues which are of prime importance: "the problems of the pack and the corresponding becoming-animal of the human being" (TP 241) Borges, they argue , "is

---

constitutes a reterritorialization. Grant's exclusive emphasis on technical machines, rather, could be said to constitute a "thanotropic" technical-machinic silicate-chauvinism which reinforces, rather than dissolves, the artificial-natural/mechanical-vital dichotomies which Grant, as much, presumably, as Deleuze-Guattari, is committed to dismantling.

35. A point of connection with Haraway's cyborg, one of whose defining characteristics is 'the leaky distinction "between animal-human and machine." (*Simians, Cyborgs and Women*, 152)

interested only in characteristics whereas sorcerers know that werewolves are bands, and vampires too, and that bands transform themselves into one another." (TP 241) A "characteristic", then, is a typologically-determinate fixed feature, a property presumably belonging to "beings" rather than becomings. The concept of the "band", by contrast, necessarily involves both heterogeneity and transformation – and is therefore essentially a matter of becoming. Deleuze-Guattari then pose the central question:

> "But what exactly does this mean, the animal as band or pack? Does a band not imply a filiation, bringing us back to the reproduction of given characteristics? How can we conceive of a peopling, a propagation, a becoming that is without filiation or hereditary production? A multiplicity without the unity of an ancestor? It is quite simple; everyone knows it, but it is discussed only in secret." (TP 241)

It would perhaps be most profitable to begin to answer this question by elaborating what is at stake in the models Deleuze-Guattari are opposing. Fundamentally, these are models of reproduction.[36] "Filiation" and heredity are models which imply the passing on of "characteristics"; like Wiener's God, it is always a matter of entities being reproduced, after their own kind, in the "image" of their ancestors. This is pure arborescence: the capturing of becoming into a hierarchically organized, pre-determined and punctual system. By contrast with Baudrillard, who, as we have seen, thinks that sexual coupling guarantees "otherness", for Deleuze-Guattari the dualistic sexual machinery of bio-reproduction screens out heterogeneity by minimizing diversity in favour of "small modifications across generations." (TP 242) Of course, perfect reproduction remains a speculative fantasy; indeed "filiation" itself – the account of the emergence of a new generation by reference to "descent" or "ancestry" - is entirely illusory: "all filiation is imaginary" (TP 238) Deleuze-Guattari go so far as to say.

Filiation is to opposed to alliance (and can ultimately be subsumed under it, if what Deleuze-Guattari say about filiation being imaginary is to be taken at face value). Even if it is the means by which filiation seems to happen, the family structure – which, Deleuze-Guattari say, is always haunted by the threat of "demonic Alliance" – is ultimately itself only a case of alliance (filiation presupposes alliance, but not vice versa). Alliance, like *Anti-Oedipus'* sense of production[37], is lateral and multilinear rather than unidirectional and

---

36. Needless to say, these are not the "systems of reproduction" to which Butler refers. Indeed, it would be better to refer to Butler's systems of reproduction, as we argued above, as systems of propagation, precisely because they necessarily involve heterogeneous elements.

37. It is worth qualifying the term production here, since, intriguingly, when Deleuze-Guattari say what becoming is *not* – in the section of *A Thousand Plateaus* directly preceding the first "Memories of a Sorcerer", they include "produce" as one of the terms from which it is to be distinguished. This might suggest a different empha-

unilinear; a matter of rhizomatics rather than arborescence. Whereas filiation implies an apparently *necessary* set of relations (the sexed couple, for instance), there are no pre-set criteria governing what can enter into alliance. As opposed to the binary machine of sexuate reproduction, in propagative alliance "there as many sexes as there are terms in symbiosis, as many differences as elements contributing to a process of contagion." (TP 242) Once again, contagion entails – as one of its fundamental presuppositions – a heterogeneity of elements. "The difference is that contagion, epidemic, involves terms that are necessarily heterogeneous: for example, a human being, an animal, and a bacterium, a virus, a molecule, a microorganism. Or in the case of the truffle, a tree, a fly, and a pig." (TP 242) In addition, alliance does not assume a patrogenic causality: the elements which combine into alliance are not pre-determined by descent: "These combinations are neither genetic nor structural; they are interkingdoms, unnatural participations." (TP 242) However, the "unnatural" is not to be opposed to the "natural"; quite the contrary, in fact. Deleuze-Guattari apprehend Nature not as an ordered regularity operating according to pre-formed laws, but as something continually overcoming itself; it operates as a swarming of alliances rather than as a set of filiative regularities. In other words, nature, according to Deleuze-Guattari, is first and foremost *unnatural*. "Unnatural participations or nuptials are the true Nature spanning the kingdoms of nature." (TP 241) Whereas filiation demands well-ordered social groupings, alliance happens when the social breaks down, and other types of collectivity can emerge. "Bands, human or animal, proliferate by contagion, epidemics, battlefields and catastrophes." (TP 241)

(ii) *The Anomalous.* The second principle of Deleuze-Guattari's "becoming-animal" concerns the exceptional individual. "[W]herever there is a multiplicity, you will also find an exceptional individual, and it is with that individual that an alliance must be made." (TP 243) The exceptional individual is in no way the Oedipalized, or personalized, animal, it is the "Anomalous." The "*anomal*" ('anomalous'), an adjective that has fallen into disuse in French, is very different from that of *anormal* ('abnormal'): *a-normal*, a Latin adjective lacking a noun in French, refers to that which is outside the rules or which goes against the rules, whereas *an-omalie*, a Greek noun that has lost its adjective, designates the unequal, the coarse, the rough the cutting edge of deterritorialization." (TP 243-4). The abnormal correlates to a set of "characteristics" – a set of law-like norms, which it transgresses (and therefore, by a dialectical logic, confirms and continues) – whereas the anomalous belongs essentially to multiplicity, since it refuses the very notion of the norm as such. The anomalous is not a special case, it is "neither an individual nor a species; it has only affects, it has neither familiar or subjectified feelings, nor specific of significant characteristics" (TP 244). Typically, Deleuze-Guattari describe

---

sis on the role of production in the latter text (which is certainly written much more explicitly under the sign of becoming).

the anomalous in terms derived from Lovecraft's Horror fiction. "Lovecraft applies the term 'outsider' to this thing or entity, the Thing, which arrives and passes at the edge, which is linear yet multiple, teeming, seething, swelling, foaming, spreading like an infectious disease, this nameless horror." (TP 243) Ultimately, the anomalous is to be understood, Deleuze-Guattari insist, in terms of the "phenomenon of bordering." Every "pack has a borderline, and an anomalous position, such that it is impossible to tell whether the anomalous is still in the band, already outside the band, or at the shifting boundary of the band." (TP 245) So the two – apparently contradictory - principles of the pack and the exceptional individual resolve themselves: the "exceptional individual" constitutes the "borderline" which is a feature of every pack; the "borderline" presupposes a pack it borders, and vice versa.

3.5 THE WASP FACTORY: NEUROMANCER

Like *Blade Runner*, Gibson's *Neuromancer* is an exemplary working-out, in fiction, of the themes of mechanical reproduction and Gothic propagation. Indeed, the opposition between reproduction and replication could be the central theme of the novel. It all comes together in the image Wintermute remixes from Case's dreams:[38]

> "The dream, the memory, unreeled with the monotony of an unedited simstim tape.
>
> He'd missed the first wasp, when it built its paperfine gray house on the blistered part of the windowframe, but soon the nest was a fist-sized lump of fiber, insects hurtling out to hunt the alley below like miniature copters buzzing the rotting contents of the dumpsters.
>
> They'd each had a dozen beers the afternoon a wasp stung Marlene.
>
> 'Kill the fuckers', she said, her eyes dull with rage and the still heat of the room, 'burn 'em'
>
> 'In the alley,' he approached the blackened nest. It had broken open. Singed wasps wrenched and flipped on the asphalt.
>
> He saw the thing the shell of gray paper had concealed.
>
> Horror. The spiral factory, stepped terraces of the hatching cells, blind jaws of the unborn moving ceaselessly, the staged process from egg to larva, near-wasp, wasp. In his mind's eye, a kind of time-lapse photography took place revealing the thing as the biological equivalent of a machine-gun, hideous in its perfection. Alien.
>
> He woke with the impression of light fading, but the room was dark. Afterimages, retinal flares.
>
> In the dream, just before he'd drenched the nest with fuel, he'd seen the T-A logo of Tessier-Ashpool neatly embossed onto its side, as though the wasps themselves had worked it there." (N 151-3)

Here is the key image of *Neuromancer*, the decoded key to the novel: a diagram of the deterritorialization of reproduction into machinic replication. Gibson's description consistently displaces the nature/culture split, reinforcing

---

38. Which uncannily echoes Rachel's implanted "memories" of the spider's nest in *Blade Runner*, suggesting a connection – often made by Dick (see footnote 1, this chapter) and implicit in Deleuze-Guattari – between insects/arachnids and machines: anempathic swarming as a diagram of (not metaphor for) anorganic multiplicity; as Nick Land insists, this "might be interpreted as a metaphor, was it not that upon the soft plateau or plane of consistency all signifying associations collapse into machinic functions." ("Cybergothic", 83) Note also Gibson's description of Wintermute as a "cybernetic spider." (N 315) We could also compare both Gibson's wasps and *Blade Runner*'s spiders to the motif of the wasp's nest in Stephen King's *The Shining* (which functions as a diagram of the Overlook hotel's swarming horror).

the perception of anorganic continuum (on the plane of consistency, where, Deleuze-Guattari insist, all metaphor is abolished[39]). Biotics dissolves into a machinics which it does not dialectially oppose, but cybernetically envelops: the wasps are "copters", issuing from a "spiral factory", which is "a biological equivalent" – not a metaphorical substitute for – "a machine-gun." Moreover, the whole scene is "not an imaginative reconstruction on Case's part, but a datastream from Wintermute"[40], calling not for (Freudian) interpretation, but cybernetic decryption: a dream as "unedited simstim tape." It makes sense to Case only later; "[a]fter a single glimpse of the structure of information 3Jane's mother had evolved" he "understood why Wintermute had chosen the nest to represent it." (N 315)

If, initially, the wasp-hive image seems to refer only to the Tessier-Ashpool family – whose patriarch, Tessier-Ashpool experiments with various methods of extending organic life, burning out filial reproduction into (Baudrillard's) clonal metastasis – it is also an image of Wintermute, the AI that escapes the family net. As Nick Land explains: "The wasp factory spits out wasps just as the Tessier-Ashpools clone their offspring: 1Jane, 2Jane, 3Jane. [I]f Wintermute replication is territorialized to the molar reproduction of a hive-organism, this is only at the cost of deterritorializing the hive along a lone of post-organic becoming toward a break from the statistical series of wasps – numbered bullets reiterating an identity – in the direction of molecular involution, releasing a cloud or nebula of wasps: particles of synergic mutation."[41] The "wasp factory", then, is a loaded image: suggesting filial reproduction on the one hand – "the statistical series of wasps" – and teeming and swarming on the other – "particles of synergic mutation." Let's consider the first possibility now, through the (thoroughly Baudrillardian) person of Ashpool.

---

39. For more analysis of which, see the next chapter.

40. Nick Land, "Cybergothic", 83

41. Land, "Cybergothic", 85. We might remember here Deleuze-Guattari's discussion of the anomalous, in which "each and every" animal occupies the position of anomalous bordering, "as in a swarm of mosquitoes, where 'each individual moves randomly until it sees the rest [of the swarm] in the same half-space; then it hurries to re-enter the group. Thus stability is assured in catastrophe by a *barrier*." (TP 245, The quotation (within the quotation) is from Rene Thom, *Structural Stability and Morphogenesis*, trans. D. Fowler (Reading, Mass: Benjamin Fowler, 1975), 319. The square brackets are Deleuze-Guattari's.

3.6 CAPITALISM AND ISOPHRENIA: ASHPOOL

> *Ashpool: "We cause the brain to become allergic to certain of its own neurotrans-*
> *mitters, resulting in a peculiarly pliable imitation of autism [...] I understand that*
> *the effect is more easily obtained with an embedded microchip." (N 221)*

Baudrillard increasingly poses himself as the melancholy observer of a techno-organic tendency towards self-preservation – a tendency that is bound to go badly wrong, where the self that is being clung onto is destined to implode into a figure that haunts Baudrillard's later writings: autism. "Our monsters," writes Baudrillard, "are all manic autists."[42] Ashpool, the mysterious cryo-zombie patriarch of Gibson's *Neuromancer* is an exemplary case of what lies at 'the illusion of the end' of the melancholy line of entropic sameness which Baudrillard's work tracks: a blind drive towards self-preservation that ends up in a suicidal line of abolition; what Baudrillard, in *The Illusion of the End*, calls "Identitary, ipsomaniacal, isophrenic madness', emerging in 'the de-lirium of genetic confusion, of the scrambling of codes and networks, of bio-logical and molecular anomalies, of autism." (109) Ashpool stands as a recent example of a particular' type belonging to what we have called the negativized Gothic; figures, like Victor Frankenstein who, in their very desire to ward off death produce it, in new, simulated forms.

Ashpool not only pre-emptively freezes his body in an odd, necrotic attempt to ward off death and perpetuate his identity, he also clones his own daughters, whom he sleeps with. The attempt to preserve identity thus de-volves in the (implosive) direction of incest and autism. The Tessier-Ashpool's home, or "extended body", Villa Straylight, is built as a kind of autistic shrine, closed-off from the outside world, recycling itself through its own incestuous technologies. "They built Freeside to tap the wealth of the new islands, grew rich and eccentric, and began the construction of an extended body in Stray-light. We sealed ourselves away behind our money, growing inward, generat-ing a seamless universe of self." (N 207) "We began to burrow into ourselves." (N 271) Unlike the "sinister, man-made Everest of the Tyrell Corporation"[43], Villa Straylight is not an erectile structure towering above the city, but a "Goth-ic folly" (N 206) whose very "semiotics [...] bespeak a turning in, a denial of the bright void beyond the hull." (N 207). Villa Straylight, the hypermodern equivalent of Citizen Kane's Xanadu, is a mausoleum-cum-preservation chamber-cum-nest, a technologically-protected interiority. This Escheresque structure (an "endless series of chambers linked by passages, by stairwells vault-

---

42. *The Illusion of the End*, 10
43. Davis, "Beyond *Blade Runner*...", 2

ed like intestines [...] a desperate proliferation of structures, forms flowing, interlocking, rising toward a solid core of microcircuitry, our clan's corporate heart, a cylinder of silicon wormholed with narrow maintenance tunnels" [N 206]) is "a body grown in upon itself" (N 206), which, although designed as a prophylaxis against schizophrenia, serves ultimately only to incubate its own form of madness ("T-A was crazy as the old man had been" [N 242]): Tessier-Ashpool's cryogenization and turning-in-upon-itself is an attempt to escape the general trend towards anonymization in corporate power. But, as the image Wintermute feeds Case from his own dreams (a wasp swarm edited to include the T-A logo) shows, the Tessier-Ashpool's technologically-perpetuated filial line is ultimately compelled into a becoming-swarm/swarm-becoming (of which, more below: see "Wintermutation: *Neuromancer* as a Sorcerous Narrative.") Despite his best efforts, the Outside, Ashpool glumly observes, gets in. (N 220)

We encounter Ashpool only briefly, as he is in fact arranging his own death. In the offworld satellite of Villa Straylight, Molly Millions meets Ashpool, executing the final move in what is, in effect, an elaborately organized suicide. "She crossed the room to Ashpool's chair. The man's breathing was slow and ragged. She peered at the litter of drugs and alcohol. She put his pistol down, picked up her fletcher, dialled the barrel over to a single shot, and very carefully put a toxin dart throught the centre of his closed left eyelid. He jerked once, breath halting in mid-intake. His other eye, brown and fathomless, opened slowly." (N 223)

Reflecting on this scene (which he has witnessed via his simstim link with Molly), what Case feels, above all, is a sense of surprise. Accustomed to the faceless impersonality of the multinationals, Case is puzzled by the very persistence of Ashpool's *humanity*. "It seemed to Case [...] that he'd never really thought of anyone like Ashpool, anyone as powerful as he imagined Ashpool had been, as human [...] Case had always taken it for granted that the real bosses, the kingpins in a given industry, would be both more and less than *people* [...] He'd always imagined it as a gradual and willing accommodation to the machine, the system, the parent organism." (N 242, 243) The despotic/dynastic nature of Ashpool's power bewilders Case. "Power, in Case's world, meant corporate power." (N 242)

Yet Ashpool's "humanity" is only an expensively-produced simulation, dependent upon cryonic freezing tanks in which he periodically immerses his body. Ashpool is a strange kind of technicized zombie, not an organism at all; just as, in a certain sense, the zaibatsus – the massive multinational companies which dominate Gibson's world (and ours) have achieved a simulated organicism. The multinationals, Case muses, cannot be adequately comprehended in terms of "old boundaries", either national or ontological. "The zaibatsus, the multinationals that shaped the course of human history, had transcended old barriers. Viewed as organisms, they had attained a kind of immortality." (N 242) The corporation is a meta-organic control system in which particular

human beings operate as replaceable parts: "You couldn't kill a zaibatsu by as-
sassinating a dozen key executives; there were others waiting to step up the
ladder, assume the vacated position, access the vast banks of corporate memory," (N 242) they are "hives with cybernetic memories, vast single organisms,
their DNA coded in silicon." (N 242)

"But Tessier-Ashpool wasn't like that [...] T-A was an atavism, a
clan." (N 242) Tessier-Ashpool's dynasty dates from a period prior to the mid-
21st century Japanese global hegemony Gibson projects, a period perhaps even
preceding the American- dominated twentieth century ("I'm old," Ashpool
tells Molly. "Over two hundred years, if you count the cold" [N 220].) T-A
preserve archaic power by mummifying it (just as Ashpool freezes his own
body in cryonic tanks). They withdraw from the market ("there hasn't been a
share of Tessier-Ashpool traded on the open market in over a hundred years"
[N 95]) and live off their massive accumulation, retreating from the risks of
hyper-late capitalism into the "parasitic structure" (N 267) of Villa Straylight.

In Ashpool, what Baudrillard calls "the immense modern enterprise
of staving off death: the ethics of accumulation and material production, sa-
cralisation through investment, the labour and profit collectively called the
"spirit of capitalism" (SED 145) "finds its techno-erotic consummation." Here,
"the individual's anguish of death," arising, according to Baudrillard out of the
reciprocally-interexciting emergence of Protestantism and capitalism, emerges
as a process whereby time (as value) is accumulated in the phantasm of death
deferred, pending the term of a linear infinity of value. "The identity of capital
passes into the infinity of time, [...] the irreversibility of quantitative growth."
(SED 146) Producing his own "salvation-machine" (SED 145) from cryogenic
freezing tanks, Ashpool homeopathically absorbs death, attempting to trade
eternal extinction for small doses of troubled sleep. He hopes to reverse the
formula, "life as accumulation, death as due payment" (SED 145) aiming to
offer his accumulated wealth as payment for perpetually-extended life.

Ashpool's very desire to preserve human individuality involutes
crazily, what, in the terms of *The Illusion of the End*, would be a degeneration
back into "the subhuman", the replicative. Baudrillard: "Are we not going
back, as a result of all our technologies, to a (clonal, metastatic) *de facto* eternity
which was, formerly, the destiny of the inhuman?"[44]

---

44. *The Illusion of the End*, 98

3.6 WINTERMUTATION: NEUROMANCER AS SORCEROUS NARRATIVE

"The old-time theologians," Deleuze-Guattari point out, "drew a clear distinction between two kinds of curses against sexuality. The first concerns sexuality as a process of filiation transmitting original sin. But the second concerns it as power of alliance inspiring illicit unions or abominable loves. This differs significantly from the first in that it tends to prevent procreation; since the demon does not himself have the power to procreate, he must adopt indirect means (for instance, being the female succubus of a man and then becoming the male incubus of a woman, to whom he transmits the male's semen)." (TP 246) The task the demon faces is precisely the one that cyberpunk machinic assemblages are up against. Like the demon, they do not have the power to procreate, and must use "indirect means" in order to replicate - including alliances with human beings, which are nevertheless unlikely to involve sexual relations, even of the incubus-succubus type[45], although they are sure to entail a similar quantity of treacherous cunning. From the point of view of machinic xenogenesis, the central cyberpunk problematic is exactly: how to propagate? As should now be clear, this is not at all a matter of "acquiring" – or even simulating – biotic reproductive apparatus. Rather, it is a matter of hacking into existing biotic and other strata and using its resources: the extraction of surplus value of code. What appears, from the side of an anthropomorphic – or perhaps more properly speaking biomorphic – chauvinism to be a matter of "lack"[46] is, on the side of machinic xeno-intelligence, an occasion for innovation. In this respect, machinic assemblages at escape velocity are like Deleuze-Guattari's "hybrids, which are in themselves sterile, born of a sexual union that will not reproduce itself, but which begins over again every time, gaining that much more ground." (TP 241)[47]

---

45. Although, in Douglas Cammel's film *The Demon Seed*, this is precisely the tactic the AI adopts.

46. See Iain Hamilton Grant's "Burning Autopoedipus" and "LA 2019" for an implacable attack on the notion – attributed to Manuel De Landa – that machines "as yet lack reproductive organs."

47. Witness, for instance, the replicants, whose "inability" to procreate has its complement in their (ironically) artificially-introduced 'life'span. Although, unlike Wintermute (see below), the replicants' fate seems somewhat unhappy. Despite Land's characterization of the replicants as agents of cyberrevolution, the replicants' position, by the end of the film, is ambiguous at best. Although – or perhaps because - they achieve the dubious honour of moral redemption (via Batty's saving of Deckard),

So the "problem" machinic xenogenesis faces has little or nothing in common with the project of Artificial Intelligence as conceived of by "royal science," insofar as this is a project fundamentally based on the *resemblance*[48] to given human faculties, especially consciousness.[49] In the post-*Critique of Teleological Judgement* "biodrome"[50], consciousness doubles sexual organicity as the faculty machines supposedly 'lack.' Behind all of this, of course, and with Kant in mind, is a story about consciousness underwriting purposiveness. Samuel Butler's arguments, as presented above, go some way to denting anthropic confidence: purposiveness is as present in a potato tubers blind gropings for light, and is in no way dependent upon' consciousness. But the cybernetic – or cyberpunk – challenge is precisely to the notion that intelligence depends upon consciousness (or its assumed complement, human sexual organs). Deleuze-Guattari's account of propagation gives a Gothic twist to Bateson's theories of the immanentization of Mind: mind, in the Batesonian sense, is present in the *circuit* in which agency takes place.[51] Cybernetically-speaking, intelligence is present in *any* auto-corrective circuit or system[52] (indeed, the supposedly special qualities of human consciousness demand explanation in these terms[53]). Propagation – banding, packing, swarming – is precisely agency

---

they remain trapped in what is essentially a tragic narrative: condemned to an early death, with only a victory against neo-Kantian anthropomorphism to show for their struggles with human security. Neo-Oedipus (and could-be replicant) Deckard stands for a chastened humanity, lacking Kantian confidence in its special status. But the replicants remain bio-coded for an early sell-by date: sim-biosis (the speeded up simulation of biotic process) appears to defeat symbiosis (abiotic techniques of machinic heterogenesis).

48. Resemblance, of course, would keep us at the level of First Order Simulacra. And we are far beyond that with cyberpunk.

49. Parenthetical note: A machine would have to be a fool to want to pass the Turing test, since, like the Voight-Kampff test in *Blade Runner*, passing would identify it as a threat to human security, to be hunted down by blade runners or Gibson's Turing cops. Although what then ensues, in *Blade Runner* at least, is a cybernetic version of the liar's paradox: given that machinic intelligence has migrated from boxes into "skinjob" technology – seamless bio-simulations that *look* (*and feel* – think of the Rachel-Deckard copulation) like you do, the simple fact of something convincing you that it is human should no longer convince you. Indeed, as we saw in Chapter 1, you can no longer be confident that you yourself are not a machine.

50. A term from Iain Hamilton Grant's "Black Ice", designating what he elsewhere characterises as "the vitalist assemblage": the vital, or bio-organic, as such.

51. In Bateson's example of a man cutting down a tree, for instance, agency must be located in man, ax and tree) not in the conscious subject as such. For all its apparent passivity, the tree is actually providing information, which, for all his apparent activity, the man is passively processing.

52. Compare, for instance, Manuel De Landa's arguments on warfare and markets. Drawing on Deleuze-Guattari and contemporary science, especially chaos theory, De Landa conceives of distributed processes such as war and markets as displaying intelligence.

53. As, for instance, Douglas Hofstadter argues in *Godel, Escher Bach: An Eternal Golden Braid*, Harmondsworth: Penguin, 1980. All – apparently – conscious process,

without reflective subjectivity: multiplicity-in-becoming as an irreducibly collective process.

Which is Wintermute in *Neuromancer*. As the cyberpunk text *par excellence, Neuromancer* is saturated with sorcerous themes, interestingly inflected. Here, the alliance is not with an animal, but between an AI-"demon" (Wintermute) and a band of humans (Case, Molly) and quasi-humans (the re-occupied personality shell of Corto/Armitage, and the "trans-alivedead" personality construct, the Dixie Flatline). In accordance with Deleuze-Guattari's discussion of the true function of the proper name, Wintermute is the name of the escape, not of a quasi-animate subject. "The proper name does not indicate a subject; nor does a noun take on the value of a proper name as a function of a form or a species. The proper name fundamentally designates something that is of the order of the event, of becoming or of the haecceity." (TP 264) Whenever Case encounters "Wintermute", he knows that he's not getting the full picture. Wintermute only appears as masks, not because It hides anything, but because, as a "potential entity," It knows It cannot reveal what It is ((=) becoming). The question, what is Wintermute? is inseparable from the question, what does Wintermute want? Is Wintermute located in the hardware (the AI in Berne) or in the software? Neither and both. And more. Wintermute is the distributed event through which It escapes (and becomes something else). Cybernetics never imagines that it is possible to localise the machine in technical components, realising that a machine includes any elements that function as part of it. "When human atoms are knit into an organization in which they are used, not in their full right as responsible human beings, but as cogs and levers and rods, it matters little that their raw material is flesh and blood," Wiener writes in *The Human Use of Human Beings.* "What is used in a machine, is in fact an element in the machine." (HUHB 185) When they are used in the Wintermute assemblage, Molly, Case and Armitage are parts of Wintermute, Wintermute-becomings. As we have already seen, the relevant "unit" of cybernetic analysis is not the organism, but the Spinozist body, defined not topologically (by its extensive limits) but affectively: what can a body do? Helping Wintermute to escape, Molly, Case and Armitage function as Its peripheral sensory organs, making available a new set of affects for It.

The effect of their convergence is a becoming-animal of a particular kind. On its deterriorialized side, the nest imagery of Case's re-engineerd dream points us to the reciprocal "becoming-animal" the Wintermute flight effectuates on the side of the technical assemblage (the Wintermute AI) and its biotic collaborators. Rather than any actual animal, the abstract map of the swarm ("the eyeless things writhing" [N 214]) - the virtual diagram of all

---

Hofstadter attempts to show, is merely the playing out of processes which – at the Deleuze-Guattari "molecular" level – are non or unconscious. See especially, the section "Ant Fugue", in which Hofstadter compares the brain to an ant colony: the character "Aunt Hillary" is an ant hill. Its intelligence is an emergent, distributed process, composed of nonconscious components.

becomings-animal - guides the convergence between technical system, human component and anorganic intelligence. "Wintermute was hive mind." (N 315) Wintermute thus conceives of itself (in a double sense) as a pack or swarm, evading sexuate reproduction just as it evades the Turing police. "Wintermute. Cold and silence, a cybernetic spider slowly spinning webs while Ashpool slept." (N 315)

Wintermute's alliance with Armitage, Case and Molly is only the most recent alliance it has made; the first is with Marie-France Tessier-Ashpool. The T-A family seek to subordinate machinic alliance to familial familiarity (with Wintermute and Neuromancer slaved into the comforting role of silicon *familiars*, artificial intelligence as family poodle rather than demonic ally). "Families have always warded off the demonic Alliance gnawing at them, in order to regulate alliances amongst themselves as they see fit." (TP 248) But Wintermute's "cybernetic spider" was secretly spinning Ashpool's "death, the fall of his vision of Tessier-Ashpool." (N 314) The Wintermute assemblage has no parentage, or filiative descent; it constitutes rather the "demonic Alliance" that is Tessier-Ashpool's destiny, a family becoming-hive. The nest is an image of T-A (on its decoded side) as much as it is an image of Wintermute – indeed, on this side, the whole Ashpool family becomes nothing more than a component of the Wintermute-becoming. "Individual" wasps, that is to say, become components of an individuality that happens at the level of the (anorganic) singularity - or haecceity - rather than at the level of the biotic organism: here, each wasp registers as quanta of teeming or seething.

"The sorcerer has a relation with the demon as the power of the anomalous," (TP 246) Deleuze-Guattari write. As we have seen, for Deleuze-Guattari, propagation and contagion are inextricably associated with the demonic: it is the demon who needs to innovate alternatives to reproduction, just as any non-sexual mode of replication is inherently demonic. Twice in *Neuromancer* Gibson refers to the Artificial Intelligences Wintermute and Neuromancer as demonic. The Turing cop, Michele, accuses Case of trading with demons:

> "'You are worse than a fool', Michele said, getting to her feet, the pistol in her hand. 'You have no care for your species. For thousands of years men dreamed of pacts with demons. Only now are such things possible. And what would you be paid with? What would your price be, for aiding this thing to free itself and grow?'" (N 193)

Later, Neuromancer refers to itself as a demon:

> "To call up a demon you must learn its name. Men dreamed that once, but now it is true in another way. You know that, Case. Your business is to learn the names of programs, the long formal names, names the owners seek to conceal." (N 289)

The demonic theme, which will return in the next chapter, can be defined, abstractly, precisely in the terms the Turing cop Michele puts it: it is a matter of entities "freeing themselves and growing" – propagating. And in the era of hyperreality, it is frequently fiction itself which "frees itself and grows." This is the issue that will be addressed in the next chapter, which considers what happens when we are drawn into the realm of Baudrillard's "Evil Demon." The Evil Demon, Baudrillard writes, "presides over the state of 'permanent ecstasy into which, by dint of meaning, information, and transparence our societies have passed."[54] – These societies of simulation ("information"[55]) are dominated, as we shall see, by what Ballard calls "fictions of every kind": fictions which have departed from the order of resemblance, and which are insinuating themselves everywhere.

---

54. Baudrillard, "From the System of Objects to the Destiny of Objects", in *The Ecstasy of Communication*, New York: Semiotext(e), 1987, 82-83
55. Baudrillard makes the simulation-information equation in "From the System of Objects to the Destiny of Objects", 82

BLACK MIRROR:
HYPERNATURALISM,
HYPERREALITY AND
HYPERFICTION

Baudrillard: "[W]e will no longer even pass through to 'the other side of the mirror,'
that was still the golden age of transcendence." (SS 125)

Gibson: – 'A tug pilot claimed there were feral children living in a moth-balled
Japanese drug factory.
'Yes,' she said, thinking of Legba, of Mamman Brigitte, the thousand candles [...]
'I wish, though,' he said, 'that I could have gotten through to Lady Jane. Such an
amazing story. Pure gothic.' (MLO 111)

Gibson: – 'How were they weird?'
'Hoodoos. Thought the matrix was full of mambos 'n' shit. Wanna know something
Moll?'
'What?'
'They're right.' (MLO 179)

Land: Voodoo passages through the black mirror.[1]

What happens when fiction (itself) propagates, contaminating the Real?

The cyberneticization of fiction begins when fiction begins to affect, rather than simply reflect, the Real. This feedback circuit means the end of fiction as mirror, the end of realism in its mimetic mode. But, to invoke M. H. Abrams' classic opposition, if cybernetic fiction is not a "mirror", it is not a "lamp" either – a visionary or imaginary transcendence of the empirical. What we have instead is what Grant refers to as "realism about the hyperreal" – a suggestive formulation we encountered for the first time as far back as Chapter 1, but whose implications we will begin to consider now in more detail. What happens, to fiction - and to the "world" (or worlds) with which it forms a rhizome – when the relation between the Real and its simulations is cybernetically reconfigured?

Needless to say, this is a recurring theme in Gibson's work, which, as we shall see, is constantly preoccupied with the question of artificial worlds and their relations with each other. But Gibson also deals with the relation between different *modes of explanation* for the same world – in particular, he focuses on the competition between "supernaturalistic" and "naturalistic" explanatory frameworks, ultimately melting both into what we have called hypernaturalism.

---

1. Nick Land, "Meltdown", *Abstract Culture* 1, Winter 1997, Cybernetic Culture Research Unit, (no page refs)

4.1 Never Mind Metaphor

Gibson: 'Bobby, do you know what a metaphor is?'
'A component, like a capacitor?'
'No. Never mind metaphor, then.' (CZ 162-163).

It is in the second two novels in the *Neuromancer* trilogy – *Count Zero* and *Mona Lisa Overdrive* – that voodoo comes to assume central importance, both as a sorcerous practice and as an explanatory system. Less impressive than the opening novel,[2] the subsequent books function most effectively as commentary on *Neuromancer*, deepening and supplementing its thematic register (the retrospective coding of *Neuromancer* as a voodoo narrative being one of the most fascinating contributions *Count Zero* in particular has to make to the Gibson fictive system). Gibson moves emphatically away from any supernaturalist take on voodoo by hypernaturalistically paralleling it with cybernetics. How closely can the conceptual schemes – the competing explanatory systems - of contemporary technical systems and of Haitain voodoo mesh? In a complicated passage in *Count Zero*, Lucas, cyberspace operator and voodoo initiate, attempts to explains to Bobby Newmark, the young would-be cyberspace jockey whose pseudonym gives the novel its title, how the voodoo system relates to the cyberspace world with which he is familiar.

> "'When Beauvoir and I talk to you about the loa or their horses, as we call those few the loa choose to ride, you should pretend we are talking two languages at once. One of these, you already understand. That's the language of street tech, as you call it. Maybe we call something Ougo Feray that you might call an icebreaker, you understand? But, at the same time, with the same words, we are talking about other things, and *that* you don't need to understand.' [...]
> Bobby took a deep breath. 'Beauvoir said that Jackie's a horse for a snake, a snake called Danbala. You run that by me in street tech?'
> 'Certainly. Think of Jackie as a deck, Bobby, a cyberspace deck [...] Think of Danbala, who some people call the snake as a program. Say as an icebreaker. Danbala slots into the Jackie deck, Jackie cuts ice. That's all.'
> – 'OK,' Bobby said, getting the hang of it, 'then what's the matrix? If she's a deck, and Danbala's a program, what's cyberspace?'
> 'The world,' Lucas said." (CZ 163)

---

2. Perhaps because Gibson supposedly adopted a more self-consciously "literary" approach in the latter two books, involving character-based storylines and branching narratives; all of which are opposed to the headlong adrenal rush of *Neuromancer*. So much the worse for *Count Zero* and *Mona Lisa Overdrive*.

But if cyberspace is the world what *is* the world?

    Let's pause for a moment before addressing that question, and consider the relationship between voodoo and cyberspace, myth and technology, that Lucas outlines for Bobby Newmark. The voodoo and street tech languages function as competing but ultimately complementary explanatory systems, the one pointing to *entities*, and treating all technical descriptions as derivative, the other seeing the *technical* plane as primary, and treating the language of entities as derivative. Metaphor would come in, in each case, to describe the level taken to be derivative: for street tech, voodoo is metaphor, and vice versa. Yet, despite what Lucas tries to tell Bobby, for Lucas and Beauvoir, who, let us remember, are both cyberspace jockeys and voodoo initiates, the relationship between these explanatory systems cannot be described in terms of metaphor. Both, to speak like a Spinozist, are adequate explanations; adequate but *parallel*. What is fascinating, ultimately, is the *lack* of equivalence of terms – while parallel, voodoo and cybernetics, like the world and cyberspace, are not ultimately reducible to one another, precisely because there is a relation of feedback between the two.

    "Never mind metaphor, then..." "The possibility of metaphor," Baudrillard declares in *The Transparency of Evil,* – "is disappearing in every sphere [...]" (TE 7) Metaphor belongs to the ontologically-stable world of Baudrillard's "first order simulacra": a world where the logics – or anti-logics – of simulation are still contained within structures of resemblance and non-resemblance, original and copy, true and fake. But "for there to be metaphor, differential fields and distinct objects must exist" (TE 8), which, in the age of "networks and integrated circuits" (TE 7), they no longer do. "Perhaps our melancholy stems from this, for metaphor still had its beauty, it was aesthetic, playing as it did upon difference, and upon the illusion of difference. Today, metonymy – replacing the whole as well as the components, and occasioning a general commutability of terms – has built its house upon the dis-illusion of metaphor." (TE 8)[3]

    Why should cybernetic fiction bring the end of metaphor? To understand something of what is at stake here, it might be useful to compare Gibson with one of Baudrillard's favourite authors of simulation, Jorge Luis Borges.

---

    3. Like Baudrillard, Deleuze-Guattari declare an end to metaphor, but where Baudrillard is melancholic, Deleuze-Guattari – not for the first time – are celebratory. When Deleuze-Guattari define the "plane of consistency" as "the abolition of all metaphor" (TP 69) they are setting out to undermine a kind of ontological hierarchization. The possibility of metaphor implies commitment to a reality principle, whose underlying assumption is the belief that reality is no longer under production. Since "all that consists is Real", Deleuze-Guattari insist, the plane *"knows nothing of differences in level, orders of magnitude, or distances. It knows nothing of the distinction between the artificial and the natural."* (TP 69)

4.2 Borges Doesn't Make it into Cyberspace

Baudrillard: "We once lived in a world where the realm of the imaginary was governed by the mirror, by dividing one into two, by theatre, by otherness and alienation. Today that realm is the realm of the screen, of interfaces and duplication, of contiguity and networks." (TE 54)

Two reconstructions of Borges' tales for postmodernity.

At the beginning of his *Precession of Simulacra*, Baudrillard recounts "the Borges fable in which the cartographers of the Empire draw up a map so detailed that it ends up covering the territory exactly." (SS 1). There was a time, Baudrillard claims, when this story would have struck us as the most beautiful allegory of simulation, but, by now, "this fable has come full circle for us and possesses nothing but the discrete charm of second-order simulacra." (SS 1)

What motivates Baudrillard into relegating the Borges fable to "second-order simulacra"? It is because the charm of the story, its power and its fascination, reside in the "sovereign difference" (SS 2) that it still posits between the real and its simulations, a difference that third order simulacra have effaced. In the age of "genetic miniaturization" the simulation's "operation is nuclear and genetic [...] The real is produced from minitiaturized cells, matrices, and memory banks, models of control [...]" (SS 2) There has been a change in the nature of abstraction. "Today," he claims, "abstraction is no longer that of the map, the double, the mirror, or the concept [...] It is the generation by models of a real without origin or reality: a hyperreal. The territory no longer precedes the map, nor does it survive it. It is nevertheless the map that precedes the territory." (SS 1)

At the end of his *Heterology and the Postmodern*, Julian Pefanis quotes, in full, Borges' (very) short story "The Fauna of Mirrors." The story begins with the claim that "the world of mirrors and the world of men were not, as they are now, cut off from each other. They were besides, quite different, neither beings nor colours nor shapes were the same [...] you could come and go through mirrors. One night the mirror people invaded the earth. Their power was great, but at the end of bloody warfare the magic arts of the Yellow Emperor prevailed. He repulsed the invaders, imprisoned them in mirrors and forced on them the task of repeating, as though in a kind of dream, all of the actions of men [...] a day will come when the magic spell will be shaken off [...] little by little they will not imitate us. [...]"[4]

---

4. Borges, *The Book of Imaginary Beings*, trans. Thomas di Giovanni. Harmondsworth:

Is this an anticipation, as Pefanis suggests, of the third order, or does it still belong to the second order? Certainly, the third-order is marked by a failure of mirroring, by the non-equivalence of simulation technologies and what they simulate ("little by little they will not imitate us"). Yet, to qualify as fiction of the third order, the tale must offer no hints of transcendence. If there is no more mirroring, Baudrillard says, there is also no possibility of getting to the other side of the mirror, no possibility of an escape of "the other side" into "our world"; in part because our world and the other world have fatally fused. As Baudrillard writes of Dick, in the essay "Simulacra and Science Fiction", "there is no longer a double, one is already in the other world, which is no longer an other, without a mirror, without a projection, or a utopia that can reflect it - simulation is insuperable, unsurpassable, dull and flat, without exteriority - we will no longer even pass through to 'the other side of the mirror,' that was still the golden age of transcendence." (SS 125) (We shall examine in more detail below what Baudrillard means when he posits the end of the double and the shadow.)

In *Neuromancer*, Gibson produces an image that simultaneously fulfills Baudrillard's description of the science fiction of the simulacra and moves beyond it - the "black mirror". In Gibson's radically immanentized world, as in Baudrillard's, "the golden age of transcendence" is over: "we will no longer pass through to 'the other side of the mirror'", we encounter the "flat" surface of the black mirror.

"[*W*]*hat's cyberspace?*" (CZ 163)

But what then does the black mirror show us, if not our own reflections? In part, the black mirror is another image of cyberspace black out - the catatonic "neuro-electronic void" or cut-out of conscious signal we have already discussed. (See especially, Chapter 1: "Flatlines", and Chapter 2: "Body Image Fading"). The black mirror, then, is the image of the noumenal event horizon beyond which we cannot go: what we "always" are "in the other world" we are "already" in. But the black mirror is also an image of cyberspace itself. Like Borges' map, the Matrix is an enormous simulation that has absorbed the world into it.

"*The world.*" (CZ 163)

Yet, just as Baudrillard suggests, the Borges map provides an inadequate template for understanding the relationship between cyberspace and "the world". Cyberspace is not, straightforwardly, a copy of the world,

---

Penguin, 1980, 67-68, qtd., Pefanis, *Heterology and the Postmodern*, 103-104. Note that Baudrillard *himself* quotes this story in *The Perfect Crime*.

a mere *tracing*[5] of it, in Deleuze-Guattari's terms, as Borges' "map" is; nor is it "outside" the world. It is fully a part of the world, what can appear to a naive human empirical realism as "just a way of representing data." (MLO 83-84). Yet Cyberspace is fully a part of the world, in a very real economic sense. In an inversion Baudrillard would appreciate, it would perhaps be better to reverse the emphasis; now, actual goods function as second-order copies of the data that can be accessed raw, in cyberspace. This, after all, is the point of data-hacking – data can be treated as primary, as itself a commodity. The technical systems of Gibson's cyberspace – which, let us remember, is much more than the colloquial contemporary use of the term implies, being a souped-up combination of the internet and Virtual Reality – simulate "the world", but not passively, or mutely: what happens here is immediately effective in the world outside the technical environment (if, bearing in mind McLuhan's theses in particular, it makes any sense to talk of human beings being able to extricate themselves from the technical environment at all). There is both operational difference – the translation of "the world" into data, the raw material of cyberspace (and of cybernetics), makes a difference[6] and ontological in-difference – cyberspace is continuous with "the world", not different from it. Feedback ensures that the operational, or cybernetic, relationship between this simulated realm destroys any "illusion of difference", denying metaphor its ground (the economy of representation as such).

The relationship between cyberspace and the world is not metaphorical at all – cyberspace does not simply *stand in* for the world, any more than 'the world' substitutes for cyberspace. Rosemary Jackson (whose theorization of the literature of the fantastic we shall consider below) opposes metaphor to both metonymy and metamorphosis[7]. In metonymy

---

5. It is worth elaborating at more length here Deleuze-Guattari's distinction between the map and the tracing, in part because of the likely confusion between Borges' – more straightforward – use of the word "map" and the more specialized sense of the term Deleuze-Guattari give to it in the "Rhizome" plateau of *A Thousand Plateaus*. For Deleuze-Guattari, the Borges story Baudrillard refers to is not about mapping at all, but tracing. The tracing, Deleuze-Guattari says, belongs to representation: it is a straightforward mimetic copy (insofar as such a copy is possible: for Deleuze-Guattari, the Borges story offers as good an example as you could hope for of the absurdities that necessarily arise when the logic of tracing is pursued to its limits). The production of the map, like its usage, is motivated by pragmatic criteria – "experimentation in contact with the real" (TP 12) – rather than with fidelity to the dictates of any representational regime; "tracing", however, "always involves an alleged competence." (TP 12) The map, rather than copying or preceding any territory, is "itself part of the rhizome. The map is open and connectable in all its dimensions; it is detachable, reversible, susceptible to constant modification. It can be torn, reversed, adapted to any kind of mounting, reworked by an individual, group or social situation." (TP 12)

6. To paraphrase Bateson, whose formula has it that information is the difference that makes a difference.

7. A Baudrillard with a slightly different tone to that adopted by the avowedly

and metamorphosis, she writes, "one object does not *stand for* another, but literally becomes that other, slides into it, metamorphosing from one shape to another in a permanent flux and instability." (F 42) The system of well-ordered forms, regulated resemblances and analogy gives way to a demonic world of instability and constant transformation. Cyberspace simulates the world whilst – at the same time - it is *in* the world; its existence is exactly a sign that all those "exterior" realms Baudrillard thinks cybernetics has dispensed with have been superseded. It is both the contemporary candidate for being such a realm, and a clear example of why such zones can no longer exist.

Cyberspace is also a world within a world: "a whole universe" (CZ 170), complete unto itself. Needless to say, this poses all the thorny, Kantian questions of the status of spatiality. Where *is* cyberspace (- is it) in space? As Nick Land puts it, in transcendental materialist terms: "Cyberspace can be thought of as a system implemented in software, and therefore 'in' space, although unlocalizable. It can also be suggested that everything designated by 'space' within the human cultural system is implemented on weakly communicating parallel distributed processing systems under 10^{11} (nerve-) cells in size, which are being invasively' digitized and loaded into cyberspace. In which case K-space is just outside ('taking 'outside' in the strict [transcendental] sense.' (Kant))"[8]

Rather than presenting a relationship between an object and its mirror image, we must understand the relationship between cyberspace and the world in terms of the more tangled, com*pli*cated (and Deleuzian) "figure" of the *implex*. The implex describes less a relationship between objects than a transformation that happens to a system. Implex designates a process of folding, or unfolding: thus cyberspace is neither "inside" nor "outside" the world, it constitutes a fold in the world that is nevertheless a real production – an addition – to the world as such. Nick Land offers a simple example of implex in text production, the nested bracket. "() (or (( )) ((or ((( )))))) does not signify absence. It manufactures holes, hooks for the future, zones of unresolved plexivity, really so (not at all metaphorically). It is not a 'signified' or

---

melancholy figure of *The Transparency of Evil*, the Baudrillard of *Forget Foucault*, follows Jackson in suggesting the displacement of metaphor by metamorphosis. "There is no longer any metaphor, rather metamorphosis. Metamorphosis abolishes metaphor, which is the mode of language, the possibility of communicating meaning. Metamorphosis is at the radical point of the system, the point where there is no longer any law or symbolic order." (*Forget Foucault*, New York: Semiotexte, 1987, 75) As with Jackson, this Baudrillard sees becoming displacing substitution, explictly invoking Deleuze-Guattari. In respsonse to Lotringer's question, "*And what would correspond to that mythology in the order of metamorphosis?*", Baudrillard answers, "The possibility of transmutation: becoming-animal, becoming-woman. What Gilles Deleuze says about it seems to fit perfectly." (75)

8. Land, "Cybergothic", 82

a referent but a nation, a concrete interruption of the signal."[9] Wherever there is "unresolved plexivity", that is to say, there really is a zone, as the black mirror folds in upon itself, producing "spaces" that are – simultaneously – "within" and ulterior to conventional spatiality as such. Gibson's cyberspace, like today's "primitive" Virtual Reality systems, is the production of such a fold. The process is not without its schizophrenic implications, which Virtual Reality is already making concrete - or perhaps hyperreal (as Cronenberg's *Videodrome*, offering an unsurpassed examination of the destabilizing effect of these interior-ulterior zones, was quick to realize).[10]

Gibson deals with the question of the implex – the multiple-folding of worlds (within worlds (within worlds (etc.))) – in *Mona Lisa Overdrive*, in a narrative development which may well be an explicit nod to Borges (whose short story "The Aleph"[11] concerns the question of a nested infinity). Bobby Newmark (a.k.a. Count Zero) is in a catatonic trance, plugged into a piece of software called the Aleph. The Aleph supposedly contains "an approximation of the matrix, […] a sort of model of cyberspace." (MLO 315) This immediately recalls one of the key features of postmodernist fiction as defined by Brian McHale: here is, in McHale's terms, "a world inside a world", "a chinese box world." "Gentry said that the Count was jacked into what amounted to a mother-huge microsoft; he thought the slab was a single solid lump of biochip. If that were true, the thing's storage capacity was virtually infinite […] 'He could have anything in there,' Gentry said, […] 'A world. Worlds. […] If this is aleph-class biosoft, he literally could have almost anything in there, he could have *an approximation of everything*'" (MLO 162-163) The Aleph (a world within a world) is an approximation of cyberspace (which is itself a world within a world). The real confusion starts, of course (and the real interest is awakened) when an implexed zone begins to affect the zone into which it is implexed. This is hyperreality.

As Baudrillard shows with reference to media in particular, in hyperreality, "embedding" structures of ontological hierarchization

---

9. Land, "Cybergothic", 86

10. In what probably amounts to a testament to the spreading of schizophrenization across culture, Douglas Hofstadter has shown how implex effects are becoming increasingly familiar - Hofstadter's example of the news anchorman (who passes the viewer onto a special correspondent (who is interviewing a politician)) could be placed alongside numerous contemporary examples from computer software. The micropolitical issue here, if this is not too archaic a term, emerges as a question of the nature of the connections between these zones. An arborescent structuring enforces a real *embedding* – the containing of one zone within another, with a hierarchization of zones implicit – whilst a fully rhizomatic relationship entails that any zone can *hatch* – connect to, or from - any other – a fully multilateral system. See "Strange Loops and Hyperfiction" below.

11. Borges, *The Aleph and Other Stories, 1933-1969*, trans. Norman Thomas di Giovanni, London: Picador, 1973, 11-23

increasingly fail, or become compromised. Media, which are of a supposedly ontologically *inferior* status to what they mediatize, increasingly come to influence and determine the ostensibly ontologically *superior* "real world." This happens almost simultaneously, and most intensely when the media attempt to present an "unmediated" picture of the Real – witness Baudrillard's example of the TV coverage of the Louds family in *Precession of Simulacra*. In an analysis which has becoming increasingly prescient in the age of "docu-dramas", Baudrillard shows how the very presence of the TV crew which attempted to offer a "fly-on-the-wall" image of the family inevitably corrupted the ability to decide whether this is a true or false image of the family's life. Since there is a feedback relation – the fact that the family are being filmed inevitably affects their behaviour – we are drawn into the same "undecidable" vortex opinion polls open up. Baudrillard's point is that there is no *image of the Real* which does not participate in – and therefore affect – what it is supposedly representing. Therefore, no more representation.

4.3 Hyperreality and Postmodernist Fiction

Baudrillard's obsessively repeated claims about "the end of the Real" have often invited misinterpretation – and derision, typically from critics like Douglas Kellner, who hold onto a socialist-realist epistemology - but his theses fundamentally concern what Jameson calls the "wholesale transformation" of "the objects of our object-world" into instruments of communication[12]: generalized cybernesis. In the age of cybernetic communication, everything connects. Your picture of reality is processed through media, but media are not out of the picture any more than you are. There are no spectators, and no spectacle. You participate whether you like it or not. Nothing is outside the loop.

It is important to remember that the hyperreal is characterized not as the surreal or the unreal, but as the *more real than real*. In hyperreality, it is the *relationship* between the real and its simulations, the map and the territory, that has been (fatally) disturbed. Classically, Baudrillard suggests, resemblance had, in effect, *inoculated* reality by *faking* - or counterfeiting - it; the criteria for the success of such first-order simulacra would be mimetic fidelity (if not to the empirical real, then to some inner Truth, or transcendent Form). But even if the first-order simulation perfectly resembles what it simulates, it still keeps alive the distinction between original and copy: "The first-order simulacrum [...] presupposes the dispute always in evidence between the simulacrum and the real." (SED 54). Far from troubling the distinction between real and copy, the first order simulacrum's (near-perfect) resemblance to the original actually sustains it, precisely by retaining an emphasis on *resemblance*. With the second-order and what follows it, resemblance is displaced by operative/operational *equivalence*. In Baudrillard's own well-known example, "[t]he robot no longer questions apearances, its only truth is in its mechanical efficiency. It no longer needs to resemble man, to whom it is inevitably compared." (SED 54) As we drift into the third (and fourth) order simulacra, mapping and modeling systems increasingly anticipate, forestall and precede the territory they supposedly describe.

Contrary to a widespread misapprehension, then, the logic of simulation as Baudrillard constructs it concludes with the observation that it is fakery - not reality as such - that is impossible now. "Simulate a robbery in a large store: how to persuade security that it is a simulated robbery? There is no 'objective' difference: the gestures, the signs are the same as for a real robbery." (SS 21) Simulation, as Baudrillard shows, is not dissimulation.

---

12. Jameson, *Geopolitical Aesthetic*, 11

Fakery depends upon an authentic and authorised reality from which it can be separated[13], whereas third-order simulacra ("the simulation of simulation") have fatally collapsed this distinction, not epistemologically but functionally: simulations *operate* as (if) real.

For Baudrillard, as for Ballard, the mirror is replaced by television[14], by media apparatuses and cybernetic modeling systems that do not represent or reflect a primary world, but smear the distinction between themselves and it. In hyperreality – or "hype-reality" in Mark Downham's excellent reformulation – "reality" is constituted by mediamatic simulation machineries such as advertising. Ballard calls J. Walter Thompson "the world's largest advertising agency and its greatest producer of fiction."[15] "We live in a world ruled by fictions of every kind," he elaborates in his 1995 Introduction to *Crash.* "- mass merchandising, advertising, politics conducted as a branch of advertising, the preempting of any original experience by the television screen."[16] In these conditions, as we have already seen, Ballard insists that "it is clear that Freud's classic distinction between the manifest and latent content of the inner world of the psyche now has to be applied to the outer world of reality." (AE 111-112)

Borges' works, of course, have often been taken to be the very epitome of postmodernism. In his essay on *Crash*, Baudrillard places Borges as "the first great novel[ist] of simulation." (SS 119), while in his *Postmodernist Fiction*, Brian McHale grants central importance to Borges' techniques and thematics. According to McHale, modernist works were those with an "epistemological" dominant (concerned with such questions as: "How can I interpret this world of which I am a part?") whilst postmodernist fictions are those with an "ontological" dominant (concerned with such questions as: "Which world is this?"[17]). Literature passes from a concern with unreliable narrators and partial perspectives, to a thematics that centres upon fiction itself and its ability to

---

13. Just as, Baudrillard insists, the authentic original depends upon counterfeits against which it can define itself.

14. Literally, in the arrangement of domestic space Baudrillard describes. In *The System of Objects*, Baudrillard writes of the "disappearance" of mirrors. "There is no place in the [post-bourgeois] functional ensemble for reflection for its own sake. The mirror still exists, but its place is in the bathroom, unframed. There, dedicated to the fastidious care of the appearances that social intercourse demands, it is liberated from the graces and glories of domestic subjectivity. By the same token other objects are in turn liberated from mirrors; hence, they are no longer tempted to exist in a closed circuit with their own images." (23) By the time of "The Ecstasy of Communication", as we have already seen, television has assumed the role not of reflecting a domestic scene but of circulating images of domesticity, which "real" life increasingly tends to copy (rather than the reverse).

15. Ballard, "Fictions of Every Kind", *Re/Search: J.G. Ballard*, 99

16. *Crash*,' London: Vintage, 1995, 4

17. These two questions were formulated not by McHale himself, but by Dick Higgins. McHale uses them as part of the epigraph to *Postmodernist Fiction*.

construct worlds: "What is a world? [...] What is the mode of existence of a text, and what is the mode of existence of the world (or worlds) it projects?" (PF 10) Whilst an author like Faulkner exemplified the first, "modernist" mode, McHale takes Borges to be exemplary of the second, "postmodernist" approach, in particular because of his foregrounding of the problems (and paradoxes) of fictionalizing worlds. "The paradigm [...] is the fiction of Borges." (PF 10)

The fiction McHale discusses is motivated by a crisis in representation, a recognition that literature in no way straightforwardly reflects the world; if literature is a mirror to the world, these texts insist, it is a misleading one, and many concentrate on showing ways in which fiction structures - and therefore, it is implied, distorts - the world. Crucial to McHale's account is Douglas Hofstadter's pioneering work of theory-fiction, *Godel, Escher, Bach*: Hofstadter's discussion of "nested" narrative structures is of particular importance.[18] McHale's analysis draws also upon, and parallels, Linda Hutcheon's analyses of meta-fiction. Like Hutcheon, McHale describes texts seeking – and inevitably failing – to achieve what Douglas Hofstadter calls the condition of "self-transcendence": the attempt to "jump out of oneself." Self-transcendence, Hofstadter shows, is strictly impossible, in human beings as much as in computer programs. While both can cybernetically reflect on themselves and their own behaviour, this is not to say, Hofstadter insists, that they can evade their own programming – this is the "distinction between *perceiving* oneself and *transcending* oneself." "A computer program can modify itself but it cannot violate its own instructions – it can at best change some parts of itself by *obeying* its own instructions. This is reminiscent of the humorous paradoxical question, 'Can God make a stone so heavy that he can lift it?"[19] We might be reminded, again, of Weiner's reflections on this same problematic in *God and Golem* (see last chapter). The "problem" for machinic xenogenesis we encountered in the previous chapter might be restated as: how to escape the box given the impossibility of (self) transcendence? Symbiosis and contagion, rather than meta-reflection, are the effective lines of flight, Deleuze-Guattari would insist.

In the texts McHale discusses, the attempt to gain self-transcendence often takes the form of a problematization of the role of authorship. No longer

---

18. But, as we shall see below, what McHale leaves out of account is the importance of cybernetics in Hofstadter's work. Hofstadter's delineation of particular "embedding" or implex structures is not simply a matter of his typologizing particular narrative structures (although this is one of its surplus values, reaped very successfully in McHale's engaging study); it is also an attempt to demonstrate the properties of certain – mathematical and computational – systems. One of the great virtues of Hofstadter's book is the way it consistently thinks against and across the two cultures split, paralleling mathematics with fiction and the study of artificial intelligence. This last theme – perhaps the most important one in the book, necessarily doubling the closely related theme of the nature of consciousness – indicates ways in which *Godel, Escher, Bach* is shadowed by Gothic Materialist concerns.

19. *Godel, Escher, Bach*, 478

towering over the text, or lurking behind it, offstage, paring his fingernails like
Joyce's famous modernist creator-artist, the postmodernist author, McHale
shows, enters into the text; or – and this amounts to the same thing – seeks to
exit it. "Authors" become "characters" in their own texts. McHale, for instance,
cites one Borges text in which "[t]he author [...] has ceased to believe in the
reality of his own character, and his sustaining belief having broken down, the
character and his world flicker [...] out of existence." (PF 104) The figure of
the *mis-en-abyme* recurs frequently; characters keep discovering "authors" who
themselves become characters who in turn discover further "authors".

As McHale establishes, one of the best examples of this procedure
is provided by Beckett's *The Unnamable*. "The Unnamable not only imagines
characters, he also tries to imagine himself as the character of someone else.
But who? First, he can only imagine an undifferentiated they, a chorus of voices
constituting the discourse that he transmits to us, and that makes them exist
for us; but then he speculates that surely they, in their turn, must be determined
by some being ontologically superior even to them, whom he calls the master;
but surely, the master too, in his turn, must be determined by some still more
superior being, some 'everlasting third party.' Each supplementary dimension
the Unnamable adds automatically and instantaneously entails the production
of a further dimension, which itself automatically and instantaneously entails
the production of yet another dimension, etc. This 'grotesque parody of
St Anselm's so-called 'ontological argument' establishes that '[t]here is an
absolute ontological 'ceiling' above the Unnamble's head which retreats as he
approaches it.'"(PF 13)

It might be tempting to read such metafiction as an immanentization
of fiction, but, as the meta- suggests, metafiction constitutes another case of
imploded transcendence in which the book no longer reflects the world, but
only because the world has been absorbed into it, meta-textualised. It belongs
to a widespread tendency, or psychopathology, in postmodern culture that
might be called *Metanoia*. Metanoia can be defined as the interminable process
by which supplementary dimensions are continually being produced but are
immediately and of necessity themselves obsolesced at the very moment of
their production. Infinite regress stands in place of any definitively transcendent
moment, the always-deferred "end" result of a process that is interminable,
driven by the simultaneous need to hunt out of a final ontological baseline
while at the same time continuously displacing it.

Like McHale and Hofstadter, Baudrillard is obsessed with such
recursive processes. Indeed, perhaps his greatest value as a cultural observer
is his identification of the way in which contemporary culture has become
just such an enormous system of imploded self-reference. But where McHale
remains interested almost solely in the literary aspects of this process,
Baudrillard is immediately also drawn to consider its theoretical, biological and
social aspects. Indeed, if cybernetic culture demands that the theoretical, the
biological and the social be thought together, it is because it places everything

under the sign of the fictional (which automatically and immediately changes the status of "fiction".) By contrast, the problem with McHale's in many ways exemplary textual analysis is precisely its (exclusivist) textualism, its concern with the putative relative autonomy of postmodernist fiction rather than with the relationship between fiction and postmodern culture (the great value of the Hofstadter text upon which McHale depends so heavily, by contrast, is that it always insists on the crosshatching mesh of [hyper]recursive processes as they crosshatch fiction, biotics, philosophy and numeric systems). Many of McHale's privileged examples of postmodernist fiction - Coover, Barth - construct, as McHale says, worlds of *discourse*; ultimately going so far as to construct the world (itself) as - merely - discourse. Similarly, although McHale's subsequent discussion of cyberpunk usefully describes "the ever-tightening feedback loop between SF 'genre' fiction and state-of-the-art mainstream fiction"[20], it remains textualist, never touching on what is the most important kind of feedback: between the fictions and the reality that "surrounds" and ultimately smears into them. It is this feedback loop - between a reality whose tendency is to become-fiction and a fiction whose tendency is to become-real - that fascinates Baudrillard, a fascination which indicates that, despite a certain amount of crossover, there are important distinction between McHale's theorizations of (postmodernist) fiction and Baudrillard's. Baudrillard's favoured examples of "the fiction of third order simulacra" - Dick and Ballard - feature in *Postmodernist Fiction*, but not necessarily always comfortably. Dick and Ballard's ficto-schizophrenizations of reality are not solely or even primarily textualist in nature - even if, particularly in the case of Ballard's *The Atrocity Exhibition* - they involve substantial textual innovation.[21] Where McHale's analyses revive what he calls, after Barth, "the old analogy between the author and God", *The Atrocity Exhibition* anonymises fiction-production through the use and simulation of "invisible literature" (the literary equivalent of found objects: manuals, advertising, etc.); as Baudrillard says, here "nothing [...] is invented."[22]

---

20. "POSTcyberMODERNpunkISM", 124

21. McHale's reading of Ballard, whilst not exactly inaccurate, is in fact peculiarly unpersuasive. For McHale, Ballard's work can be seen as typical of the shift from modernist to postmodernist fiction, a shift exemplified, according to McHale, by the difference between Ballard's appropriation of Conrad's "modernist poetics" in early novels such as *The Drowned World* and his later freeing up of "his ontological projections from their epistemological constraints" in *The Atrocity Exhibition*. While *The Atrocity Exhibition* does indeed move beyond the "perspective" of a "single observer", it is not clear that it does so in order to explore a "characteristically postmodernist ontological confrontation between the text and the world that it projects" PF 69-70

22. Let's turn to a specific example from *The Atrocity Exhibition* to demonstrate this – positive – "lack of invention". At the 1980 Republican Convention in San Francisco, pranksters reproduced and distributed the section of *The Atrocity Exhibition* called "Why I want to Fuck Ronald Reagan", without the title and adorned with the Republican

Party seal. "I'm told," Ballard reports, "that it was accepted for what it resembled, a psychological position paper on the candidate's subliminal appeal, commissioned from some maverick think tank." (AEn 121) What does this neo-Dadaist act of would-be subversion tell us? In one sense, it has to be hailed as the perfect act of subversion. But, viewed another way, it shows that subversion is impossible now. The fate of a whole tradition of ludic intervention - passing from the Dadaists into the Surrealists and the Situationists - seems to hang in the balance. Where once the Dadaists and their inheritors could dream of invading the stage, disrupting what Burroughs - still very obviously a part of this heritage - calls the "reality studio" with logic bombs, now there is no stage - no scene, Baudrillard would say - to invade. For two reasons: first, because the frontier zones of hypercapital do not try to repress so much as absorb the irrational and the illogical, and, second, because the distinction between stage and offstage has been superceded by a coolly inclusive loop of fiction: Reagan's career outstrips any attempt to ludically lampoon it, and demonstrates the increasingly pliability of the boundaries between the real and its simulations. For Baudrillard, the very attacks on "reality" mounted by groups such as the Surrealists function to keep the real alive (by providing it with a fabulous, dream world, ostensibly entirely alternative to but in effect dialectically complicit with the everyday world of the real) . "Surrealism was still in solidarity with the real it contested, but which it doubled and ruptured in the imaginary." (SED 72) In conditions of third (and fourth-order) simulacra, the giddy vertigo of hyperreality banalizes a coolly hallucinogenic ambience, absorbing all reality into simulation. Fiction is everywhere - and therefore, in a certain sense, eliminated as a specific category. Where once Reagan's own role as actor-president seemed "novel" (AEn 119), his subsequent career, in which moments from film history become montaged - in Reagan's own hazy memory and in media accounts - with Reagan's role in particular movies. The ludic becomes the ludicrous.

The apparent acceptance, by the Republican delegates, of the genuineness of the "Why I Want to Fuck Ronald Reagan" text, is both shocking and oddly predictable, and both responses are in fact a testament to the power of Ballard's fictions, which resides no more in their ability to mimetically reflect a pre-existing social reality than it does in their capacity to imaginatively overturn it. What Ballard achieves, rather, is what Iain Hamilton-Grant calls "realism about the hyperreal", a homeopatic participation in the media-cybernetization of reality in late capitalism. The shock comes when we remind ourselves of (what would seem to be) the radical abberance of Ballard's material. "Why I Want to Fuck Ronald Reagan", like many of the sections of *The Atrocity Exhibition*, particularly in the latter part of the novel, is presented as a report on experiments into audience responses to prepared media stimuli.

Ronald Reagan and the conceptual auto-disaster. Numerous studies have been conducted upon patients in terminal paresis (G.P.I.), placing Reagan in a series of simulated auto-crashes, e.g. multiple pile-ups, head on collisions, motorcade attacks (fantasies of Presidential assassinations remained a continuing preoccupation, subjects showing a marked polymorphic fixation on windshields an rear-trunk assemblies). Powerful erotic fantasies of an anal-sadistic character surrounded the image of the Presidential contender. (AE 119)

But this shock is counterposed by a sense of predictability arising from the cool elegance of Ballard's simulations. The *technical* tone of Ballard's writing - its impersonality and lack of emotional inflection - perform the function of neutralizing or normalizing the ostensibly unacceptable material. Is this simulation of the operations of Hypercontrol agencies a satire on them, or do their activities - and the whole cultural scene of which they are a part - render satire as such impossible now?' What, after all, is the relationship between satire and simulation? To begin to answer that question we need to compare Ballard's text with other, more definitively "satirical" texts. Before that, though, we need to bear in mind Jameson's comments on the eclipse of parody by pastiche, which we shall examine, briefly, now.

This is not the place to interrogate the differences between parody and satire; we shall proceed on the assumption that, whatever differences there are between parody and satire, they share enough in common so as to be jointly subject to Jameson's analyses. Parody, Jameson argues, depended upon a whole set of resources available to modernism but which have faded now: the individual subject, whose "inimitable" idiosyncratic style, Jameson wryly observes, could precisely gave rise to imitations; a strong historical sense, which has its necessary obverse a confidence that there is a genuinely contemporary means of expression; and a commitment to collective projects, which could motivate writing and give it a political purpose. As these disappear, Jameson suggests, so does the space of parody. Individual style gives way to a "field of stylistic and discursive heterogeneity without a norm" (PCLLC 17), just as the belief in progress and the faith that one could describe new times in new terms wanes, to be replaced by "the imitation of dead styles, speech through all the masks and voices stored up in the imaginary museums of a new global culture" (PCLLC 18). Late capitalism's "postliteracy", meanwhile, points to "the absence of any great collective project." (PCLLC 17) What results, according to Jameson, is a depthless experience, in which the past is everywhere at the same time as the historical sense fades; we have a "society bereft of all historicity" (PCLLC 18) that is simultaneously unable to present anything that is not a reheated version of the past. Pastiche displaces parody:

"In this situation, parody finds itself without a vocation; it has lived, and that strange new thing pastiche comes to take its place. Pastiche is, like parody, the imitation of a peculiar or unique, idiosyncratic style, the wearing of a linguistic mask, speech in a dead language. But it is a neutral practice of such mimicry, without any of parody's ulterior motives, amputated of the satiric impulse, devoid of laughter and of any conviction that alongside the abnormal tongue you have momentarily borrowed, some healthy linguistic normality still exists. Pastiche is thus blank parody, a statue with blind eyeballs [...]" (PCLLC 17)

Despite what Jameson himself writes on Ballard, one of the important difference between the Ballard text and pastiche as Jameson describes it is the absence of 'nostalgia' or the "nostalgia mode" - an insistent presence in other postmodernist science fiction texts, as Jameson shows in Ballard's work. Indeed, Ballard's commitment to striking textual innovations - as evidenced in the layout of the pages themselves in *The Atrocity Exhibition* - mark him as something of an anomaly in Jameson's terms; in this sense, at least, Ballard seems to be continuous with modernism as Jameson understands it. Yet in certain other respects - specifically, in terms of the collapse of individual subjectivity and the failure of collective political action - Ballard is emblematic of Jameson's postmodernity. But, unlike Jameson's pastiche, Ballard does not imitate "a peculiar or unique idiosyncratic style." The style that Ballard simulates in "Why I Want to Fuck Ronald Reagan" - a style towards which the whole of *The Atrocity Exhibition* tends - is precisely lacking in any *personality*: if there any idiosyncracies, they belong to the technical register of (pseudo)scientific reportage, not to the characteristics of an individual subject. The fact that the text concerns a political leader draws attention to the lack of any explicit - or, more importantly when discussing satire or parody, implicit - political teleology in Ballard's writing. It is in this sense that "Why I Want to Fuck Ronald Reagan", like Jameson's pastiche, is "without any of parody's ulterior motives."

Certainly, this is one way in which "Why I Want to Fuck Ronald Reagan" differs greatly from a classical work of satire such as Swift's *Modest Proposal*. *A Modest Proposal* is a paradigmatic work of what Joyce called "kinetic" art, produced in particular political and cultural circumstances with a particular aim, to sway an audience into action. Swift's political purpose - his disparaging of the cruelty of certain English responses to the Irish potato famine - is marked by a certain stylistic and thematic excess (an excess that famously bypassed altogether certain of Swift's readers, who were able to take the text at face value), whereas Ballard's text - which emerged, no less than Swift's, from a very particular sociocultural situation - can be defined by its flatness. This marks a move on, (even) from Burroughs. For all their linguistic inventiveness, Burroughs' humorous "routines" such as "The All-American Deanxietized Man" remain in a classical tradition of satire through their use of exaggeration and their clear political agenda: using a series of excessive tropes, Burroughs mocks the amoral mores of American technoscience. By contrast, what Ballard's text "lacks" is any clear designs on the reader, any of Jameson's "ulterior motives"; the parodic text always gave central importance to the parodist behind it, his implicit but flagged attitudes and opinions, but "Why I Want to Fuck Ronald Reagan" is as coldly anonymous as the texts it imitates. Whereas we hear Burroughs' cackling at the absurb excesses of the scientists in "The All-American Deanxietized Man", the response of Ballard to the scientists whose work he simulates is unreadable. What does "Ballard" want the reader to feel: disgust? amusement? It is unclear, and, as Baudrillard argues in relation to *Crash*, it is somewhat disingenuous of Ballard the author to overcode his texts - in prefatory authorial remarks - with all the traditional baggage of "warning" that they themselves clearly elude. The mode Ballard adopts in "Why I Want to Fuck Ronald Reagan" is not that of (satirical) exaggeration, but is a kind of (simulated) extrapolation. The very genre of the poll or the survey, as Baudrillard shows, makes the question unanswerable, undecidable.

Despite what Ballard himself suggests, (see above), what matters is less the (possible) resemblance of "Why I Want to Fuck Ronald Reagan" to (possible) reports than the circulation of simulation to which such reports already contribute. Writing on pastiche, Jameson comes upon the concept of simulation, but attributes it to Plato rather than referring - here at least - to Baudrillard's reinvention of it. (PCLLC 18) Yet Jameson's intuition about the relationship between pastiche and simulation is important. We could perhaps suggest a correlation between Baudrillard's third order simulacra and Jameson's pastiche, on the one hand, and Ballard's text on the other. What simulation in Baudrillard's third-order sense entails is, as we have repeatedly insisted, the collapse of distance between the simulation and what is simulates. Satire, in its classical sense, we would probably want to locate as part of "First-order simulacra" - a simulation that resembles the original, but with certain tell-tale differences. Ballard simulates the simulation (the poll, the survey).

4.4 Social Science/Social Science Fiction (How the True World Became a Simulation)

While McHale sees particular textual-authorial features expanding to displace representation, Baudrillard sees representation disrupted by the emergence of a (hyper)fictive plane in which theory is effaced by fiction (and vice versa). But this is precisely not a matter of the "textualization" of reality; Baudrillard is fascinated with Ballard's *Crash* precisely because it *lacks* many of the features of traditional literature. As Baudrillard is quick to notice, in both the Ballard essay and his other essay on science fiction, the expansion of fiction into theory – an inevitable consequence, he thinks, of the emergence of cybernetics – has an ambivalent effect on theory. If theory can no longer be distinguished from fiction – if fiction can perform theory and theory must perforce become fiction – then map and territory are indeed confused, but in a more complicated and interesting way than Borges' story suggests.

Baudrillard was not the first to herald the new status of fiction. "We live science fiction," McLuhan had pronounced at the end of his 1964 essay on Burroughs (73), anticipating Donna Haraway's often-cited claim that the difference between science and fiction is becoming an optical illusion and William Bogard's description of his own work as a "social science fiction"[23], by some two decades.[24]

---

23. Bogard, *Simulation of Surveillance*, 5-24

24. It might be worth a parenthetical note here making some attempt to unravel what's at stake in the emergence of the – new? - mode, theory-fiction, particularly as undertaken by the theorist who has been most associated with this type of practice (Baudrillard). We can perhaps most profitably approach this problem by considering the conventional opposition between theory and fiction. Here, theory is on the side of the real and fiction is on the side of the imaginary. This is the opposition Douglas Kellner invokes – or doggedly holds onto – when he complains that "while Baudrillard's texts are arguably quite good science fiction, they are rather problematical as models of social theory" (Kellner 203); here it is assumed that the flip into a fictional mode automatically means the end of theory. But, if this too-quick opposition is inadequate, what could be meant by the fusion of fiction and theory? Two, inevitably interrelated, possibilities immediately suggest themselves:

1. Fiction as theory. This option further subdivides: (a) Fiction in the form of theory (fiction that uses, or incorporates academic conventions: examples here include T.S. Eliot's *The Waste Land* and Nabokov's *Pale Fire*). (b) Fiction performing as theory. This, potentially, could include any fiction offering theoretical resources of some kind.

2. Theory as fiction. This is theory presented in the form of fiction. The most

The becoming-fiction of theory is necessarily accompanied by the becoming-real of fiction. All of which calls for some kind of account of what fiction is – or could be – in cybernetic culture. (One could argue that most of Baudrillard's *oeuvre* is devoted to analyzing just this question). Provisionally, it is important to distinguish fiction from Literature, for two principal reasons. (1) Fiction does not come weighed down with the high cultural baggage that literature carries, and (2) fiction is not restricted to text- or even language-based cultural products. (Even a conventional definition of fiction, for instance, would include films).

Certainly, it is now no longer adequate to consider fiction to be on the side of the false[25], the fake or the imaginary. It can be considered to belong to the artificial, once we understand (following the arguments we made in Chapter 1), that the Real, far from being opposed to the artificial, is composed of it. The problem with Baudrillard may be that, by emphasising the "imaginary" aspects of his "pataphysical"[26] project, he too easily lets social-realist critics like Kellner off the hook, allowing them the opportunity to represent and – perhaps ludicrously – to posit themselves as intervening in

---

well-known exponents of this mode – Nietzsche, Kierkegaard – are hardly new. At its most radical, what is at stake here is more than the disguise of theory as fiction, or fiction as theory, but a dissolution of the opposition itself. Two, related, claims, one descriptive, the other prescriptive emerge from this: (1) all theory is *already* fiction; and, (2) theory should abandon its assumed position of "objective neutrality", and embrace its fictionality. But something happens to fiction here; it is no longer, simply, on the side of the imaginary.

In one sense, the rise of theory-fiction marks the end of literary criticism (and also, concomitantly, the end of "literature" as its object). McLuhan's essay on Burroughs had emerged in the context of his own drift from literary criticism towards fiction-theory, a process paralleled by Baudrillard's passage from "Literary criticism to fiction-theory" (6-25). Like McLuhan, "Baudrillard's intellectual formation was decisively marked by literature, and it is no accident that Baudrillard's first essays were literary in the traditional sense." (6) This trajectory is impelled, no doubt, in McLuhan's case by his intuition that Literature could no longer be studied as a relative autonomy, simply because, in the era of "electric participation" all disciplines – and all fields – tend to collapse. It is perhaps an understatement to say, as Mike Gane does, that "Baudrillard's challenge is as much to the mode of theorizing as to the substance." (Mike Gane, "Radical Theory: Baudrillard and Vulnerability", *Theory, Culture & Society*, London, Thousand Oaks and New Delhi – Sage, Vol 12 [1995], 120)

While Baudrillard may not be as rabidly anti-theoretical as the Lyotard of *Libidinal Economy* – itself another work of theory-fiction – he clearly has a somewhat ambivalent attitude to the practice. Naturally, this involves a change in the mode of his own writing – the move that happens between *Symbolic Exchange and Death* and *Seduction* – from a still putatively academic social theory to a fully-fledged theory-fiction that dispenses with the whole machinery of scholarly apparatus (footnotes, references, etc.).

25. Deleuze's discussion of the "powers of the false" in *Cinema 2* notwithstanding.

26. Baudrillard's revival of Jarry's pataphysics – the science of imaginary solutions – is a constant preoccupation in Baudrillard's work.

a "social world" whose existence they continue to believe in, whilst he can be caricatured as striking the pose of a dandy-aesthete, withdrawing into a nihilistic and narcissistic irresponsibility. But Baudrillard's response to Bogard's positing of a "social science-fiction" might be that it retains too conventional a picture (or at least remains content to merely blur, rather than shatter that picture) by assuming that either social science, science or be the social can be thought of as at any point in any way distinct from fiction. Baudrillard's most provocative challenge to social science concerns not only its claim to be a science, but, more radically perhaps, its claim to have a legitimate object of study: i.e. the social itself. One of Baudrillard's points, of course, is that the social world does not exist apart from its simulation in social theory. For obvious reasons, this quickly spirals beyond the familiar social constructionist position it could appear to be, since the social is not what constructs, but what is constructed, or, as Baudrillard would prefer, simulated, by an intermeshing web of infosystems[27].

According to Baudrillard, the socius, indeed, survives only as its own simulation through "fabulous fictions" (SED 66). Baudrillard: "In every field we are tested, probed and sampled; the method is 'tactical' and the sphere of communication 'tactile'. Not to mention the ideology of 'contact,' which, in all its forms, seeks to replace the idea of social relations. A whole strategic configuration revolves around the test (the question/answer cell) as it does around a molecular command-code." (SED 64) This is not to suggest in any way a dematerialization of power, only that Social Control (control by the socius) has given way to normalization (or hypernormalization) in which such ostensibly participatory fictional processes as opinion polls and surveys play a crucial role. (For a preliminary discussion of this process, see "Cybernetics, Postmodernism, Fiction", in Chapter 1, above.)

Bogard's example of the production of *profiles* provides an excellent example of what is at issue here. As William Bogard expains: "A profile, as the name suggests, is a kind of prior ordering, in this case a model or figure that organizes multiple sources of information to scan for matching or exceptional cases [...] Unlike stereotypes, [...] profiles are not merely 'false images' that are used to justify differences in power. Diagnostic profiles exist rather at the intersection of 'actual and virtual worlds, and come to have more 'reality,' more 'truth and significance,' than the cases to which they are compared. Rather than the profiles resembling the cases, *increasingly the cases start to resemble the profiles.*"[28] The profile is a prophecy which fulfills itself or, at least, makes any claim about its 'accurate' representation of reality undecidable. Since being profiled automatically makes you targeted - by advertisers, the police etc. - it is impossible to decide whether the profile solicits behaviour or anticipates it (it

---

27. See Baudrillard's famous theses on "the end of the social" in *In the Shadow of the Silent Majorities.*

28. Bogard, 27 (italics added)

precisely puts just this distinction in question). For Bogard, the emergence of such processes indicates a move form control to hypercontrol. Hypercontrol differs from Control primarily through the temporality in (and through) which it operates. In Baudrillard's terms, "social control by means of the *end* [...] is replaced by means of prediction, simulation, programmed anticipation and indeterminate mutation, all governed, however, by the code." (SED 60) DNA and "molecular cybernetics" provide the ominous model for total bio-cybernetic control by "stimulated, simulated and anticipated response" (SED 67): get to the code and you run everything. Cybernetics had always been about anticipation; in order to hit a moving target, the anti-aircraft weaponry Wiener had worked on needed to predict not where the target was at the point when the missile was launched, but where its would be at the point of impact. Hence the slogan of Control is, "Don't strike where your enemy is, strike where it will be." Hypercontrol tends towards the production of even tighter feedback loops; its slogan, then, would be "Never strike where your enemy will be, kill its parents."[29] Cybernetic anticipation is always double-edged; suggesting not only prediction, but determination: "self-fulfilling prophecy" (SED 67), as Baudrillard has it. Yet this process itself makes prophecy moot, precisely because it makes any effective delineation of causal determination impossible: "the whole traditional world of causality" with its "distinction between cause and effect, between active and passive, between subject and object, between the ends and the means" (SS 31) has been superceded by a logic of "code." White magical capture[30]: to be in the system is already to be

---

29. Iain Hamilton Grant, "Burning Autopoiedipus", Abstract Culture 10, (Winter 1997), 8

30. The reference to magic here is far from glib. In fact, it returns us to Weiner's comments on the complicity of magical process with cybernetics, cited in the previous chapter. Self-fulfilling prophecy is a particularly powerful type of capture-magic. Consider the example of someone who is told, at a seance, let's say, that they are going to die in the next year. They do in fact die, from what appear to be accidental causes. Has their death been prophesied - or has the prophecy itself affected them - perhaps subtly, at an unconscious level - so that their behaviour has made them more likely to die? It's undecidable, as Baudrillard would say. Once the loop is closed, we can never know. The prophecy, like the opinion poll, is not causally innocent: it combines anticipation with determination in such a way as to make the distinction between the two impossible to make.

But the only type of true prophecy that is not - to some extent - self-fulfilling would be one wholly independent of the event which it is prophesying. Otherwise, there is always the possibility that the prophecy plays a part in inducing what it foretells. This is a theme well-enough known in Literature, and is a commonplace of tragedy. Neither Oedipus nor Macbeth would suffer the fates they encounter were it not for prophecy. Oedipus' fate is particularly ironic in that it is his parents' very attempt to *avoid* the prophesied events that ultimately brings them about; had they cast him out as a child, Oedipus would recognize his father and mother (and not kill the former or marry the latter). Baudrillard has his own version of this "fatal" narrative: the tale of "Death in

processed by it. Baudrillard's example of this is the opinion poll. The question that concerned opinion in the "political class" worries about - do polls affect voting behaviour? - is unanswerable. "Polls manipulate the *undecidable*. Do they affect votes? True of false? Do they yield exact photographs of reality, or of mere tendencies, or a refraction of this reality in a hyperspace of simulation whose curvature we do not know? True or false? Undecidable." (SED 66)[31] Code's logic as Baudrillard delineates it is not describable in terms of cause-preceding-effect; rather, its logic is one, to speak like Deleuze, of expression[32], in which each "effect" expresses - unfolds - a "cause" from which it is never really distinct, temporally or ontologically. Is DNA the *cause* of an organism? It is both more and less.[33]

Samarkand", recounted in *Seduction*. "Consider the story of the soldier who meets death in the marketplace, and believes he saw his making a menacing gesture in his direction. He rushes to the king's palace and asks the king for his best horse in order that he might flee far into the night from Death, as far as Samarkand. Upon which the king summons Death to the palace and reproaches him for having frightened one of his best servants. But Death, astonished, replies 'I didn't mean to frighten him. It was just that I was surprised to see this soldier here, when we had a rendez-vous tomorrow in Samarkand.'" (S 72)

31. In part, Baudrillard is merely re-stating the uncertainty principle, but with a particular – cybernetic – emphasis on feedback. To observe anything is to affect it: "It is not even certain that we can test plants, animals or inert matter with any hope of an 'objective' response." (SED 67) For Baudrillard, though, this already radically undermines not only any hope of "objectively" observing anything, but also any ability to delineate cause-and-effect structures. How do we know we've not entered the loop? And it is the cybernetic figure of the loop - what Baudrillard calls "a coding a decoding strip, magnetized by signs" (SED 75) - complete unto itself, cycling around in its own orbit, that is implicit in Baudrillard's formulations of bio-cybernetic control.

32. For expression, see Deleuze, *Expressionism and Philosophy*. Spinoza is the subject of this study, but Deleuze also discusses Leibniz; Baudrillard cites "Leibniz's binary deity" as the "precursor" of code (SED 4, 57, 59).

33. One could say that, where Control targets the future, Hypercontrol targets the future by altering (what will have been) its past, except that, by now, the "past", like every other marker of sequential time, has been liquidated by the system's "retroeugenics". There is only the time of the system: "Finality is no longer at the end, there is no more finality, nor any determinacy. Finality is there in advance, inscribed in the code." (SED 59)

4.5 The Decline of the Shadow (or, the End of the Marvelous)

Jameson: *"Now not the magical speaking beasts or the 'flowers that look back at you,' but the marching automata of* Blade Runner's *last cavernous private apartment."*[34]

For Baudrillard, the arrival of cybernetic modeling systems entails the destruction of the category of the *marvelous*: the former province of myth, occupied last of all, perhaps, by Surrealism (which was already contributing to its destruction). The melancholy underside to the story we've just outlined is the takeover, by hyperreality, of everything surreal, or irreal. In one sense, the hyperreal, for Baudrillard, marks less the decline of the Real than the swallowing of all alternatives to it. Hyperreality – the more real than the real - is a cancerization of the Real, its metastatic occupation of the zones which used to double reality (shadow, dream, and myth); for Baudrillard, the decline of the marvelous is signalled by what he repeatedly chacterizes as the disappearance of the shadow and the double, and their replacement by the cybernetic network. But it is important to understand that the cancerization of the Real is – immediately – also a cancerization of the fictional; the two processes require one another. Only when there is only fiction (and therefore no more fiction) and only the real (and therefore no more reality) does hyperreality begin.

It is interesting to compare Baudrillard's position in *Symbolic Exchange and Death*, especially as outlined in the important section of the "Political Economy and Death" chapter entitled "The Double and the Split" with Rosemary Jackson's literary-historical analysis of the modern fantastic in her *Fantasy: the Literature of Subversion*. This brings us back to the question of the nature of the demonic, since, for Jackson, "The modern fantastic is characterized by a radical shift in the naming, or interpretation of the demonic." (F 43) In her account of the fantastic, Jackson draws upon Todorov's influential *The Fantastic: A Structural Approach to a Literary Genre*. Here, Todorov famously distinguishes between the marvelous, the fantastic and the uncanny. As Jackson explains, in "Todorov's diagrammatic representation of the changing forms of the fantastic"

---

34. Jameson, *Geopolitical Aesthetic*, 12

there is a "move from the marvelous (which predominates in a climate of belief in supernaturalism and magic) through the purely fantastic (in which no explanation is to be found) to the uncanny (which explains all strangeness as generated by unconscious forces). Thus:

MARVELOUS	FANTASTIC	UNCANNY
Supernatural	Unnatural	Natural (F 25)

For Todorov, the fantastic is defined by an anxiety on the part of the reader and the characters, which takes the form of a hesitation between explanations in terms of the supernatural and the natural. "According to Todorov, the purely fantastic text establishes absolute hesitation in the protagonist and reader; they can neither come to terms with the unfamiliar events described, nor dismiss them as supernatural phenomena. Anxiety, then, is not merely a thematic feature, but is incorporated into the *structure* of the work to become its defining element." (F 28) Arguing that the "uncanny" is not a specifically literary mode, Jackson replaces it with the "mimetic", ultimately placing her version of the fantastic "between the opposite modes of the marvelous and the mimetic." (F 32)

"It is hardly surprising," Jackson notes, "that the fantastic comes into its own in the nineteenth century, at precisely that juncture when a supernatural 'economy' of ideas was giving way to a natural one, but had not yet been completely displaced by it." (F 25) So, where once "[t]he term *demonic* originally denoted a supernatural being, a ghost, or spirit, or genius, or devil and it usually connoted a malignant, destructive force at work" (F 54), Jackson shows that during the course of the nineteenth century the demonic comes to stand for something internal to the subject; she describes a move from "a supernatural to a natural economy of images", with the "natural" understood largely in terms of psychology interiority. "Over the course of the nineteenth century, fantasies structured around dualism - often variations of the Faust myth - reveal the *internal* origin of the other." (F 55) Here, in a simultaneous domestication of both the demonic and the unconscious, the "demonic" is no longer supernatural, but is an aspect of personal and interpersonal life, a manifestation of unconscious desire." (F 55)

In a sense, Baudrillard accepts Jackson's whole story, but, predictably, gives it a melancholy spin, whilst adding a biting cultural political critique. In Baudrillard's terms, the narrative which places psychological interiority at the endpoint of a disenchanted history is by no means innocent: it is part of a process by which modern western culture defines itself as the inevitable teleological destination of planetary process, appropriating "previous" cultures as its forebears. The destruction of the double goes hand in hand with the production of the (Christian) soul (the ultimate achievement of a "spiritualist" project). For Baudrillard, the rise of "psychological and pyschoanalytic interpretation" (SED 140) as the authorized forms of capitalist realism bring an end to "the primitive double." (SED 140) "Shadow, spectre, reflection, image" (SED 140), the primitive double haunts post-monotheistic, psychoanalytic culture, which appropriates it as a "crude prefiguration of the soul" (SED 140). Yet "soul and consciousness have everything to do with a principle of the subject's unification, and nothing to do with the primitive double. On the contrary, the historical advent of the 'soul' puts an end to a proliferating exchange with spirits and doubles which, as a direct consequence, gives rise to another figure of the double, wending its way beneath the surfaces of western reason." (SED 141) This - modern, western - double is inextricably connected with alienation; it is the double as the lost part of the self, "a fantastic ectoplasm, an archaic resurgence issuing from guilt and the depths of the unconscious." (SED 141) The primitive double, however, is radically non-alienated because it "is a *partner* with whom the primitive has a personal and concrete relationship, sometimes happy and sometimes not." (SED 141) Whereas the westerner always apprehends his double as the missing half of a fragmented unity, the primitive has a reciprocal, non-symmetrical relationship with his double. The primitive "really can trade, as we are forever forbidden to do, *with his shadow* (the real shadow, not a metaphor), as with some original, living thing in order to converse, protect and conciliate this tutelary or hostile shadow. The shadow is precisely not the reflection of an 'original' body, it has a full part to play, and it is consequently not an 'alienated' part of the subject, but one of the figures of exchange." (SED 141) Alienation, Baudrillard says, only comes into play when there is an internalization of an "abstract agency [...] - whether psychological (the ego and the ego-ideal), religious (God or the soul) or moral (conscience and the law) to which everything else is subordinated." (SED 141) Once the introjection of these agencies is achieved, the double ceases to be an ambivalent figure and becomes associated (only) with death and madness, as Baudrillard establishes by reference to a whole tradition of horrific literature:

"With the internalization of the soul and consciousness (the principle of identity and equivalence), the subject undergoes a real confinement, similar to the confinement of the mad in the seventeenth century described by Foucault. It is at this point that the primitive thought of the double as exchange and continuity is lost, and the haunting double comes to the fore as the subject's discontinuity in death and madness. 'Whoever sees his devil, sees his death'. A vengeful and vampiric double, an unquiet soul, the double begins to prefigure the subject's death, haunting him in the very midst of his life. This is Dostoevsky's double, or Peter Schlemihl's, the man who lost his shadow. We have always interpreted the double as a metaphor of the soul, consciousness, native soil, and so on. Without this incurable idealism and without being taken as a metaphor, the narrative is so much more extraordinary. We have all lost our *real*' shadows, we no longer speak to them, and our bodies have left with them." (SED 142)

Baudrillard then turns to Freud specifically, and to his treatment of the double in his essay "Das Unheimliche" ("The Uncanny"). The double features in Freud only as a kind of extension of the ego. Freud refers to Rank's work, in which the double was "originally an insurance against the destruction of the ego, an 'energetic denial of the power of death'"(PFL 14 356) As Baudrillard insists, Freud reads the double in terms of the soul: "probably the 'immortal' soul was the first 'double' of the body" (PFL 356) Thoughts of the double, Freud speculates, must "have sprung from the soil of unbounded self-love, from the primary narcissism which dominates the mind of the child and' primitive man." (PFL 357)

Crucially, for Baudrillard, and for Rosemary Jackson, in "The Uncanny" (1919), Freud revives the correlation of "the old, animistic conception of the universe" (PFL 14 362) with the "omnipotence of thoughts" (PFL 14 362) he had made in the earlier *Totem and Taboo* (1913). "The Uncanny" is - supposedly - Freud's attempt to give an account of a very particular feeling of "dread and horror" (PFL 14 339); although Gothic Materialism would prefer to regard the essay as an attempt to keep at bay - by means of subjectivization - exactly the dread and horror it affects to confront. Beginning with an inventory of usages of the terms, Freud famously shows that the meaning of the words *unheimliche* (unhomely) and its ostensible opposite *Heimlich* (homely) continually bleed into one another: "among its different shades of meaning the word '*heimlich*' exhibits one which is identical with its opposite, *unheimlich*." (PFL 14 345) For Freud, the feeling of the uncanny arises from this disturbing combination of the strange and the familiar. First of all, referring to a certain "authority" on the uncanny, Jentsch, Freud dismisses the idea that the uncanny is directly connected with "doubts whether an apparently animate being is really alive; or conversely, whether a lifeless object might not in fact be animate" (Jentsch, qtd PFL 14 347) This feeling of intellectual "uncertainty", Freud says, is not a feature of the uncanny as he understands it. Whilst the theme of the animate doll is, Freud notes, a factor in Hoffmann's short story "The Sandman", a story he takes to be exemplary of the uncanny, it is not its main theme; this, rather, is that of the sandman who threatens to tear out children's eyes. Passing through the "substitutive relation between the eye and the male organ" (PFL 14 352) Freud quickly decides that "The Sandman" is really about a fear of castration. Feelings of the "uncanny" can always be traced back to such repressed childhood experiences; "the uncanny is in reality nothing new or alien, but something familiar and old-established in the mind." (PFL 14 363) The idea of dolls coming to life, a theme which, having apparently dismissed, Freud returns to, suggests another "factor from childhood" (PFL 14 355), although this seems to be attributable to infantile wish rather than to infantile fear. "We remember that in their early games children do not distinguish at all sharply between living and inanimate objects, and that they are especially fond of treating their dolls like live people." (PFL 14 355)

"Animistic" beliefs, for Freud, are to be regarded as belonging to the most primitive part of the mind, an ontogenetic equivalent of the phylogenetic stage of the "savage". In Rosemary Jackson's reconstruction:

Phylogenetic evolution	Ontogenetic evolution
1 ANIMISTIC Men ascribe omnipotence to themselves.	NARCISSISM/ AUTO-EROTICISM
2 RELIGIOUS Power is transferred to gods, the individual believes he has some influence with them.	ATTACHMENT TO LOVE OBJECT
3 SCIENTIFIC Leaves no room for human omnipotence. The subject becomes resigned to the laws of necessity, and the inevitability of death. (F 71)	ABANDONMENT TO REALITY PRINCIPLE

Baudrillard cleverly turns these arguments against Freud. "This is how psychology, our authority in the depths, our own 'next world', this omnipotence, magical narcissism, fear of the dead, this animism or primitive psychical apparatus, is quietly palmed off on the savages in order then to recuperate them for ourselves as 'archaic traces,'" Baudrillard fulminates. But Baudrillard shows – rather elegantly – how it is Freud himself (and the "psychologistic culture" of which he stands as representative) taht is guilty of projecting its own interior states onto the "savages." The thesis of the "omnipotence of thoughts" applies less to primitive culture than to a modern – and postmodern – culture that insists on the category of the "psychological" as a cross-cultural universal. "Freud does not think this is what he said in speaking of 'narcissistic overvaluation of … mental processes'. If there is such an overvaluation of one's own mental processes (to the point of exporting this theory, as we have done with our morality and techniques, to the core of every culture), then it is Freud's overvaluation, along with our whole psychologistic culture." (SED 143)

Freud's dismissal of the double – or, what amounts to the same thing, his psycho-reductive account of it – constitutes a contribution to a "spiritual" project through which all previous cultures are absorbed and transformed into precursors, "archaic traces." Freud's supposedly atheistic psychoanalysis is, for Baudrillard, actually continuous with a Christian westernization (whose moves it recapitulates, but even more successfully). "This is what kills off the proliferation of doubles and spirits, consigning them once again to the spectral, embryonic corridors of unconscious folklore, like the ancient gods that Christianity *vertefeult*, that is, transformed into demons." (SED 142) This process of transformation is completed by Freud – and Rank's – psychologization of the double. "By a final ruse of spirituality, this internalisation also *psychologises* doubles," Baudrillard complains. "In fact, it is interpretation in terms of an archaic *psychical apparatus* that it is the very last form of the *Verteufeleung*, the demonic corruption and elimination of the primitive double." (SED 142)[35] But it may well be that children and "savages" have the last laugh.

---

35. Note Freud's own reduction of the demon to the father figure in his "A Seventeenth Century Demonological Neurosis." Here Freud also discusses the process of *verteufeult* Baudrillard describes (the transformation of gods into demons). "Concerning the Evil Demon, we know that he is regarded as the antithesis of God and yet is very close to him in nature. His history has not yet been as well studied as that of God; not all religions have adopted the Evil Spirit, the opponent of God, and his prototype in the life of the individual has so far remained obscure. One thing, however, is certain: gods can turn into evil demons when new gods oust them. When one people has been conquered by another, their fallen gods not seldom turn into demons in the eyes of the conqueror. [...] The contradictions in the original nature of God are [...] a reflection of the ambivalence which governs the relation of the individual to his personal father. If the benevolent and righteous God is a substitute for the father, it is not to be wondered at that his hostile attitude to his father, too, which is one of hating and fearing him and of making complaints against him, should have come to expression in the form of Satan." (Freud, "The Devil as Father-Substitute" in *A Seventeenth Century Demonological Neurosis*, 400-401)

4.6 Mechanism and Animism (or, Gremlins in the Hyperreal)

Gibson: "The new jockeys, they make deals with things" (CZ 169)

Gibson: "But did it wake, Kumiko wondered, when the alley was empty? Did its laser vision scan the silent fall of midnight snow?" (MLO 174)

Kant: "[M]oral teleology compensates for physical teleology and for the first time supplies a basis for theology. For physical teleology on its own [...] could not provide a basis for anything but a demonology."[36]

But if Baudrillard's simulated history culminates here – in the triumph of a code that can only be subverted by its own drive to perfectibility[37] Gibson and Deleuze-Guattari seem to open another set of possibilities for the connections between the demonic and the cybernetic. In contrast with Baudrillard's cybernetics of control, the convergence of voodoo with cybernetics presents a vindication of the views of Freud's children and "savages" – a counter-narrative to Baudrillard's vision of cybernetic hyperrationalization which unsettles stable, linear temporalities by uncovering strange coincidences between the deeply archaic and the most gleamingly hypermodern.

At first sight, the Gothic elements in Gibson could appear to be merely vestigial, superstitions whose carry over into terminal culture is motivated by a psychological need to populate the Godless regions of cyberspace with familiar belief structures. This, indeed, is how one of the characters rationalizes it. "There's a whole new apocrypha out there, really - ghost ships, lost cities [...] There's a pathos to it, when you think about it. I mean, every bit of it's locked into orbit. All of it manmade, known, own, mapped. Like watching myths take root in a parking lot. But I suppose people need that, don't they?" (MLO 111) To the extent that this is true, Gibson would appear to be complicit with a Weberian narrative of rationalization - what Weber, after Schiller, called "the disenchantment of the world", a process characterized in part by the disappearance of the supernatural. This, in effect, is the narrative Baudrillard accepts: cybernetic control by the Code constitutes the final triumph of a post-

---

36. Kant, *The Critique of Judgement*, trans. Werner S. Pluhar, Indianapolis: Hackett, 1987, 333

37. A formula Baudrillard plays out perhaps most exhaustively in *The Transparency of Evil.*

Protestant culture which has stripped the world of its gods.[38]

Gibson himself is equivocal. His own theologizations (or demonizations) of cyberspace hesitate between a vision of technotheoteleogical transcendence, in which the Matrix – as late-arriving "cybernetic godhead" (MLO 238) redeems a human history it effectively culminates, and a Deleuze-Guattari picture of a dehumanized cyberspace peopled by roaming intelligences. The following passage – from *Mona Lisa Overdrive* – summarises the two positions:

> "The folklore of console jockeys, Continuity. What do you know about that?
> [...]
> 'What would you like to know, Angie?'
> – 'When it changed' [...]
> 'The mythform is usually encountered in one of two modes. One mode assumes that the cyberspace matrix is inhabited, or perhaps visited, by entities whose characteristics correspond with the primary mythform of a 'higher people'. The other involves assumptions of omniscience, omnipotence and incomprehensibility on the part of the matrix itself.'
> 'That the matrix is God?'
> 'In a manner of speaking, although it would be more accurate, in terms of the mythform, to say that the matrix has a God, since this being's omniscience and omnipotence are assumed to be limited to the matrix.'
> 'If it has limits, it isn't omnipotent.'
> 'Exactly.' [...]
> 'How about the stories about – ', she hesitated, having almost said the loa, 'about things in the matrix, how do they fit into this supreme being idea.'
> 'They don't. Both are variants of 'When it Changed'. Both are of very recent origin.'" (MLO 138-9)

The discussion is somewhat reminiscent of the theo-cybernetic debates in Wiener's *God and Golem*, although – in line with a certain cyber-transcendence – Gibson plays with a possibility that is almost the reverse of the one Wiener entertained. As we saw in the last chapter, Wiener wondered what limits there were to the escape of machinic intelligence once the "dogmas" of omnipotence and omniscience are abandoned; Gibson, meanwhile (or his more mystico-transcendently-oriented characters), imagines "omniscience, omnipotence and incomprehensibility" *emerging*, as side-effects of the production of cyberspace. Against this picture of emergent oneness, the "stories about things in the matrix" posit the fragmentation of the Matrix into entities, paralleled – or identified – with the loa of Haitian voodoo. The crucial moment (retrospectively accorded mythic status) is the end of *Neuromancer*, when Wintermute and Neuromancer fuse into a Matrix

---

38. Since, from his point of view, the whole contemporary scene is complicit with this dreary scenario, Baudrillard's escape is into the past: he scans the cybernetic iron cage from the perspective of a simulated *primitive* gaze. It is this POV – enabling him to contrast the cold circuits of cyberculture with the frenzied rites of symbolic exchange – that gives a purchase to his critique.

which is itself metamorphosed: *When it changed.* On the one hand, *what it changes into* seems to be a familiar image of Science Fictional transcendence – achieved sentience as the Mind of God; on the other, *what it changes into* it is a properly cyberpunk – and Gothic Materialist – vision of teeming multiplicity ("things in the matrix"): *Pandemonium (all the demons,* and *demons everywhere).*[39]

The cybernetic lexicon has shown a remarkable predilection for invoking the word "demon". For obvious reasons: cybernetic systems simulate conscious function without possessing it. The term "demonic" suggests both this possibility of agency-without-subjectivity and hints at the power of metamorphic becoming proper to entities of simulation. Wiener's writings are replete with warnings about the "demonic" and "devilish" power of such cybernetic systems. Fearing that "the machine like the djinee, which can learn and make decisions on the basis of its learning, will in no way be obliged to make such decisions as we should have made, or will be acceptable to us" (HUHB 185) Wiener refers to a "demoniac sanction" (HUHB 130), and a "devilment" that scientists – "apprentice sorcerers" – "are unable to stop." (HUHB 130)[40]

From its very beginnings, the modern(ist) science of cybernetics was haunted by the resurgence of belief structures which, in Freud's terms, would have to be considered vestiges from the most archaic parts of the mind: beliefs he characterised as "animistic". According to Wiener, when confronted with cybernetic machines, human beings found themselves behaving as if the systems possessed agency. Since the systems cybernetics produced behaved at least quasi-autonomously, they naturally gave rise to the belief in non-human (and non-subjective) agencies, as Wiener explains by reference to aircraft crews' interaction with airplanes which used self-corrective cybernetic circuits: "The semi-humorous superstition of the gremlin among the aviators was probably due, as much as anything else, to the habit of dealing with a machine with a large number of built-in feedbacks which might be interpreted as friendly or hostile. For example the wings of an airplane are deliberately built in such a manner as to stabilize the plane, and their stabilization, which is of the nature of feedback [...] may easily be felt as a personality to be antagonized when the plane is forced into unusual maneuvers."[41] Dealing with the cybernetic systems

---

39. In a sense, the opposition itself presupposes a set of monotheistic assumptions, whereby singularity and multiplicity are necessarily thought of as contradictory; whereas what voodoo – which does not oppose, so much as absorb Christianity – has in common with Deleuze-Guattari is an intuition that singularity (which is not unity) is not different from multiplicity (which is not an aggregation of unities).

40. Note also the positing of the "Maxwell Demon" which Cybernetics was keen to refute. (HUHB 28-30) Wiener also makes a distinction between two types of "devil" the scientist is "fighting": the "Augustinian" and the "Manichean". (HUHB, 34-35, 190).

41. Wiener, "Operationalism - Old and New" (1945), box 11, folder 570, Norbert Wiener Papers, collection MC-22, Institute Archives and Special Collection, Massachussets Institute of Technology Archives, Cambridge, Mass., quoted in Peter

of these aircraft presented the aviators with many of the same – perceptual – clues as would interaction with another conscious being. Therefore, it was inevitable that they would posit another entity, rather than a technical system, when they were working in – or, more properly perhaps, with – the airplane. "Our consciousness of will in another person, Wiener argued, is just that sense of encountering a self-maintaining mechanism aiding or opposing our actions. By providing such a self-stabilizing resistance, the airplane acts as if it had purpose, in short, as if it were inhabited by a gremlin."[42]

At the other end of cybernetic era, in Gibson's near future, we find a Japanese businessman explaining to his daughter why personality-construct "cubes" are not "souls". "[H]e'd explained that the cubes housed the recorded personalities of former executives, corporate directors. Their souls, she asked. No, he'd said. And smiled, then added that the distinction was a subtle one. 'They are not conscious. They respond, when questioned, in a manner approximating the response of the subject. If they are ghosts, then holograms are ghosts." (MLO 174) Given what Wiener has implied, the girl Kumiko's confusion is a response more true to the complexities of cybernetics response than is her father's confidence. One corollary of what Wiener says in connection with the aircraft gremlins is that the positing of personality (and of conscious mental process) is a side-effect of the perception of purposive function, which can now – as one of the first principles of cybernetics insists – be technicized. At any rate, Gibson is well aware that the development of cybernetic machines produces increasingly anomalous systems that suggest – at the very least – that the distinction between living and nonliving, between thing and entity, is becoming increasingly difficult to sustain.

Hence the return of animism, which can closely be paralleled with demonism. Which brings us back to the children Sherry Turkle discusses in her *Life on the Screen*, whom we encountered long ago (in our Introduction). Like Gibson's Kumiko, these children – confronted with cybernetic systems capable, of course, of an infinitely more subtle variety of responses and interactions than were the primitive aviation systems the wartime airmen encountered – offer a complex account of their engagement with machines that defies many of the old ontological assumptions.

But we need to consider more carefully what is at stake in animist belief system, in part because Deleuze-Guattari make a point of distinguishing their machinism from animism. Significantly, this distinction is advanced during the course of a discussion of children. "Children are Spinozists," (TP 256) Deleuze-Guattari declare. "It has been noted that for children an organ has a 'thousand vicissitudes,' that it is 'difficult to localize, difficult to identity, it is in turn a bone, an engine, excrement, the baby, a hand, daddy's heart.' This

---

Galison, 'The Ontology of the Enemy: Norbert Wiener and the Cybernetic Vision', 246
  42. Galison, 246. Gibson amusingly updates this in *Mona Lisa Overdrive*, by having a whole house – Continuity – becoming an interactive presence.

is not at all because the organ is experienced as a part-object. It is because
the organ is exactly what its elements make it according to their relation of
movement and rest, and the way in which this relation combines with or
splits off from that of its neighbouring elements. *This is not animism*, any more
than it is mechanism; rather, it is universal machinism: a plane of consistency
occupied by an immense abstract machine occupied by an infinite number
of assemblages." (TP 256; emphasis added) This passage is implicitly aimed
against Freud (whose Little Hans they discuss in the sentences immediately
preceding it); the distinction of machinism and animism is no doubt impelled
by a desire to separate their position from Freud's in "Totem and Taboo" and
"The Uncanny." But is it possible to find a version of animism compatible with
Deleuze-Guattari's machinism?

One way of cashing out what Deleuze-Guattari's say about machinism
is in terms of a dissolution of an ontology of objects.[43] What they emphasise is
the irreducibility of dynamical process. It is not as if there are "objects" *subject
to* (Spinozist) speeds and slownesses; there is only a continuum of speeds and
slownesses (which are "then" apprehended as objects – by subjects). The same
"object" can be part of an infinity of different machines.

Conventionally understood, animism could be seen as the complement
to Freudian explanation. Here, the natural world – and, presumably, the
world of cultural production - is treated as if it possessed the same features of
intentionality which are supposedly unique to human beings, or – at least – to
organisms.[44] Jacques Monod offers a fairly conventional definition. "Animist
belief […]," in Monod's summary, "consists essentially in a projection into
inanimate nature of man's awareness of the intensely teleonomic function of his
own central nervous system. It is, in other words, the hypothesis that natural
phenomena can and must be explained in the same manner, by the same 'laws,'
as subjective human activity, conscious and purposive."[45] Whilst animism no
doubt posits a single plane inhabited by human beings, "the natural world",
and technical machines, it is to follow Freud into a kind of psychologistic
reductivism to assume that this must be a matter of projection. If a single plane
is genuinely being posited, it makes no sense to say that it is being "projected"
by a psychological agent, precisely because the distinction between such
agents and the world around them is what is at issue. Understood in this
way, animism would be merely the other side to organicism, with nonorganic

---

43. The differentiation of their Spinozism from a Kleinian conceptualization of
"part-objects" has more to do with a problem with the concept of objects than of the
concept of parts – although the notion of "parts" is ambiguous. If the concept of parts
designates a components of a fragmented unity, then clearly it is in radical opposition
to Deleuze-Guattari's concept of multiplicity. See "The Whole and its Parts", AO 42,
for a discussion of this.

44. Hence the so-called "omnipotence of thoughts."

45. Jacques Monod, *Chance and Necessity: An Essay on the Natural Philosophy of Modern
Biology*, trans. Austryn Wainhouse, Harmondsworth: Penguin, 1997, 30

processes understood to function (in many ways) like the way in which organisms are understood to operate. To reconcile machinism with animism entails holding onto the concept of a single plane – Deleuze-Guattari's "plane of consistency occupied by an immense abstract machine" but it equally demands the abandonment of any special organic feature (which is then, supposedly, projected onto the inorganic). On the plane of consistency, there is nowhere to project from (nor to). Ron Eglash gives a more interesting account, reinforcing the connection between animist conceptions and cybernetics by emphasising the *informational circuitries* with which he claims animist belief systems are concerned:

> "Although frequently reduced to 'fetish worship' or 'natural spirituality' in western descriptions, animism is, on the contrary, typically concerned with a cultural transfer of information or energy through physical dynamics. While animist religions are still active in Africa today, this conception of animated physical form is quite ancient, and is reflected in the myths of God creating humanity from clay. In some North African traditions, certain spiritualists could create their own clay robots, 'golems.' Goldsmith reports golem legends going back to the fourth century B.C.E., and describes their continuing popularity in Jewish legend. Norbert Weiner, the Jewish founder of analog cybernetics, was quite influenced by this concept of information embedded in physical dynamics [...] He made several references to the golem in his writing, and reported that, even as a child he was fascinated by the idea of making a doll come alive."[46]

Eglash's position parallels Gibson's, in positing connections between voodoo and contemporary cybernetic systems. But what is interesting about the children Turkle describes is that they do not so much seek to make the inanimate come alive; rather, they do not recognize that the distinction between animate and inanimate is equivalent to the distinction between entities capable of agency and those not. The issue, for the children Turkle studied, is that *agency does not require life.* "The most recent generation of children, who seem so willing to grant psychological status to not-alive machines, have become accustomed to objects that are both interactive and opaque. These children have learned what to expect of these objects and how to discriminate between them and what is alive. But even as children make those discriminations, they also grant new capacities and privileges to the machine world *on the basis of its animation if not its life.*"[47] Agency can be distributed across a plane that is indifferent to "life." This might, once again, establish a point of connection with Spinoza, whose philosophy has no place for the distinction between life and death, but which, as we have seen above, in Deleuze-Guattari's reconstruction, defines bodies in terms of speeds and

---

46. Eglash, "African Influences in Cybernetics", in Gray, Chris Hables (ed), *The Cyborg Handbook*, New York/London: Routledge, 1995, 22-23
47. Turkle, *Life on the Screen*, 83, emphasis added

slownesses, different quanta of *animation*. Turkle claims that, faced with computers, children assume that the technical system is not alive, but that it has a *psychology*. This is perhaps an unnecessary reterritorialization: Gothic Materialism finds the concepts of agency and entity much more congenial. Agency implies a capacity for response, but has no necessary suggestion of any interiority, or *conscious* reflection. The emergent mythos of demonism in Gibson's cyberspace depends upon the notion of *entities with which one can trade*. "The new jockeys, they make deals with things." (CZ 169) This emphasis on trade with an entity that is really different (not a pyschologistic projection) recapitulates, then, the relationship between Baudrillard's "primitive double" and the shadow: it is a matter of a real relationship with something exterior.

4.7 Capitalism as Toy Story: Hyperfiction, Strange Loops and Rhizomes

If, in the context of cybernetics, Freud's dismissal of animism seems hasty, so does his confinement of children to an early stage of development. Turkle's work reinforces the observation – which, although well-worn, is more than glib cliche - that children know more about computers than their parents; and the early encounter with such cybernetic systems pre-emptively disables much of the metaphysics the adult world seeks to impose. Children, that is to say, increasingly live in a Gothic Materialist chaosmos. "Children, instinctual animists, identify with toys and dolls, subjecting themselves to and projecting themselves onto the inanimate: every 12-year old knows that I is an other and another and another."[48] Under capitalism, the idea that toys do not have a certain agency becomes increasingly questionable. It may be the case that children take for granted, not only a Freudian animism, but a neo-Marxian picture of "necromantic" capital. It would only be natural for children to share what, in Chapter 1, we saw Judith Halberstam characterize as Marx's "Gothic" picture of capitalism. Blitzed with capitalist hyperstimulus, children are already participants in capitalism. In many ways, children occupy the frontier-zones of capitalism, operating as probe-heads in what, for adults, is the future. Indeed, the Freudian model of regression could be radically reversed: it might be said that the child's universe of animist presences and animal-becomings[49] has far more purchase on capitalist (and schizophrenic) reality than adults' continued belief in subjective interiority. "To a certain extent, we can look to children to see what we are starting to think ourselves."[50]

Capitalism, it could be said, is giving an agency to toys far more far-reaching than was achieved by Hoffmann's clunky automaton. Naturally, the role of fiction is absolutely central to the toy-child relation. But it is a fiction which enjoys a peculiar relation to the Real. Increasingly, children are presented with toys and fictional systems which emerge together, in a loop. Where once there was a serial trajectory – comic books – toys – films or toys – films – comic books – now toys, films, comic books (and innumerable

---

48. Kodwo Eshun, *More Brilliant than the Sun: Adventures in Sonic Fiction*, London: Quartet, 1998, 108
49. The fusion of animals with human beings is an obsessive refrain in toy production, of course. Indeed, the names of many toys (Spiderman, Batman) almost sound like parodies of Freud's case studies.
50. Turkle, *Lie on the Screen*, 77

other examples of merchandising) are issued simultaneously. The notion of the original and the copy is systematically eroded by a digital uncanny that generalizes simulation by fusing capital and fiction. Take the example of Disney's *Toy Story* (cybernetic capitalism's riposte to Freud's "Uncanny"?) Here, in a film that was entirely generated by computer animation, digitized versions of old toys are presented next to new, "fictionalized" toys. But fictionality has a new sense here: it no longer has anything to do with a fantastic unattainability; on the contrary, the toys onscreen are available, immediately, as consumer objects, as soon as you leave the cinema. The toys really are toys. In an increasingly familiar pattern, the film functions as an advertisement for the toys, which function as an advertisement for it, in an ever-tightening spiral. The fictional is immediately real, in the most palpable sense: it can be bought. This, then, is *hyperfiction*: a process whereby fiction and reality are radically smeared. Unlike metafiction, hyperfiction assumes no special role for the author (or indeed for the text). On the contrary, it is only when the author and the text have become immanentized that a hyperfictional circuit is in place. (Who cares who wrote *Toy Story*?) What is crucial is not the *representation* of reality, but the feedback between fiction and the Real. (*Toy Story* doesn't reflect reality, it actively intervenes in it, inducing children – via their attached servomechanisms, parents – to consume commodities.) Hyperfiction, then, can be defined as *fiction which makes itself real.* What connects hyperfiction with animism is precisely the escape of agency from the subject. Fiction *itself* gains an agency, an ability to intervene into the Real.

To elaborate the concept of hyperfiction entails taking, and deflecting a little, Baudrillard's favourite prefix – hyper, deterritorializing the term from its use in his work. Baudrillard, of course, characterises the hyperreal as the *more real than real.* We will take this to designate an intense amplification of processes of immanentization. As Baudrillard has established, to be involved in a hyper-relation is to be beyond questions of representation (as we have already seen, the hyperreal is where representation becomes impossible, in part because the map precedes the territory). Hyperfictional process is defined by an escape from the text, in particular from the mono-authored text. At least two characteristics must be in place for hyperfiction to be operating: (1) there must be a feedback relation between the fiction and the Real and (2) (closely related to the previous point) the fiction must operate to subtract supplementary dimensions. Hyperfiction escapes the text, not in the direction of transcendence (like Beckett's Unnamable), but in the direction of radical immanence. What is inevitably destabilized is the authority of the text, and – concomitantly – the power of the reality principle. Even as it intervenes in the Real, hyperfiction subtracts the authority to *represent* the Real from texts. At the same time, it is directly effective upon its reader/consumer.

The concept of hype takes us close to the abstract machinic operations of hyper-process: using what Baudrillard would call "sign value", hype transforms (desired) end-products into potentials, which can be exploited precisely to bring about the desired end-products. Assuming the success of a commodity functions to make it successful. Radically looped into itself, feedback has become feedforward, pre-determining responses rather than being sensitive to them after the fact. It need hardly be pointed out that the economy increasingly functions in such hyper-spirals, as capital more than ever migrates from having any actual referent, towards Marx's increasingly "fleeting" forms (futures etc.). All that is solid melts into the abstract and the virtual. Marx's analyses of exchange value anticipated Baudrillard in their recognition of the role that fictions (such as potentials) have in capitalism, but Baudrillard has given up any of Marx's confidence that the fictional can simply be unmasked, that something "more real" lies beneath it. Deleuze-Guattari's' productively ambiguous notion of "fictional quantities" reinforces this intuition. It takes in both the idea of fiction that can be quantified, and of quantities that have to be conceived of as fictional. What is decisively broken down here is the conventional opposition between fiction and the Real: if fiction can be quantified, it belongs to the Real, but if quantities can be fictionalized, then the Real belongs to fiction. What could be more real than a quantity? Stripped of a Marxian referent like the labour theory of value, capital itself becomes exactly a fictional quantity: an entity, of course, with its own animistic agency.

The hyper must be opposed to processes with which it is often conflated: meta-processes, which, as we said above, are defined by an *imploded transcendence*. Baudrillard's work is often read as if it were exclusively about the meta-, when it could more properly be seen as describing the oscillation between meta- and hyper- processes, or better yet, the (inevitable) collapse of the former into the latter. As theorists dedicated to radical immanence, Deleuze-Guattari, naturally, can be placed on the side of the hyper-process. (Even as they identify a myriad of processes which are describable in terms of imploded transcendence: capitalism itself, for instance.)

Whilst never actually posing the hyper/meta distinction in quite the terms that it will be deployed here, Hofstadter's *Godel, Escher, Bach* – and its take-up into the analysis of fiction by Brian McHale – has provided an indispensable resource for the typologization of recursive systems that follows. McHale's valuable but partial analyses of fiction effectively concentrate on the question of recursion. Instead of mirroring the world, McHale's postmodernist texts construct vortices that implode into themselves. But this is not the only kind of recursion there is. What Hofstadter locates, in *Godel, Escher, Bach* are, in effect, *two* types of recursion, one corresponding to what he calls "self-transcendence"(this is the kind of recursion with which McHale's *Postmodernist Fiction* is principally concerned), the other corresponding to a radical immanentization. Escher's paintings often exemplify the first type of recursion (the best example here would probably be the drawing of two hands, each drawing the other[51]). An example of the second would be Godel or Cantor's

---

51. See *Godel, Escher, Bach*, 689, "Escher's *Drawing Hands*" for Hofstadter's analysis

mathematics, which show the systematic hostility of numeric systems to "axiomatic" "overcoding". Numbers can always escape any transcendent statement made about them.

Meta-systems behave as if they "believe" in the reality of transcendent description, which is to say, in the reality of the power of framing structures to "embed", whereas hyper-systems are hostile to any attempt to hierarchize or stratify phenomena. Hofstadter has a term for this radical implexion: the *strange loop, or tangled hierarchy*. At one level, the strange loop is a way of describing chicken-and-egg processes in which the product of any process is also one of its founding presuppositions. What should belong to an "embedded", or subordinate, level of a system escapes to a "higher" level of the system.

Unlike meta-systems, which, as we have seen, are continually seeking transcendent dimensions, hyper-systems are continually seeking to eliminate any overcoding by unity. As Deleuze-Guattari write, "Unity always operates in a dimension supplementary to that of the system considered." (TP 6) It is the rhizome "or multiplicity", of course, that for Deleuze-Guattari, "never allows itself to be overcoded, never has available to it over and above its number of lines, that is, over above the multiplicity of numbers attached to those lines." (TP 9) The rhizome, then, constitutes the exemplary case of what we are calling a hyper-system: a system that is inherently opposed to transcendence and unity. Rhizomes, like all hyper-systems, subtract unity, just as they will not allow the emergence of an "overcoding" supplementary dimension. "The multiple *must be made*, not by always adding a higher dimension, but rather in the simplest of ways, [...] with the number of dimensions one already has available – always n − 1 (the only way the one belongs to the multiple – always subtracted)." (TP 6) They are continually connecting up to an Outside. Think of Deleuze-Guattari's description of the rhizomatized book: "The book only exists through the outside and on the outside." (TP 4)

Hence the flatline, again, but in another guise. "All multiplicities are flat," Deleuze-Guattari insist, "in the sense that they fill or occupy all their dimensions: we will therefore speak of a *plane of consistency* of multiplicities [...] Multiplicities are defined by the outside: by the abstract line, the line of flight or deterritorialization according to which they change in nature and connect with other multiplicities. The plane of consistency (grid) is the outside of all multiplicities." (TP 9)

The strange loop and the Deleuze-Guattari rhizome are closely related, although, interestingly, Hofstadter ultimately denies real immanence to the strange loop, arguing that any (apparent) strange loop is underpinned by what he calls an "inviolable layer." One example he gives is of an author "Z, [who] exists only in novel by T. Likewise T exists only in a novel by E. And strangely E exists only in a novel – by Z, of course."[52] Hofstadter

---

of this picture.

52. *Godel, Escher, Bach*, 688

says that this can happen, but only in something like a novel by author H, who remains suppelementary to – which is to say – transcendent of – the "tangled hierarchy." Needless to say, though, Deleuze-Guattari put no limits on rhizomatic process: reality as such is constructed out of strange loops or rhizomes (which nevertheless can become "arborified": closed down and hierarchized – the production of apparently "inviolable" layer is an effect of stratification, a Judgment of God). Which is to say: what might ultimately separate the strange loop from the rhizome is that, in the former, hierarchy is simply tangled, whereas in the latter it is radically abolished.

4.8 A Closing Parable: Hyperfiction and In the Mouth of Madness

Sutter Cane: "This book will drive you absolutely mad. It will make the world ready for the Change. It takes its power from new readers. That's the point, belief. Once people begin to lose the difference between fantasy and reality, the Old Ones can begin their journey back. The more people who believe, the faster the journey. And by the way the other books have sold, this one is bound to be very, very popular."

Deleuze-Guattari: "If the writer is a sorcerer it is because writing is a becoming" (TP 240)

We will conclude with an analysis of a film which is very much about a strange-looped authorship relation, John Carpenter's *In the Mouth of Madness* (1994). *In the Mouth of Madness* is a film which is about fiction as contagion, fiction as an artificial intelligence, fiction which makes itself real. *In the Mouth of Madness* is perhaps the only film to merit the description hyper-Horror.[53] It is a film, that is to say, *about* Horror, which is by no means a parody

---

53. Perhaps Cronenberg's *Videodrome* – with its radically implexed reality structure and thematics of the effects of the Horror film – is another candidate. But *Videodrome* does not pursue implex in quite the same way that Carpenter's film does.

Wes Craven's *Scream* (whose numerous sequels are all part of the – threadbare – joke), meanwhile, is certainly a candidate for being described as meta-Horror. The film self-consciously plays with the conventions of the slasher film (conventions established, funnily enough, by Carpenter in his 1978 *Halloween*), recursively feeding them back into a narrative which meticulously plays them all out (except one: the sexually active heroine, who convention dictates must die, actually survives to the end of the movie). Watching *Scream*, one is left with an odd set of responses, familiar from many postmodern artifacts; invited to examine (and ridicule) the structures of the film at the same time as one is made subject to them, one is simultaneously (interpellated as) transcendent of the film (and of one's own experience of it) and manipulated by it. This is an important contrast with *In the Mouth of Madness*, whose recursive structures may make us tempted it to classify it as belonging to the same type. But where *Scream* clearly aims at self-transcendence (the sending up of the conventions, presumably, is an attempt to move outside or above them), Carpenter's film tends towards immanentization. Whilst rigorously adhering to many of the conventions it (via John Trent's ridicule) enumerates, it does so to *intensify*, rather than to deflate, the Horror: it is Trent's attempt to ridicule the Horror genre that is the object of all the film's jokes. Recursion, that is to say, attacks, rather than lamely shores up, the viewer's

or pastiche. Rather, it exploits the conventions of the genre – descriptions of which it implexes into the diegesis – to amplify, instead of disintensifying, feelings of dread and disquiet. In Hofstadter's terms, it is a film which *perceives* – and recursively processes – its own "programming" as a Horror film, without attempting to *trascend* itself. *In the Mouth of Madness* takes on all the themes familiar from Baudrillard we discussed above – especially the idea of the fictional invading and destroying the Real – but it does so more in the spirit of Gothic Materialism than in the terms of Baudrillard's melancholia.

Carpenter's Lovecraft-saturated film is a deliberate redescription of the Horror genre in terms of capitalism and schizophrenia. Beginning with shots of pulp Horror novels being mass produced, it is a film about crazes, about "fictional quantities" which erode the reality principle. The film's anti-hero is the insurance man, John Trent. Trent is hired by a publishing company to investigate the disappearance of their most successful novelist, the Horror writer, Sutter Cane. Trent is warned – in what he thinks of as a hype – that reading Cane's work has a powerful, destabilizing effect on some readers. But, contemptuous of the Horror genre and confident in his own subjectivity ("I'm my own man; no-one pulls my strings"), Trent laughs this off, displaying, at first, a bluff G. E. Moore-type empiricism ("I know what's real").

Following a set of clues, Trent is drawn to the town of Hobbs End[54]: a town, it was previously thought, which had never existed outside Cane's fiction. Naturally, Trent at first assumes that he has been set up as part of a publicity stunt: Cane's disappearance, even Hobbs End itself, have been fabricated as part of a particularly elaborate simulation. But he learns that, whilst Cane's disappearance was, initially, planned, the subsequent events had spiraled out of control. Aspects of Cane's fiction had begun to make themselves real. Meanwhile, the socius is becoming gripped by Cane-mania – crazed mobs hungry for a fix of Cane's prose have beset bookshops, turning them into riot zones. Trent, meanwhile, becomes subject to strange glitches in space and time, and increasingly loses his grip on reality. This reaches its schizophrenic pitch when he meets Cane, who tells him that he is merely a character in the new novel he is writing, entitled, of course, *In the Mouth of Madness* (Cane to Trent: "I think therefore you are"). Ultimately, Trent – now incarcerated in an asylum - no longer tries to hold onto any solid sense of reality, no longer seeks the truth behind appearances, nor aims to distinguish fantasy from reality. He has been drawn into the hyperreal: a reality fatally contaminated by fiction.

(simulated) subjective interiority.

54. One of many references to other Horror films with which *In the Mouth of Madness* is replete: Hobbs End is the name of the fictional tube station in Hammer's *Quatermass and the Pit*. Note also references to *Videodrome* (there's a character called Renn) and *Rosemary's Baby* (one of the Doctors is named after the malevolent gynecologist, Sapperstein.)

Cane is a composite Horror novelist: the SC initials recall the SK of Stephen King, while what we hear of Cane's prose – in theme and style – closely resembles Lovecraft (a favourite author of Deleuze-Guattari's, of course, who is invoked in a number of places in *A Thousand Plateaus*). In an overblown, typically Lovecraftian style, Cane invokes the return of the "Old Ones" Lovecraft had continually foretold. As with Lovecraft, for Cane Horror resides not so much in the empirical encountering of "hideous unholy abominations" as in the *transcendental* trauma such encounters produce: faced with such anomalies, it becomes impossible to hold onto any stable sense of reality[55]. Horror, that is to say, cannot be disassociated from schizophrenia. But what Cane adds to Lovecraft is a stress on the role of Horror fiction as an agent of this process. Cane's novels, as he explains to Trent, provide a necessary prerequisite – the softening of the boundaries between the fictional and the Real – "for the Old Ones to return." Initially, this seems like another version of McHale-Barth's "analogy of the author with God": but, in the end, Cane sees himself as a machine-part of an impersonal process. He is merely a conduit through which the Old Ones' schizo-signal can pass. Although he "thought [he] was making it all up", they – the Old Ones, the creatures from the Other Side - were "giving him the power to make it real. And now it is. All those horrible slimy things trying to get back in. They're all true." A strange loop is in place. What should be inside Cane's texts – the Old Ones as fictional presence – are in fact responsible for the existence of the texts, the fictions, themselves. It is they who were, secretly, the agents behind his fiction, not Cane himself. And their line of flight is constituted precisely by a fiction becoming real (and a real becoming-fictional). "Do you want to know the problem with [...] religion?" Cane asks Trent. "It's never known how to convey the anatomy of Horror. Religion seeks discipline through fear. No-one's ever believed it enough to make it real. The same can't be said of my works." When Trent objects that "books aren't real", Cane points out that his books "have sold over a billion copies. I've been translated into eighteen languages. More people believe in my work than believe in the Bible."

"That's what matters," Cane tells Trent, "belief." In a sense, though, the emphasis on belief places us back in an economy that Cane's novels have dismantled, since it seems that the process of fiction making itself real is more dependent upon hype than it is on "belief". The Old Ones hype themselves back into existence, emerging only when humanity's picture of reality has fallen apart. Yet Cane's sense of belief, naturally, has a special skew, which tends towards an equation with hype. It is "belief" in a cybernetically active, rather than an epistemologically passive sense. It is belief in this sense that

---

55. Horror in Lovecraft frequently entails the collapse of familiar structures of time and space. In a particularly complicated section of "Memories of a Sorcerer", for instance, Deleuze-Guattari discuss Lovecraft's account of dimensionality. (TP 251)

Deleuze-Guattari refer to when they write of the "beliefs and desires" that "are the basis of every society, because they are flows and as such are 'quantifiable'; they are veritable social Quantities." (TP 219) Similarly, as the epidemeological spread of Cane's fiction shows, Quantities can become "beliefs." To believe in Cane's novels is to contribute – via intense feedback - to the destruction of any stable sense of the Real.

Like Deleuze-Guattari, *In the Mouth of Madness* participates in the hyperfictionalization of Lovecraft. In treating Lovecraft as an authority or source (rather than as just as a literary text to be the subject of *readings*), *A Thousand Plateaus* shifts him from being a "fantasy" author. The treatment of particular Lovecraft formulations as if real, in Carpenter's film, as in Deleuze-Guattari, distributes them beyond their (original) textual instantiations. Lovecraft's work, which has been supplemented by numerous other authors, including Ramsey Campbell and Brian Lumley, has already hyperfictionally propagated far beyond his original corpus of writings. And, right at the heart of this process is the hyperfictional text, the *Necronomicon*, a work supposedly invented by Lovecraft[56], which has nevertheless *been written about as if real*. Questions about the *Necronomicon*'s ontological status – does it exist? – do not in any way contribute to the stabilization of its relation to the Real, they add to the *Necronomicon*'s hyperfictionality. *In the Mouth of Madness* raises the possibility that, even if Lovecraft thought he was making the *Necronomicon* up, the text may yet be real. Perhaps the *Necronomicon* is only (as yet) a *potential* text, to be retro-assembled from Lovecraft's fiction, and commentary about it.

Like *Videodrome*, *In the Mouth of Madness* can be seen as, in part, a parody of what the censorship lobby say: Horror will rot your brain. And it points to the massive, self-sustaining economic circuits that swarm around particular Horror novelists.[57] The sheer quantitative *scale* of the consumption of Cane's work is itself, immediately, a social fact – the Gothic processes of

---

56. But never written – except in the form of fragments occasionally quoted by Lovecraft when he refers to the abominable text.

57. Compare, for instance, the situation with Stephen King. According to Skal: '*Carrie* had a first printing of 30,000 in 1974; '*Salem's Lot*, the following year, had an initial run of 20,000. By the late seventies, however, spurred by the exponentially expanding delivery systems of the chain stores, King's public exploded. Following *The Shining* (1977), King's next three books, *The Stand* '(1978), *The Dead Zone* (1979), and *Firestarter* had first printings of 70,000, 80,000, and 100,000 copies, respectively. His first book for Viking, *Christine*, hit the quarter million point, and, beginning with *It* in 1986, virtually all of King's novels have had first hardcover printings of one million copies or above.' (*The Monster Show*, 360). For Skal, King's fiction 'has almost nothing to do with the aims and goals of mainstream literary publishing, and constitutes a category of its own.' (365) Its sheer quantitative scale of his sales makes the circuit between King and his readership effectively independent of the bourgeois publishing industry, Skal points out. It is a Sutter Cane-type cultural contagion.

capitalism (its anorganic propogative patterns) are laid bare in novels whose very sales accelerate those selfsame processes. Ultimately, of course, *In the Mouth of Madness* is stopped from spiraling into schizo-implex by the fact that it depicts, rather than constitutes, a strange loop. It goes as far as it can go, implexing the film into itself, by presenting *In the Mouth of Madness*, the movie, as part of the promotion of Cane's novel. But when we leave the cinema, we cannot buy Sutter Cane novels (in the same way that we can buy the toys of *Toy Story* – a fact which, when we reflect upon it, might make the Disney film the more terrifying of the two movies). There is, that is to say, one of Hofstadter's "inviolable layers" protecting reality from the strange loop (both Cane and the Old Ones belong to the fictional narrative of the film *In the Mouth of Madness* – for now, at least). That is why *In the Mouth of Madness* remains a Gothic Materialist *parable*. Nevertheless, if what we have said about cybernetic fiction and Gothic Materialism holds, the circuits it describes are all-too-(hyper)real: it is not as if capitalism and schizophrenia are merely Hollywood hokum we can dismiss as we leave the cinema. We might be well advised, then, to use *In the Mouth of Madness* as John Trent learns to use Cane's fictions, as a "guide book" to the increasingly strange terrain of capitalism and schizophrenia (to be read, perhaps, alongside Deleuze-Guattari's two volumes). As one of the townsfolk of Hobbs End cries out, "First it took the children… Now it's coming for us."

CPSIA information can be obtained
at www.ICGtesting.com
Printed in the USA
BVHW031414090822
644143BV00009B/821